THE Teenager's
GUIDE TO THE Law

Gabrielle Jan Posner, LLB, LLM, Barrister

Cavendish
Publishing
Limited

First published in Great Britain 1995 by Cavendish Publishing Limited, The Glass House, Wharton Street, London WC1X 9PX

Telephone: 0171-278 8000 Facsimile: 0171-278 8080

British Library Cataloguing in Publication Data

Posner, Gabrielle
Teenager's Guide to the Law
I Title
344.200835

ISBN 1-874241-00-7

Printed and bound in Great Britain

This book was written with my two favourite teenagers in mind, Lizzie Bloom and her brother, Richard, who actually became an adult in the time it took me to finish the book.

It is dedicated to my parents, Ann and Sidney Posner, who have always acted in a *parentally responsible* manner for me and whom I have never wanted to *divorce* (well, hardly ever!)

ACKNOWLEDGMENTS

I would like to express my gratitude to the following people for their help and guidance

- Nicola Wyld of the Children's Legal Centre;

- Emma Knights of Child Poverty Action Group;

- Tamara Lewis, Solicitor, Central London Law Centre;

- Catherine Perez Phillips, Drugs Adviser for Release;

- Ed Cape, Solicitor and Law Lecturer;

- Neville Harris, Reader in Law, Centre for the Study of the Child, the Family and the Law, Faculty of Law, University of Liverpool;

- Ole Hansen, Solicitor;

- Keith Richards, Barrister and Senior Lawyer to the Consumers Association;

- Jim Newey, Solicitor to SHAC, housing aid for London; and to

- Everyone at the National Youth Agency, supporting working with young people.

I would also like to thank Jillian Hurworth and Victoria Wilson for undertaking some of the preliminary research, my mother for her painstaking proof reading, everyone at Cavendish Publishing for their patience and efficiency, and somebody else who is too modest to accept any credit, but without whose considerable input and support, I would never have completed this book.

Gabrielle Jan Posner
May 1995

INTRODUCTION

If you are aged between 12 and 18, this book is aimed at you. It is designed to be a handy reference guide setting out your legal rights and how the law treats you as a young person. It tells you in language you can easily understand about the different aspects of the law that may affect you in your daily life and how to go about enforcing your rights.

(a) The structure of the book

The book is in five parts:

- *Part One*   The main areas of law affecting young people.
- *Part Two*   Table of minimum ages: what the law says young people are allowed to do and when.
- *Part Three* Where to go for information and help: a list of useful addresses and telephone numbers.
- *Part Four* Making the law work for you: tips on things you can do to protect your position.
- *Part Five* Quiz: test your knowledge of the law.

(b) Some preliminary warnings

(1) The law is not always clear cut

You will appreciate this when you read through this book.

A good example of this is, how do you define a 'child' for the purposes of the law? The Children Act 1989 states that a child means a person under the age of 18. Since 1969 the age of majority in this country has been fixed at 18, in other words, on your 18th birthday you become an adult in the eyes of the law.

However, it does not necessarily follow that all young people under the age of 18 will always be treated by the law as children. This can be illustrated by certain examples

■ At any age you may be able to give consent to medical treatment on your own behalf, if you are considered to have sufficient maturity and intelligence to understand what is involved.

■ Until you have reached the age of 10 you are treated as incapable of committing a criminal offence.

■ If you are aged 10 or over, but have not yet reached 14, you can only be convicted of a criminal offence if the prosecution can prove that you actually knew that what you were doing was seriously wrong.

■ Once you are 14 you have full criminal responsibility for your actions in the same way as an adult.

■ At 16 you can leave school and get a full-time job, you can get married with the consent of your parents and you can be served beer or cider with a meal in a restaurant.

■ At 17 you can hold a licence to drive a car and you can no longer be made the subject of a *care order*.

■ At 18 you are an adult. Having said that, there are certain respects in which those aged 18 or over, but who have not yet reached 21, are treated differently from adults who are aged 21 or over. For instance, until you are 21 you cannot become a Member of Parliament or adopt a child.

Criminal law and procedure is perhaps the most confusing area of all.

■ If you are under the age of 18 you are referred to, generally, as a 'juvenile'.

■ If you are aged 10 or over, but have not yet reached 14, you are classified as a 'child'.

■ If you are aged 14 or over, but have not yet reached 18, you are classified as a 'young person'.

■ If you are aged 18 or over, but have not yet reached 21, you are classified as a 'young adult'.

However, people falling within a particular age group are not necessarily all treated in the same way. For instance

■ Somebody under the age of 17 must only be interviewed by the police about their involvement in a criminal offence in the presence of an *appropriate adult*.

■ If you are aged 14 or over, but are under 17, the police generally require your written consent, as well as the written consent of a parent, before taking body samples, fingerprints and photographs. If you are aged 17 or over only your written consent is required.

■ You cannot be sent to a young offender institution until you have reached the age of 15.

■ Until you have reached the age of 18 you will usually be dealt with in the youth court and not in the adult courts.

■ Once you are 18 you will be dealt with in the adult courts, but the adult courts cannot send a young adult to prison, only to a young offender institution.

Even more confusingly, the law is not always the same for boys and girls. For instance

■ A girl can consent to heterosexual intercourse once she has reached the age of 16, but a man cannot consent to a homosexual act until he has reached the age of 18.

■ A boy can join the armed forces when he is 16, but a girl has to wait until she is 17.

(2) 'Young people'

Where it is necessary to make a distinction, this book refers to somebody under the age of 14 as a 'child' and somebody aged 14 or over, but who has not yet reached 18, as a 'young person'. Generally, I have used the expression 'young people' to refer to teenagers.

(3) Parental responsibility

This is explained in Part One, Chapter 38. Basically, it includes the power to make a wide range of decisions about your life and your upbringing until you become an adult.

In situations in which formal consent (in other words permission) is needed, for example to get married if you are aged 16 or over, but are under 18, such consent must be given by all those people who have *parental responsibility* for you.

Who has *parental responsibility* for you depends on your own particular circumstances which, in this day and age, can be varied. If you think about what family life was like 40 years ago, most children in those days grew up in families where their mother and father were married to one another. Now, for instance:

■ Your parents may be divorced or separated or not married to one another or married to somebody other than your mother or father.

■ You may be living with another adult family member or friend under a *residence order.*

■ You may be being looked after by the local authority because you are in care as a result of a *care order*, or because you are being *accommodated.*

In different parts of this book where the issue of consent arises, I have sometimes used the expressions 'parental consent' or 'the consent of your parents', even though the person who has to give that consent may not actually be a parent but somebody else who has *parental responsibility* for you.

(4) Changes in the law

The law stated in this book applies only to England and Wales (Scotland and Northern Ireland have their own legal systems) and is current to 1 May 1995.

Where changes have recently been introduced, but are not yet fully in force, for example in criminal law and procedure, I have attempted to give an outline of what the law will be when the relevant changes are brought into effect.

Be warned, the law changes quickly. By the time you read this book some parts of it may no longer be up to date although many of the principles will remain the same.

Contents

Part Two: Table of Minimum Ages

Part Three: Where to Go for Information and Help

Part Four: Making the Law Work for You

Tips on Things You Can Do to Protect Your Position 352

Part Five: Quiz 362

Test your Knowledge of the Law 362

The Main Areas of law Affecting Young People

HOW TO USE PART ONE

The object of Part One is to outline the law that applies in different situations which could happen to you. It is important to bear in mind that the legal problems you may meet in your daily life can be endlessly varied and that the law doesn't always provide one straightforward answer. A book like this can only set out the position in very general terms and sometimes you may have to go to your local *Citizens' Advice Bureau, law centre* or *neighbourhood advice centre* or to see a solicitor for advice and assistance in solving your problem.

In addition, there are various specialist organisations and bodies that may be able to give you information and help with a particular problem. You will find their addresses and telephone numbers, together with brief details about what they do, listed in Part Three.

This book isn't designed to be a textbook either. If you want to find out more about a particular area of the law, there are specialist works in the reference section of most libraries, and your nearest university bookshop should stock a full range of textbooks.

The sources of law

In this country our law cannot be found in one code. Instead it comes from two main sources, *Parliament* and the *courts*. From time to time, Parliament passes *statutes* to deal with the legal aspects of our lives. This is called *legislation*. The judges sometimes have to consider and interpret such legislation and their decisions set precedents for the future. This is called *case law*. Quite often, Parliament has not made any legislation at all and it is left to the courts to establish guidelines in the case law. In addition, rules for the protection of personal and human rights made by the *United Nations* and the *European Parliament* may apply in this country.

Although this book tries to avoid using technical language, some pieces of legislation are so significant that I have felt it necessary to mention them. This isn't meant to alarm you, but *it is important to know what you're talking about if you want to use the law to your advantage.*

In Part One the various areas of the law are dealt with in alphabetical chapters. Look up the particular area that interests you in the contents section which begins on page ix. When you have found the right chapter, the page number it begins on is given opposite. If a chapter deals with a large area it is divided into headings. Frequently, there is an overlap between different areas of the law and, in each chapter, you'll find cross references to other related chapters and the relevant headings of those chapters.

If you do not know very much about the legal system in this country and the various courts, it may help if you start by reading Chapter 15.

If I haven't put you off so far, hopefully, you'll now be able to make a start in finding out where you stand!

Chapter 1

It will help you to understand this chapter if you first read Chapter 35, Medical Treatment, headings (a) and (b) which deal with your say in decisions, your consent and confidentiality.

● Once a girl is 16 she can legally decide for herself whether to have an abortion without her parents' knowledge and consent.

● It is possible in theory for a girl under the age of 16 to have an abortion legally without her parents' knowledge and consent, but it is highly unlikely that any doctor would agree to this.

● The Abortion Act 1967 makes it legal for a doctor to carry out an abortion if two doctors are of the opinion that

  ○ the mother is less than 24 weeks pregnant and carrying on with the pregnancy would involve a greater risk to the mother's physical or mental health than having an abortion; *or*

  ○ an abortion is necessary to prevent grave permanent injury to the mother's physical or mental health; *or*

○ carrying on with the pregnancy would involve a greater risk to the mother's life than having an abortion; *or*

○ there is a substantial risk that the baby would be born suffering from a physical or mental abnormality that would make it seriously handicapped.

● If a girl is under the age of 18 it is possible that her parents could make an application to the High Court (*see Chapter 15, The Courts and the Legal System, heading (b)(4)*) either

○ to stop her from having an abortion if she has decided to end the pregnancy; *or*

○ to force her to have an abortion against her will.

The court should listen very carefully to the views of the girl and will only make an order if it is plainly in her best interests.

● The father of the baby is not entitled to make such an application.

● National Health Service hospitals are not generally keen to perform abortions after 12 weeks, but there are private clinics which charge a fee.

● Free pregnancy tests can be obtained from a GP, a family planning clinic or a Brook Advisory Centre. Anyone can buy pregnancy testing kits over the counter in chemists.

If you are pregnant and don't want to be, you must act quickly! Details of organisations providing advice, counselling and practical help are given in Part Three, Where to Go for Information and Help, under heading (E), Abortion and Contraception.

See also Chapter 13, Contraception; Chapter 38, Parental Responsibility and Decisions About Your Life and Your Upbringing; Chapter 56, Wardship.

Chapter 2

(a) Your right not to be sexually, physically or emotionally abused

● The law will not generally interfere with what happens in the privacy of the family home. However, there is an exception if something done to you amounts to a criminal offence or if you are being harmed or are at risk of harm.

● If you are under the age of 16 any person over that age who is looking after you (which may include a parent, step-parent or other family member) could be committing a criminal offence if he or she assaults, ill-treats, neglects or abandons you so as to cause you unnecessary suffering or injury to your physical or mental health.

● Boys can be sexually abused as well as girls. Sexual abuse may take various forms, including being touched indecently or being invited to touch somebody else indecently or being forced to have vaginal or anal intercourse. If a parent, step-parent or other family member (who is over the age of 10) behaves in this way towards you, they may be committing a sexual offence *(see further Chapter 45, Sexual Intercourse, heading (c))*.

● Assault on any person of any age is a criminal offence. It includes being hit or punched. Your parents and those who have care of you are entitled to use physical punishment against you if you have done something wrong, but they must not use excessive force or cause you injuries *(see further Chapter 42, Punishment and Discipline)*. Other forms of physical abuse include not being given enough to eat or being denied medical treatment.

● If, for example, you are being constantly picked on or deprived of love and affection this may be emotional abuse. It is unlikely to amount to a criminal offence. However, it is upsetting and can affect your health and development.

● If you are under the age of 18 the social services department of your local authority has a duty to safeguard and promote your welfare. Once they have been made aware of your situation they must make an investigation and take whatever steps they consider necessary to protect you. These could result in your being removed from home temporarily or permanently.

● If you are being abused in any way at home you should try to talk about this to a sympathetic adult whom you trust, for example, your teacher or doctor (or social worker if you have one).

If you feel too embarrassed and upset to do this and would rather talk to somebody who doesn't know you and your family, Childline and the NSPCC run free, confidential helplines with experienced counsellors available 24 hours a day to discuss your problems. Their telephone numbers are given in Part Three, Where to Go for Information and Help, under heading (B), Children and Young People in Danger or Distress. If you need to talk to a social worker about something, you should telephone or visit the social services office covering your area. You will find the details in your local telephone directory under the name of your local authority; the listing will usually be 'Social Services, Children and Families'.

● If you say something to a teacher or doctor, they should keep it confidential and not tell your parents. However, if you are considered to be in danger, they must inform the social services department, but your teacher or doctor will generally ask your permission first.

● Usually, the first stage is that a social worker will visit you and your family at home to discuss the concerns and to obtain the views of everyone involved.

(b) Child assessment orders (CAOs)

● A social worker does not have the right to enter your home for any purpose without the permission of your parents. If your parents are not prepared to co-operate in the investigation, provided there is reasonable cause to suspect that you are suffering, or are likely to suffer, 'significant harm', the local authority or the NSPCC may apply to the family proceedings court *(see Chapter 15, The Courts and the Legal System, heading (b)(2))* for a *child assessment order* (CAO).

● This involves an assessment of the state of your health and development or the way in which you have been treated.

● A CAO can be made if you are under the age of 18, even if you are aged 16 or over and married.

● It lasts for up to 7 days.

● The court can direct that you live away from home for all or part of the period of the assessment, if this is necessary.

● The court can also direct that you undergo a medical or psychiatric examination or other assessment but, if you have sufficient understanding to make an informed decision and you do not want this, you can refuse to agree.

(c) Child protection conferences and the Child Protection Register

● It is likely in these sorts of situations that a child protection conference will be organised. This is a meeting of all the people involved with you and your family, including social workers, teachers, doctors, health visitors and the police, to allow them to exchange information and assess the degree of risk to you.

● Your parents will be invited to attend. If you are old enough to express your views, you should also be given the opportunity to attend. You do not have to go, instead, you could send a letter stating what you want. If you do attend, parts of the conference may be held in your absence. You can request that you be allowed to have your say without your parents being present if you would find it too frightening or distressing to speak in front of them. It may be possible to arrange for a solicitor to represent you at the conference.

If you are uncertain or confused about whether to attend a child protection conference, and what will happen, it is a good idea to contact one of the organisations listed in Part Three, Where to Go for Information and Help, under heading (P), Children and Young People in Care.

● The aim of the conference is to find a way to solve the problem so as to enable you to remain at home safely, and without the need for court proceedings. The decisions and recommendations of the conference are called the *child protection plan*. This must be reconsidered at regular intervals at *child protection review meetings*.

● It may be that the conference will be put off to another date while further investigations are being carried out.

● The result of the conference could be that everyone involved enters into an agreement about what is to happen to you in the future. This may include a promise by your parents not to treat you in a particular way, attendance at a family centre or the family undergoing 'family therapy' *(see further Chapter 47, Social Services and Children in Need, heading (a))*.

● The conference may make a decision to include your name on the *Child Protection Register*. This is a register of the names of all the children in the area who have been, or are suspected of having been, abused or neglected in some way.

● If your name is included, a social worker will be appointed. He or she will make regular visits and ensure that you are safe.

● Whether or not to keep your name in the register must be reviewed at a *child protection review meeting* once every 6 months.

(d) Police protection

● It may be that the problem is too urgent to wait for a conference. For example

○ you arrive at school with a black eye caused by your step-father punching you and you tell your teacher that you are too frightened to go home that afternoon.

● Where the police have reasonable cause to believe that you would otherwise be likely to suffer 'significant harm', they have the power to place you in suitable accommodation and keep you there for a period of up to 72 hours. This is known as being taken into police protection. Wherever possible, the police prefer to remove the abuser from your home rather than you.

● The police must immediately inform the social services department.

● If you appear capable of understanding, the police must immediately tell you about the steps that have been taken, the reasons, and about any further steps that may be taken.

They must also find out your wishes and feelings.

● It is possible that you will be placed with temporary foster parents or in a children's home. If you request it, this address can be kept secret from your parents.

● However, the police must inform your parents, all those with *parental responsibility* for you *(see Chapter 38, Parental Responsibility and Decisions About Your Life and Your Upbringing)* and anyone with whom you were living immediately before being taken into police protection, that you are in police protection and the reason for this.

(e) Emergency protection orders (EPOs)

● It may be that the social services department consider that you will require further protection once the 72 hours has finished. In these circumstances an application may be made to the family proceedings court for an *emergency protection order* (EPO). There must be reasonable cause to believe that you are likely to suffer 'significant harm' if an EPO is not made.

● An EPO can be made if you are under the age of 18, even if you are aged 16 or over and married.

● This enables you to be removed to accommodation provided by or on behalf of the local authority (usually temporary foster parents or a children's home), or to be kept in the place where you are presently being accommodated.

● EPOs are also applied for in some cases where a child or young person has not previously been in police protection. For example

   ○ if your parents were unable to cope with you and arranged for you to be accommodated *(see further Chapter 9, Care Orders and Accommodation, heading (b))*, but they then change their minds and try to remove you from the foster home where you are settled and doing well; *or*

   ○ if you are in hospital receiving treatment for a particular condition (for example, an eating disorder) and your parents attempt to discharge you from the hospital against medical advice.

● An EPO lasts initially for any period of up to 8 days (including the day you were taken into police protection).

● If it is a real emergency, you and your parents need not be told that the application is being made. However, you and your parents must be informed immediately once an EPO has been granted.

If you and/or your parents were not present at the first hearing, an application can be made to end the EPO after 72 hours.

● An EPO can be extended only once, for a further period of up to 7 days, if the court considers it necessary to keep you safe.

● If somebody obstructs an EPO, the police can be granted a warrant to enter and search any premises.

● An EPO gives the local authority *parental responsibility* for you *(see Chapter 38, Parental Responsibility and Decisions About Your Life and Your Upbringing).*

● On an application for an EPO, the court will appoint a *guardian ad litem* to represent your interests. The *guardian ad litem* or the court will appoint a solicitor for you. *(The functions of the guardian ad litem and your solicitor, and your ability to have a say, are the same in applications relating to EPOs as they are in all care proceedings and are dealt with in Chapter 10, Care Proceedings, under heading (b)).*

● The court can also direct that you undergo a medical or psychiatric examination or other assessment but, if you have sufficient understanding to make an informed decision and you do not want this, you can refuse to agree.

● At the end of the EPO the local authority must decide whether to apply for a *care order (see Chapter 11, The Children Act 1989, heading (c)(5)),* or a *supervision order (see Chapter 11, heading (c)(6)).* If they do not, you must return home unless there is an agreement for you to remain accommodated or an agreed arrangement for you to go and stay with an adult family member or friend.

(f) Other remedies for abuse

● Assuming that the local authority does decide to apply for a *care* or *supervision order,* the court can make such an order if it is satisfied that you are suffering, or likely to suffer, 'significant harm' because your parents are not looking after you properly *(see further Chapter 10, Care Proceedings, and Chapter 52, Supervision Orders).*

● It may be possible to obtain an injunction for your personal protection against a physically abusive parent *(see further Chapter 21, Domestic Violence and Harassment).*

● If you have been, or are being, sexually or physically abused, the police may wish to make an investigation. It is likely that they will ask you to agree to a full medical examination in a hospital.

They may also ask you to agree to being interviewed. If you do agree, you will be asked questions by a specially trained police officer and a social worker and the interview will probably be videoed.

There are guidelines about how you should be asked questions so as to try to make it less upsetting for you.

● If the abuser is prosecuted, you may have to give evidence at the trial. *(Being a witness in a criminal case is dealt with in Chapter 45, Sexual Intercourse, under heading (d).)*

● If the abuser is convicted, an order for compensation may be made by the criminal courts or you may be able to apply to the Criminal Injuries Compensation Board for compensation. *(This is further dealt with in Chapter 12, Compensation, under heading (a), Victims of crime.)*

● It may also be possible to *sue* the abuser for damages in the civil courts. *(See further Chapter 51, Suing and Being Sued, heading (a); Chapter 12, Compensation, heading (b); Chapter 48, Solicitors and Legal Aid.)*

See also Chapter 9, Care Orders and Accommodation, Being Looked After by the Local Authority; Chapter 10, Care Proceedings; Chapter 11, The Children Act 1989; Chapter 21, Domestic Violence and Harassment; Chapter 33, Leaving Home and Running Away; Chapter 42, Punishment and Discipline; Chapter 45, Sexual Intercourse; Chapter 47, Social Services and Children in Need; Chapter 52, Supervision Orders. Your right to access to information about you held in social services files is dealt with in Chapter 43, Records and Access to Information, under heading (c).

Chapter 3

● We all owe a duty to the people around us to take 'reasonable care' so that we do not cause personal injury to them or damage their property.

● If a person should have been more careful and should have appreciated that their carelessness would lead to the sort of harm that occurred, they are negligent. For example

  ○ a person who drives too fast down a busy high street, without keeping a proper look out, and knocks somebody else over is negligent.

● Negligence is a civil wrong (known as a *tort*), rather than a criminal offence, although the same conduct may in certain circumstances be a crime as well *(see Chapter 15, The Courts and the Legal System, heading (a))*.

● A person whose negligence causes an accident can be *sued* in the civil courts *(see Chapter 15, The Courts and the Legal System, heading (b))* for compensation called *damages (see Chapter 51, Suing and Being Sued; Chapter 12, Compensation, heading (b))*.

● If you are under the age of 18 and your negligence causes an accident, you must take responsibility for your actions and for the payment of any *damages* that may be awarded against you, not your parents.

● Until you reach 18 your behaviour is not looked at in the same way as a model adult citizen, but the judge will consider what another ordinary young person of your age would have done, or would not have done, and whether they would have foreseen the consequences.

● In fact, it is improbable that you would be *sued* as you are unlikely to have the money to pay any *damages*, unless you have insurance.

Insurance plays a large part in deciding whether or not it is worthwhile to sue somebody.

● If you are under the age of 18 and somebody else causes an accident involving you, you may be able to sue them for *damages* for negligence through one of your parents, or another responsible adult, acting as your *next friend (see further Chapter 51, Suing and Being Sued, heading (a))*.

● One of the main situations in which this could happen is a road traffic accident.

● Also, if you go to any premises, the occupier has a duty to ensure that you are reasonably safe in using them for the purpose for which you are invited or permitted to be there. There is also a duty to ensure that you are reasonably safe at school and at work. For example

○ if you are in a supermarket doing your shopping and something is spilt on the floor and not cleared up, and you slip and twist your ankle, you may have a claim for *damages* against the owner of the supermarket; *or*

○ if you are in a gym lesson at a state school and the apparatus collapses, and you fall and break your arm, you may have a claim for *damages* against your local education authority; *or*

○ if you work, say, as a mechanic and are required to do some welding without being supplied with goggles, and you harm your eyes, you may have a claim for *damages* against the owner of the garage who employs you.

● The *damages* you would otherwise be awarded could be reduced even though the other person was at fault, if you were less careful than you should have been. This is called *contributory negligence.* Again, your behaviour is judged by the standards of somebody of the same age as you. Therefore, while a small child might not be expected to look before running out from behind a parked car, somebody in their teens would be expected to do so.

● If you we were the driver of, or a passenger in, a car which was involved in a road traffic accident and you were not wearing a seat belt and as a result you suffered more serious injuries, you are likely to be treated as contributorily negligent.

● If you are driving a motor vehicle and are involved in an accident there are certain things you should do *(see further Chapter 22, Driving, heading (c)).*

If you do have an accident you should go to your local Citizens' Advice Bureau, law centre or neighbourhood advice centre, or see a solicitor, without delay.

Details of the Law Society's Accident Line are given in Part Three, Where to Go for Information and Help, under heading (U).

You should also read Part Four, Making the Law Work for You, heading (4), which deals with personal injuries.

See also Chapter 12, Compensation; Chapter 48, Solicitors and Legal Aid; Chapter 51, Suing and Being Sued. Accidents at school are dealt with in Chapter 25, Education, under heading (i); accidents at work are dealt with in Chapter 58, Working, under heading (f).

Chapter 4

ADOPTION

(a) Being adopted

● A child or young person who is under the age of 18 can be adopted provided that they are not, or have not been, married.

● You can only be legally adopted as a result of a court order.

● The moment you are adopted, the legal link with your birth family (the law uses the term *natural* family) is broken completely and permanently. You are treated in law as no longer being a part of your natural family.

● Unless your adoptive parents give their consent, your natural parents cannot remove you from your adoptive parents' care and they and other members of your natural family do not have any right to continue to see you.

● You are treated in law for all purposes as the child of your adoptive parents and they have *parental responsibility* for you *(see Chapter 38)* in the same way as natural parents. They are able to make all the major decisions such as where you will live and go to school. Also if your adoptive parents divorce or separate, the court can make the same range of orders as for natural parents and their children, and if your adoptive parent dies and leaves you out of their will, you can make an application to the court as his or her child.

● If you are not a British citizen by birth and are legally adopted in the United Kingdom by a British citizen, you will automatically become a British citizen from the moment you are adopted.

● Your adoptive parents can change your surname to their surname, and also your first name or names. It is usual for them to include the name by which they wish you to be known in their application for an adoption order. The change will be made at the time of the adoption order.

● You can be adopted by a married couple or a single person provided that the intended adoptive parent (or parents) are aged 21 or over, but a person aged 18 or over can adopt their own child *(see further below)*.

● In the case of unmarried couples, only one of the partners can adopt.

● You must already have been living with your intended adoptive family for a trial period before an adoption order can be made.

● Under the Adoption Act 1976, the court must listen to your wishes and feelings regarding the decision and take them into account according to your age and understanding. In other words, the older you are, the more important your say in whether an adoption order will be made.

● If your mother remarries (for example after a divorce), you can be adopted by your mother and step-father, although it may be a condition of such an adoption order that you have the right to continue to see your natural father and paternal grandparents. It is more likely in this kind of case that the court would make a *residence order (see Chapter 11, The Children Act 1989, heading (c)(1))*, in favour of your mother and step-father.

(b) Finding your natural family

● When a child is adopted, the Registrar General enters the adoption in the *Adopted Children Register*. This sets out the date and place of the child's birth, the child's new name, the names, addresses and occupations of the adoptive parents, the date the adoption order was made and the court that made it. This is the adopted child's new birth certificate. You can get hold of a copy of this at any time, but the copy you receive does not give your real name or any reference to your natural parents and does not mention the fact that you have been adopted.

● Once you reach the age of 18 you can find out your real name, and the names and details of your natural parents by applying for a copy of your original birth certificate.

● This right only applies if you are aged 18 or over but, if you are aged 16 or 17 and intending to get married, you can be given certain information so that you can establish whether your intended husband or wife is a blood relative.

● If you were adopted before 12 November 1975, the information will be given to you only after you have seen a counsellor. Counselling is provided by the Registrar General's office, local authorities and adoption agencies.

● The Children Act 1989 creates the *Adoption Contact Register*. People who have been adopted, once they have reached 18, and members of their natural family (including parents, brothers and sisters, grandparents, aunts and uncles) can apply to have their names and addresses put on the Register.

● The person who has been adopted can use the Register to trace their natural family. If the natural family themselves register, any details left by them will be passed on to the person who has been adopted. However, the natural relatives cannot use the Register to obtain information or trace the adopted person without his or her knowledge and consent.

● The *Adoption Contact Register* is therefore highly valuable in putting adopted people and their natural relatives in touch with each other if this is what everyone wants.

● You have no actual right to be told that you have been adopted so you may never discover the truth.

The address for the Adoption Contact Register and details of organisations providing counselling and practical help for those who have been adopted are given in Part Three, Where to go for Information and Help, under heading (O), Adoption.

See also Chapter 20, Divorce and Separation; Chapter 32, Inheritance and Wills; Chapter 36, Names; Chapter 37, Nationality; Chapter 50, Step-parents.

Chapter 5

The law in this area puts much of the responsibility for protecting children and young people from the effects of alcohol upon adults. There are various statutes which control the sale and supply of alcohol in licensed premises, for example off-licences, supermarkets, pubs, wine bars, restaurants and discos. In certain circumstances, both the adult and the child or young person may be committing criminal offences.

(a) Licensees

● The licensee, for example the publican or shopkeeper, will commit a criminal offence if he or she

- ○ allows a child under the age of 14 into a bar (it is not an offence if the child is the licensee's own child; children can go into the gardens and separate family rooms of pubs); *or*

- ○ sells alcohol to a person under the age of 18 (young people aged 16 or over can lawfully be served beer or cider with a meal in a restaurant); *or*

- ○ knowingly allows a person under the age of 18 to drink alcohol in a bar.

The licensee is entitled to refuse to serve you if you have no proof that you are over 18 and can ask you to leave the premises.

● Under a recent change in the law, pubs and wine bars wishing to encourage families to go there are able to apply for a special *children's certificate*. If such a certificate is in force, a child under the age of 14 is allowed into a bar without a criminal offence being committed provided that the child is accompanied by an adult.

(b) Other adults

● A parent or other adult will commit a criminal offence if he or she

- o gives alcohol to a child under the age of 5 except on properly justifiable medical grounds; *or*

- o takes a child under the age of 14 into a bar (except where the bar has a *children's certificate*; *see above*); *or*

- o buys, or attempts to buy, alcohol for a person under the age of 18 to drink in a bar; *or*

- o sends a person under the age of 18 to buy alcohol from an off-licence or supermarket on his or her behalf.

(c) People under the age of 18

● A person over the age of 10 but who has not yet reached 18 will commit a criminal offence if, in any licensed premises, he or she

- o buys alcohol; *or*

- o attempts to buy alcohol; *or*

- o drinks alcohol.

If you are aged between 14 and 17 you can be fined up to £1,000. If you are aged between 10 and 13 you can be fined up to £250.

● Young people aged 16 or over can lawfully be served beer or cider with a meal in a restaurant.

● Young people aged 14 or over can lawfully go into a bar, but can only be served soft drinks. You cannot drink alcohol in a bar until you have reached 18.

- There is no age limit for going into an off-licence, provided you are not buying, or attempting to buy, alcohol.

- At 16 you can buy liqueur chocolates.

- There are various rules about alcohol at league and cup football matches. You can commit a criminal offence if you have alcohol with you (and also if you are drunk)

  - in the areas of the ground open to the public during the match and within 2 hours before the start and 1 hour after the finish; *or*

  - while entering or trying to enter the ground during the same period; *or*

  - while in a coach or train on a journey to or from a match.

- No offence is committed if a child aged 5 or over drinks alcohol in their own, or somebody else's, home.

Raiding your parents' drinks cabinet is not a recommended course of action.

Drinking alcohol regularly at any age can seriously affect your health. If you have a problem with alcohol see Part Three, Where to Go for Information and Help, under heading (K), Alcohol.

The rules about working in licensed premises are dealt with in Chapter 58, Working, under heading (a)(4).

Chapter 6

BANK, BUILDING SOCIETY AND POST OFFICE SAVINGS ACCOUNTS

Holding your own account

● A bank account, building society account or National Savings account (with the post office) can be opened in a child's name from the moment he or she is born. The child cannot draw money out himself or herself but parents can do so on the child's behalf.

● From the age of 7 onwards, a child can open his or her own National Savings account or Trustee Savings Bank account and pay money in and draw money out himself or herself.

● It is up to the particular bank or building society at what age they will let you open an account with them in your own right, and how much you need to put in to start the account. Most banks and building societies now have special accounts aimed at the 10 to 18 year old age bracket (the actual ages and the range of advantages offered depend on the particular bank or building society).

● As a general rule, you will not be able to get a cash dispenser card until you are at least 12 and, usually, not until you are 13 or 14. You will be able to draw money out up to a set limit, provided that you have enough money in your account.

● Because of the rule that you are not legally responsible for your debts until you have reached the age of 18, it is unlikely that you would be given an overdraft or a cheque guarantee card if you are under 18, although this may be allowed if one of your parents acts as a *guarantor*, this means that they agree to pay if you do not.

● Complaints about banking and building society practices can be made to the *Banking Ombudsman* and the *Building Societies Ombudsman* in certain situations, for example, if all your money is credited to somebody else's account. However you cannot complain if it is a matter for the manager's own judgement, for example if you're an unemployed 17 year old who has been refused an overdraft.

● You must first ask the bank, or building society, to correct their mistake, if necessary, by writing to the head office before going to the relevant ombudsman. *(The role of ombudsmen is dealt with in Chapter 15, The Courts and the Legal System, under heading (d).)*

Details of the various ombudsmen are given in Part Three, Where to Go for Information and Help, under heading (V), Consumer Protection.

See also Chapter 8, Borrowing Money, Getting Credit Cards and Making Hire Purchase Agreements; Chapter 14, Contracts.

Chapter 7

- A person under the age of 18 cannot

  ○ enter a betting shop; *or*

  ○ place a bet; *or*

  ○ collect somebody else's winnings; *or*

  ○ work in a betting shop.

- It is a criminal offence for an adult to

  ○ have a betting transaction with somebody under the age of 18; *or*

  ○ receive or negotiate any bet through them; *or*

  ○ employ them in a betting shop.

- A person under the age of 18 can go into a bingo club, but cannot play bingo.

- You have to be a member to go into a casino and you cannot join until you have reached the age of 18.

- You must be aged 16 or over to take part in the National Lottery. If you do buy a ticket before you are 16, you will not be able to collect any winnings.

● The law does not appear to restrict people under the age of 18 from going into amusement arcades where there are slot machines which pay out cash, tokens or prizes. However, the management may have a rule preventing anybody under 18 from playing on such slot machines.

In any event, forget making your fortune by hitting the jackpot because, unlike Las Vegas, the maximum you can win in this country is presently £3 in money or a prize worth £6.

If you have a problem with gambling see Part Three, Where to Go for Information and Help, under heading (N), Gambling.

Chapter 8

BORROWING MONEY, GETTING CREDIT CARDS AND MAKING HIRE PURCHASE AGREEMENTS

● You are not legally responsible for your debts until you have reached the age of 18 and, generally, you cannot be *sued* in the civil courts to recover money that you owe. Therefore, it is highly unlikely that any bank or building society would agree to lend money to somebody who is under the age of 18.

● They may be prepared to agree to a loan if one of your parents is prepared to act as a *guarantor*, this means that they agree to pay if you do not.

● Similarly, you cannot ordinarily hold a credit card, charge card or store card in your own right until you are 18 unless you have a guarantor but, just because a parent is prepared to act as a *guarantor*, it doesn't mean you will get a card.

● Furthermore, you cannot ordinarily buy goods (generally large or expensive items such as a car or a TV) on hire purchase or any other form of credit agreement in your own right until you are 18. Again, it is a matter for the finance company whether they will accept one of your parents as a *guarantor*.

See also Chapter 6, Bank, Building Society and Post Office Savings Accounts; Chapter 14, Contracts.

Chapter 9

It will help you to understand this chapter if you first read Chapter 11, heading (a), which sets out the thinking behind the Children Act 1989, and Chapter 47, Social Services and Children in Need.

If you live away from home with foster parents or in a children's home, this may be because you are being *accommodated* by your local authority, or because you are in the care of your local authority as a result of a *care order*. In both cases you are referred to as *being looked after* by the local authority. The main difference is that if you are *accommodated*, the local authority does not have *parental responsibility* for you *(see Chapter 38, Parental Responsibility and Decisions About Your Life and Your Upbringing, and see further below).*

(a) Being in care as a result of a care order

See generally Chapter 10 which deals with care proceedings and the grounds for care orders.

● If you are the subject of a *care order*, whether it is a *full care order* or an *interim care order*, you are placed in the care of the social services department of your local authority.

● The local authority will share *parental responsibility* for you with your parents *(see Chapter 38, Parental Responsibility and Decisions About Your Life and Your Upbringing)* and has the power to decide where you will live and make other decisions about your life and your upbringing.

● A *full care order* lasts until you are 17 unless you get married at 16, or it is discharged, in other words brought to an end by the court.

● At any time while a *full care order* is in force, an application may be made to the court to discharge it.

● Such an application can be made by

   ○ you; *or*

   ○ any person who has *parental responsibility* for you; *or*

   ○ the local authority.

● On an application for discharge, the court will appoint a *guardian ad litem* to represent your interests. The *guardian ad litem* or the court will appoint a solicitor for you. *(The functions of the guardian ad litem and your solicitor, and your ability to have a say, are the same on applications to discharge a care order as they are in all care proceedings, and are dealt with in Chapter 10, Care Proceedings, under heading (b).)*

● Discharge will be ordered if the *threshold criteria* no longer exist (in other words 'significant harm', *see Chapter10, Care Proceedings, heading (c)*) and a *care order* is no longer considered to be in your best interests.

(b) Being accommodated by the local authority

● The social services department of the local authority have certain duties to provide accommodation for *children in need* within their area.

● A *child in need* is somebody under the age of 18 who is unlikely to achieve or maintain a reasonable standard of health or development or whose health or development may suffer if he or she does not get the help required, and includes disabled children *(see further Chapter 18, Disability, heading (b))*.

● The social services department must provide accommodation if you are a *child in need* who appears to require accommodation because

○ there is nobody with parental responsibility for you *(see Chapter 38, Parental Responsibility and Decisions About Your Life and Your Upbringing)*; or

○ you are lost or have been abandoned; *or*

○ the person who has been caring for you is prevented (whether or not permanently, and for whatever reason) from providing you with a suitable home.

● They must also provide accommodation if you are a 16 or 17 year old in need and your welfare is likely to be seriously prejudiced if no accommodation is provided.

● They may provide accommodation in any other case if they consider that this would be in your best interests (although they are not under a duty to do so).

● The effect of these rules is that if your parents cannot look after you, for example because they are unable to cope through ill-health or because they are going abroad without you, they may ask the social services department of your local authority to take over caring for you for a certain period.

● Before providing accommodation, the social services department must find out your views and take them into account.

● The social services department cannot provide accommodation if there is an objection from a person with *parental responsibility* for you and who is willing and able to offer you a home, except if you are aged 16 or 17 and ask to be received into *accommodation*.

30

● The social services department should draw up a written agreement regarding the nature, purpose and length of the proposed *accommodation*. This should be signed by your parents and by you, if you are old enough.

● If you are accommodated, the local authority does not have *parental responsibility* for you *(see Chapter 38, Parental Responsibility and Decisions About Your Life and Your Upbringing)*. This means that even though you are living away from home, it is still your parents who decide what happens to you.

● While you are being accommodated, anyone with *parental responsibility* for you may remove you at any time, except if you are aged 16 or 17 and asked to be received into accommodation. However, if the local authority considers that a removal is not in your best interests, they may apply to the family proceedings court *(see Chapter 15, The Court and the Legal System, heading (b)(2))* for an emergency protection order (EPO) *(see Chapter 15, heading (c)(7)) and further Chapter 2, Abuse and Child Protection Procedures, heading (e))*.

The provision of accommodation is further dealt with in Chapter 31, Housing and Homelessness, heading (a)(1), Your rights if you have nowhere to live; see also Chapter 33, Leaving Home and Running Away.

(c) The care plan

(1) Consultation

● If you are being looked after, before making any decision about you, the social services department has a duty to find out

○ your wishes and feelings; *and*

○ the wishes and feelings of your parents, any person who has *parental responsibility* for you and anybody else whose views are considered to be relevant.

● Due consideration must be given to your views having regard to your age and understanding and to your religion, racial origin, language and cultural background.

● Within 4 weeks of your beginning to be looked after, there must be a *statutory review meeting* so that full consideration can be given to your case by everyone involved including social workers, your teachers and doctor, and your foster parents (if you have them).

● The object is to make a *care plan*, in other words an outline of how you should be cared for while you are being looked after. You should generally be allowed to attend any review meetings and have a say if you want to although you may prefer to tell your social worker your views or put them in a letter.

● Your parents will be invited to attend review meetings. You can request that you be allowed to have your say without your parents being present if you would find it too frightening or distressing to speak in front of them.

● You also have a right to be represented by you own *advocate*.

Organisations like ASC, Voice for the Child in Care and Irchin provide this service. Their details are given in Part Three, Where to Go for Information and Help, under heading (P), Children and Young People in Care.

● Further *statutory review meetings* must take place within 3 months of the first meeting and thereafter at 6-monthly intervals. At these meetings the *care plan* will be reconsidered and there will be a discussion about your health, general welfare and any major developments in your life. At all stages the possibility of your returning home to your parents must be fully explored.

● The social services department can decide to hold *planning meetings* in-between statutory reviews to deal with any urgent issues that may arise.

● You should receive full written details of the decisions taken at all meetings and a copy of the *care plan*.

(2) Placement

● Where you will live while you are being looked after is, clearly, an important aspect of the *care plan*.

● The social services department may place you

○ with a foster family; *or*

○ in a community home; *or*

○ in a voluntary home; *or*

○ in a registered children's home; *or*

○ at a special school which is a boarding school; *or*

○ with a suitable adult family member or friend who is willing to have you.

● Foster families must have obtained special approval from the local authority and be registered with them.

An attempt should be made to find a family having the same racial origins as you.

● All other adults will have to undergo a formal assessment to make sure they are suitable to care for you and that their home, including the proposed sleeping arrangements, is suitable. The social services department will look at their household as a whole and the suitability of all the members who are aged 16 or over.

● There are detailed rules regulating the different kinds of children's homes listed above, but these are outside the scope of this book.

● The social services department have a duty, wherever possible, to place you near your home and to keep brothers and sisters who are being looked after together.

● The details of the placement must be recorded in writing and you should receive a copy.

(3) Punishment and discipline

● *Corporal punishment*, for example slapping, hitting and shaking, is forbidden in all residential homes for children and local authority foster placements.

You must not be deprived of food and drink or prevented from seeing your family and friends.

● All children's homes must have a written list of the kinds of punishments that can be imposed. You are entitled to see this list. *(The circumstances in which you can be locked up are dealt with under heading (f), below.)*

(4) Leaving care

● The social services department of the local authority has a duty to advise, assist and befriend children being looked after by them with a view to promoting their welfare when they stop being looked after.

● If you are under the age of 21 and at any time while you were aged 16 or 17 you were being looked after by the local authority, the social services department have a duty to continue to advise you and may additionally provide you with assistance.

● Assistance may be in kind or, exceptionally, in cash and may take the form of

  ○ a contribution to the expenses of living near the place where you work or receive education or training; *or*

  ○ a grant to enable you to meet expenses connected with your education or training.

(d) Contact with family members

● While you are being looked after, the social services department must, unless it is not reasonably practicable or consistent with your welfare, try and promote contact between you and

  ○ your parents; *and*

  ○ any person who has *parental responsibility* for you; *and*

  ○ any relative or friend or other person connected with you.

● Contact can be by visits, overnight stays, telephone calls and letters. If any person poses a danger to you, but you still want to see them, your social worker can be present throughout the visit.

● Before making a *care order*, the court must give consideration to the arrangements for contact between you and

  ○ your parents*;

○ your guardian* (if you have one, *see further Chapter 30, Guardians*); *and*

○ any person* with whom you were living under a *residence order (see Chapter 11, The Children Act 1989, heading (c)(1))* immediately before the *care order* was made.

● Once you are in care as a result of a *care order*, applications can be made to the court by both you and the social services department for orders

○ allowing contact between you and any named person; *and/or*

○ authorising the social services department to refuse contact between you and any of the people listed above marked *.

● Unless the social services department have been granted the necessary order, they can only refuse to allow contact between you and any of the people listed above marked * if it is

○ necessary to safeguard or promote your welfare; *and*

○ a matter of urgency; *and*

○ the refusal does not last for more than 7 days.

If you have sufficient understanding, you must be notified in writing of such a refusal immediately the decision is taken.

● The people listed above marked *, and any other person who has obtained *leave* (in other words, permission) of the court, can make an application for an order allowing contact between you and them.

● In all applications relating to contact, the court will appoint a *guardian ad litem* to represent your interests. The *guardian ad litem* or the court will appoint a solicitor for you. *(The functions of the guardian ad litem and your solicitor, and your ability to have a say, are the same in contact applications as they are in all care proceedings and are dealt with in Chapter 10, Care Proceedings, under heading (b)).*

● If appropriate, an arrangement can be made for you to see an *independent visitor* where you are not seeing your parents. You can ask this person for advice on any aspect of being looked after and discuss with them things that you're not happy about. *The independent visitor* may be able to go to *statutory review meetings* with you *(see heading (c) above)*, or approach your social worker to try and sort out a problem you're having, or help you put any complaint into writing *(see further heading (g) below)*.

(e) Decisions about your life and your upbringing

● If you are being accommodated, the local authority does not have *parental responsibility* for you *(see Chapter 38, Parental Responsibility and Decisions About Your Life and Your Upbringing)*. This means that even though you are living away from home, your parents still make all the major decisions about your life and your upbringing.

● In all cases the social services department must do whatever is necessary to safeguard and promote your welfare, as well as advise, assist, befriend and maintain you.

This includes paying your travel expenses where you would not otherwise be able to visit those people with whom you are allowed to have contact *(see heading (d) above)*.

● A *care order* gives the local authority *parental responsibility* and also the power to determine the extent to which a parent (or guardian) may meet their own *parental responsibility*.

● However, there are certain restrictions on how the local authority can exercise its *parental responsibility*. Notably, while a *care order* is in force

   ○ the local authority cannot cause you to be brought up in any religion other than the one you were being brought up in before the care order was made;

   ○ the local authority cannot have you adopted without a proper application to the court for an adoption order being made *(see Chapter 4, Adoption)*;

   ○ no person can cause you to be known by a new surname without the written consent of every person who has *parental responsibility* for you or leave of the court;

   ○ no person can remove you from the United Kingdom, other than if the local authority arranges for you to go on holiday for less than a month, without the written consent of every person who has *parental responsibility* for you or the leave of the court;

○ the local authority may only make arrangements for you to live outside England and Wales with the approval of the court. The court must not give its approval unless

– this would be in your best interests; *and*

– suitable arrangements have been made in the new country; *and*

– you have consented; *and*

– every person who has *parental responsibility* for you has consented.

(f) Secure accommodation and running away from care

● A child or young person who is being looked after by the local authority may not be locked up unless certain conditions exist. It must appear that

○ he or she has a history of absconding (this means running away) and is likely to do so again; *or*

○ he or she is likely to suffer significant harm, or injure himself or herself or other people.

● You can only be locked up in secure accommodation that has been approved by the *Secretary of State for Health.*

● A child under the age of 13 must not be placed in secure accommodation without the prior approval of the *Secretary of State for Health.*

● You may not be kept in secure accommodation without the approval of the court for more than a total of 72 hours in any 28 day period.

● A court can authorise you to be kept in secure accommodation for any period up to 3 months from the date of the order, and after that for further periods not exceeding 6 months at a time.

● The application will be made to the family proceedings court *(see Chapter 15, The Courts and the Legal System, heading (b)(2)).*

You must be given the opportunity to be legally represented at the hearing and a *guardian ad litem* will be appointed for you by the court *(see further Chapter 10, Care Proceedings, heading (b))*.

You may be allowed to be present in court but you have no right to attend the hearing if it would not be in your best interests.

● If the court makes a secure accommodation order, the reasons for doing so and the length of the order must be clearly stated.

● The local authority must appoint at least 3 people, one of whom must be completely independent, to review the placement in secure accommodation within 1 month from its commencement and after that at 3-monthly intervals.

The object of the review is to see whether

○ the original conditions still exist; *and*

○ the placement continues to be necessary; *and*

○ there is a placement somewhere else that would be more suitable.

Your views must be sought and taken into account.

● You have a right to be represented at these reviews by your own *advocate*.

Organisations like ASC, Voice for the Child in Care and Irchin provide this service. Their details are given in Part Three, Where to Go for Information and Help, under heading (P), Children and Young People in Care.

● If you run away from care you cannot be arrested. However, if you are in care as a result of a *care order* and you run away, stay away, go missing or are abducted, an application can be made to the family proceedings court for a *recovery order*.

● This operates as a direction to any person who has you in their care to give you up to the person named in the order or a police officer. It permits you to be removed by the person named in the order or a police officer and entitles the police to enter any premises named in the order and search for you, using reasonable force if necessary.

(g) Complaints

● Local authorities must establish and publicise a procedure for considering representations (including complaints) about the way in which they carry out their duties.

● Complaints can be made by various people, including you if you are being looked after, about any decision that affects you.

You may wish to make a complaint if, for example

- ○ you are not being permitted to visit those people with whom you are allowed to have contact; *or*

- ○ you are staying in a children's home and you are being ill-treated; *or*

- ○ your foster mother is not giving you enough to eat; *or*

- ○ your views are being ignored and you are not being invited to *statutory review meetings*.

● A complaint should be put into writing.

● The complaints procedure must involve a least 1 independent person.

● A complaint should be investigated within 28 days of it being received.

● You should be notified in writing of the result.

● If you are dissatisfied with the result, you have a right, within 28 days of receiving it, to have the complaint referred to a special panel.

You are entitled to attend this meeting and make representations. You must be told of the outcome within 24 hours.

● The local authority must have due regard to the findings and recommendations of those considering the complaint and must inform you of any action it proposes to take in response.

● The local authority is not, however, bound to act on the decision although failure to do so might result in *judicial review* in the High Court *(see Chapter 15, The Courts and the Legal System, heading (b)(4))*.

● In addition, the *Secretary of State for Health* may make an *order declaring the authority to be in default*, where satisfied that it has, without reasonable excuse, failed to comply with any of its duties under the Children Act 1989.

Directions may then be given to ensure that the local authority does comply with the duty within a specified period.

Such directions may be enforced by judicial review.

● A complaint can also be made to the *Local Government Ombudsman (see Chapter 15, The Courts and the Legal System, heading (d))* in certain circumstances. You may also wish to refer the matter to your local councillor or your local MP.

● You should also consider whether your rights under the United Nations Convention on the Rights of the Child and the European Convention on Human Rights have been infringed *(see further Chapter 55)*.

The addresses of the Local Government Ombudsmen for different parts of the country are given in Part Three, Where to Go for Information and Help, under heading (V), Consumer Protection.

Details of various organisations providing assistance to children and young people being looked after with the aim of safeguarding their interests, are also given in Part Three, Where to Go for Information and Help, under heading (P), Children and Young People in Care.

See also Chapter 2, Abuse and Child Protection Procedures; Chapter 10, Care Proceedings; Chapter 11, The Children Act 1989; Chapter 26, Emigrating, Going to Live Abroad and Holidays; Chapter 31, Housing and Homelessness; Chapter 33, Leaving Home and Running Away; Chapter 34, Marriage; Chapter 36, Names; Chapter 38, Parental Responsibility and Decisions About Your Life and Your Upbringing; Chapter 44, Religion; Chapter 47, Social Services and Children in Need. Your right to access to information about you held in social services files is dealt with in Chapter 43, Records and Access to Information, under heading (c).

Chapter 10

The basis for making care orders is the same as for making supervision orders. On an application for a care order, the court may make a supervision order, and on an application for a supervision order, the court may make a care order.

The procedures for making care orders and supervision orders are identical. For convenience, the procedure will be dealt with in this chapter, while Chapter 52 deals with the nature and effect of supervision orders.

(a) What happens in court?

● Only local authorities and the NSPCC can apply for *care orders* and *supervision orders*.

● No *care order* or *supervision order* can be made once you have reached the age of 17, or 16 if you are married.

● Applications are made to the family proceedings court *(see Chapter 15, The Courts and the Legal System, heading (b)(2)).*

● Once the application is made, the court will fix a hearing within a few days.

● At this hearing the court usually decides whether to make an *interim* (ie temporary) *care order*, or an *interim supervision order*, or no order *(see further heading (d) below)*.

● The court will give other directions about what is to happen in the case in the future, such as

   ○ whether it should be transferred to a care centre *(see Chapter 15, heading (b)(3))*;

   ○ what evidence is needed in the case;

   ○ whether all the correct people are parties to the proceedings.

● You and your mother are always parties to the proceedings.

Your father will automatically be a party if your parents are married or divorced, or if your parents are unmarried and your father has *parental responsibility* for you *(see Chapter 38, Parental Responsibility and Decisions About Your Life and Your Upbringing)*.

Fathers who do not have *parental responsibility*, step-parents and other adult family members (for example grandparents, aunts and uncles) and friends can apply to be joined as parties if they have been sufficiently involved in your life and wish to continue playing a part in the future.

● By this stage, you should have a *guardian ad litem* and a solicitor *(see further heading (b) below)*. They are appointed to represent your interests and so it is not necessary for you to actually come to court. You are allowed to attend if you wish to hear what is going on. Older teenagers do sometimes sit in court for some or all of the case if they feel strongly about something.

● The court can make a direction that you should not be present when certain evidence is being given that might upset or distress you.

● It may be some months before the case is ready for a final hearing. In the meantime there will be *directions appointments*, to enable the court to ensure that the case is progressing without delay.

● The final hearing could take a few days if it is a complicated case and there are a large number of parties all of whom wish to give evidence and call their own witnesses, for example social workers, teachers, doctors, psychiatrists and psychologists.

● The *guardian ad litem* will produce a detailed report to the court which should deal with every aspect of your life and contain your views.

● The proceedings are held in private at every stage and members of the public and the press are not allowed into court. The lawyers and the magistrates (or the judge, if the case is transferred) do not wear wigs and gowns. Some courts look more like conference rooms with everyone sitting round a large table.

(b) Your representation – the guardian ad litem and your solicitor

● As soon as care (or supervision) proceedings are started, a *guardian ad litem* will be appointed by the court for you. The *guardian ad litem* is an independent social worker from a specialist panel whose function is to safeguard your best interests and inform the court of your wishes and feelings. *(This is not the same person as the guardian ad litem in civil proceedings; that kind of guardian ad litem is dealt with in Chapter 51, Suing and Being Sued, under heading (b)).*

● The *guardian ad litem* should see you regularly and will make a full investigation into your circumstances. This may include looking at social services' files and your school records, interviewing you, your family and everyone involved with you and your family and seeking opinions from experts, such as a doctor, psychiatrist or psychologist.

● The *guardian ad litem's* report will contain recommendations about what orders would be in your best interests.

● Either the *guardian ad litem* or the court will appoint a solicitor for you who must be a solicitor from the *Law Society's Children Panel* who specialises in this kind of work.

● Your solicitor should do what the *guardian ad litem* thinks is in your best interests. If you have sufficient understanding to be capable of giving *instructions* in relation to the proceedings, in other words you are able to tell your solicitor what you want, decide which parts of the evidence you challenge, make decisions as matters arise, give evidence yourself and be cross-examined, your solicitor should take his or her instructions directly from you.

● If you are capable of giving instructions and you and the *guardian ad litem* disagree about what is in your best interests, the *guardian ad litem* will remain involved in the case but will no longer speak on your behalf.

The court has the final power to decide the question of your understanding.

● An application may be made by one of the parties for you to be medically or psychiatrically examined or otherwise assessed. *Leave* (in other words permission) of the court is required before this can happen. It is not considered desirable for children and young people to be seen by different experts and the court will encourage all the parties to agree on one expert.

If you have sufficient understanding to make an informed decision and do not want this to happen, you can refuse to agree to any examination and/or assessment.

(c) The threshold criteria and 'significant harm'

● The grounds on which *care orders* and *supervision orders* can be made are identical. These are known as the *threshold criteria*.

● Orders can only be made if the court is satisfied that

    ○   you are suffering, or are likely to suffer, 'significant harm'; *and*

    ○   that harm, or the likelihood of it, arises because either

    –   your parents are not capable of caring for you properly; *or*

    –   you are beyond parental control.

● Harm includes

    ○   ill-treatment, including sexual, physical and emotional abuse;

    ○   any damage to your physical or mental health; *and*

    ○   any damage to your physical, intellectual, emotional, social, or behavioural development.

● In order to decide whether any damage to your health or development is significant, the court compares your health or development with that of a similar child or young person.

● Even if the court is satisfied that the *threshold criteria* exist, it must then go on to consider whether a *care order* or a *supervision order* is necessary before making such an order. In reaching a decision, the court must apply the basic principles upon which it must act in every case under the Children Act 1989 *(see further Chapter 11, heading (b))*.

(d) Interim orders

● It takes some time to prepare a case for a final hearing. The court may have to make a decision about where you will live in the meantime.

● If an *interim care order* is made, you will usually be placed with temporary foster parents or in a children's home.

● If an *interim supervision order* is made, you may remain at home.

● It is possible that the court could make a temporary *residence order (see Chapter 11, The Children Act 1989, heading (c)(1))*, for example if you would be out of danger if you went to stay with your grandparents, rather than an *interim care order*, and it is usual for such an order to be coupled with an *interim supervision order*.

● It is also possible, even if the local authority does obtain an *interim care order*, that you could return home or go to stay with your grandparents.

● In order to make an *interim care order* or an *interim supervision order*, the court must be satisfied that there are reasonable grounds for believing that the *threshold criteria* exist.

● The first *interim order* can last up to 8 weeks and the court can make further orders lasting for no more than 4 weeks at a time.

● The rules about contact with family members apply to *interim care orders* in the same way as they do in respect of all children who are being looked after by the local authority *(see further Chapter 9, Care Order and Accommodation – Being Looked After by the Local Authority, heading (d))*.

See also Chapter 2, Abuse and Child Protection Procedures; Chapter 9, Care Orders and Accommodation – Being Looked After by the Local Authority; Chapter 11, The Children Act 1989; Chapter 47, Social Services and Children in Need; Chapter 52, Supervision Orders.

Chapter 11

(a) What the Children Act 1989 is about

For children and young people, the most significant Act of Parliament in modern times is the Children Act 1989 which came into force on 14 October 1991. It is about how you should be brought up and cared for. It rests on the belief that children are generally best looked after within their families with both parents playing a full part and without the courts becoming involved unless there is no alternative. It aims to strike a balance between your right to express your views on decisions about your life, the rights of parents to exercise their responsibilities towards their children and the duty of the state (in other words the courts and the social services department of the local authority) to intervene where your welfare requires it. It encourages co-operation between parents, and between parents and social services, in order to promote the welfare of all children and young people *(see further Chapter 47, Social Services and Children in Need)*. It introduces the new concept of *parental responsibility (this is dealt with in Chapter 38)*. Terms which you may have heard of, such as 'custody', 'care and control' and 'access', are no longer used. Instead, the Children Act 1989 introduces a range of *orders* (in other words instructions saying what must or must not be done).

> These are described under heading (c) below. The particular orders will keep on appearing throughout this book and it will help you to understand other chapters if you are familiar with their meanings.

(b) Principles upon which the courts act

(1) Your welfare is the paramount consideration

● In all decisions to do with your upbringing your welfare is *the court's paramount consideration*. This means that it must be placed above all the other circumstances.

● The court must also apply 2 other important principles

    ○ a decision must be made as quickly as possible; *and*

    ○ an order must not be made unless it is really necessary, and it is positively better for you than making no order at all.

(2) Your right to be heard and other factors

● In both private and public law family cases *(see Chapter 15, The Courts and the Legal System, heading (a) for the distinction)* the court must take into account a list of factors, each of which is equally important. They are

    ○ your wishes and feelings, considered in the light of your age and understanding *(how you have your say in private law family cases is dealt with in Chapter 20, Divorce and Separation, under heading (b), and your representation in public law family cases is dealt with in Chapter 10, Care Proceedings, under heading (b))*;

    ○ your physical, emotional and educational needs;

    ○ the likely effect on you of any change in your circumstances;

    ○ your age, sex, background and any other relevant characteristics you have;

    ○ any harm which you have suffered or are at risk of suffering;

○ the capability of your parents, and any other adults who may be involved, in meeting your needs;

○ the range of powers available to the court.

● The court can also take into account any other circumstances which it considers to be relevant.

(c) The range of orders the courts can make in family cases

(1) Residence orders

These orders decide with whom you will live. It is usual for you to have your main home with one parent (who will be the parent with the *residence order*) and to visit the other parent. If your parents do not live together and you divide your time between your mother's and father's homes, the court can make a *residence order* in favour of both of them, stating how much time you will spend in each household. A *residence order* can be made in favour of an adult other than a parent if you live with them, for example a grandparent. Anyone with a r*esidence order* who doesn't already have *parental responsibility*, obtains it upon the making of the *residence order* while it remains in force *(see Chapter 38, Parental Responsibility and Decisions About Your Life and Your Upbringing)*.

(2) Contact orders

These orders allow you to visit or stay overnight with the parent with whom you don't live, or some other person, and to keep in touch by telephone, letters, cards and presents.

(3) Specific issue orders

These orders enable a particular question to be decided about your upbringing, for example which school you should go to or whether you should receive medical treatment.

(4) Prohibited steps orders

These are orders stopping one of your parents or somebody else from doing something without first obtaining the permission of the court, for example taking you abroad or changing your surname.

These 4 orders are known as *section 8 orders*.

● Generally, they cannot last beyond your 16th birthday.

● A fresh *section 8 order* should not be made after that date unless the circumstances are exceptional, for example severe disability, although an existing order can be varied.

● Parents, whether married, divorced or unmarried, and other adult family members, for example grandparents and step-parents, and friends can apply for *section 8 orders*.

● You, yourself, can apply for a *section 8 order (see further heading (d) below)*.

(5) Care orders

These are orders under which you are placed in the care of the social services department of your local authority. If you are the subject of a *care order*, the local authority will share *parental responsibility* for you with your parents *(see Chapter 38, Parental Responsibility and Decisions About Your Life and Your Upbringing)* and has the power to decide where you will live and to make other decisions about your life and your upbringing. *(Care proceedings are dealt with in Chapter 10; being in care and the consequences of a care order are dealt with in Chapter 9.)*

(6) Supervision orders

These are orders under which you live at home with your parents, or with another adult family member or friend, and you have a social worker to advise, assist and befriend you. The social worker should make regular visits and ensure that you are safe. *(See further Chapter 52, Supervision Orders.)*

These 2 orders are known as *Part IV orders* or *public law orders*

● They can only be made on the application of the local authority or the NSPCC.

● No *care order*, or *supervision order*, can be made once you have reached the age of 17, or 16 if you are married.

(7) Emergency protection orders (EPOs)

Anyone can apply to the court for an EPO which enables a child or young person to be taken somewhere safe or not to be removed from somewhere safe for up to 15 days. The object of an EPO is to prevent real and immediate danger.

(8) Child assessment orders (CAOs)

If a social worker is concerned about you, but it is not an emergency, an application can be made to the court for an assessment of the state of your health and development, or the way in which you have been treated. A CAO lasts for up to 7 days and the court can direct that you live away from home.

(EPOs and CAOs are dealt with in the context of abuse and child protection procedures; see further Chapter 2.)

(d) Making your own application to the court

● You can make your own application to the court for 1 or more of the 4 *section 8* orders described above.

● You must have *leave* (in other words permission) of the court to make the application. To obtain leave the court must be satisfied that you have sufficient understanding to make the proposed application.

Before you launch into an application, you should try, if possible, to discuss the problem with your parents to see whether you can sort it out, or you could approach a sympathetic adult family member or friend to act as a go-between. Court proceedings are stressful and often cause a great deal of bitterness. There are also trained mediators and conciliators who work with families to try and help them to resolve their problems without going to court. Details of organisations that may be able to assist in overcoming a conflict within the family are given in Part Three, Where to Go for Information and Help, under heading (D), Family and Personal (Support and Counselling Services).

● If you really cannot reach an agreement with your parents and the dispute is about something important, the first stage is to find a solicitor. Solicitors specialising in this kind of work are often members of the *Law Society's Children Panel* and/or the *Solicitor's Family Law Association* (SFLA).

You can contact the Law Society and/or the SFLA to help you find a suitable solicitor in your area; their addresses and telephone numbers are given in Part Three, Where to Go for Information and Help, under heading (A), Legal and General.

- The solicitor will then apply for leave of the court. Leave will not be given if it is a minor disagreement, for example your parents will not allow you to stay out past 9 pm or to go on holiday with a friend.

- The case will usually be brought in the High Court *(see Chapter 15, The Courts and the Legal System, heading (b)(4))*.

- The application for leave should be in writing, setting out the grounds for the application. The court may grant the application for leave without a hearing, or may fix a date for all the parties to attend with their lawyers so that the judge can decide whether leave should be given.

- Normally, you require a *next friend* in order to bring the proceedings. The role of the *next friend* is to safeguard your interests. In most cases the *Official Solicitor to the Supreme Court* acts as your *next friend*, but any suitable and willing adult can be a *next friend*. (*This is not the same person as the next friend in civil proceedings; that kind of next friend is dealt with in Chapter 51, Suing and Being Sued, under heading (a).*)

- If you wish to participate directly without a *next friend*, you can do this with leave (in other words permission) of the court.

- Alternatively, you do not need a *next friend* if your solicitor considers that you have sufficient understanding to be capable of giving *instructions* in relation to the proceedings, and has accepted those instructions from you. Being able to give instructions means telling your solicitor what you want, deciding which parts of the evidence you challenge, making decisions as matters arise, giving evidence yourself and being cross-examined.

- The court has the final power to decide the question of your understanding.

- If, during the course of the proceedings, you and the *next friend* disagree about what is in your best interests, you can apply to the court for their removal so that you continue being represented only by your solicitor. The court must grant you leave if you have sufficient understanding to participate as a party in the proceedings without a *next friend*.

See also Chapter 2, Abuse and Child Protection Procedures; Chapter 20, Divorce and Separation; Chapter 26, Emigrating, Going to Live Abroad and Holidays; Chapter 33, Leaving Home and Running Away; Chapter 36, Names; Chapter 38, Parental Responsibility and Decisions About Your Life and Your Upbringing; Chapter 48, Solicitors and Legal Aid; Chapter 56, Wardship.

Chapter 12

(a) Victims of crime

(1) Compensation orders through the criminal courts

● If you have suffered personal injury because of a crime (for example if you have been assaulted or if something belonging to you has been stolen or damaged) and if the offender is prosecuted and convicted, the criminal courts can make a compensation order against him or her in your favour.

● The criminal courts must always consider making a compensation order.

● This does not cover road traffic offences, unless your car was stolen and recovered in a damaged state.

● It is not for you to make the application. The *Crown Prosecution Service* will do it on your behalf.

You should pass on to the police the necessary information, such as receipts for repairing or replacing your property.

● Compensation orders are intended for straightforward cases where there is not a large amount at stake.

The cost of the repair or replacement must be clear before a compensation order can be made.

● There are guidelines as to suggested compensation orders for personal injuries. For instance

Injury	Amount
bruising	up to £75
black eye	£100
cuts	£75–£500, depending on size and whether stitched
loss of a front tooth	£1,000
broken nose	£750–£1,750, depending on whether treatment required

● A compensation order is a separate penalty imposed by the court as well as any other punishment that the offender may receive.

● The court decides the correct level of the compensation order and takes into account the ability of the offender to pay. Therefore if, for example the offender is unemployed and gets income support, the court might not make an order, or may reduce the amount of compensation.

● The offender pays the compensation to you through the court. He or she may be given a period of time to pay, or be ordered to pay in weekly instalments. If he or she is fined and ordered to pay compensation, you will receive the compensation first out of the payments that are made.

See also Chapter 16, Criminal Proceedings, under heading (f), Sentencing and penalties.

(2) The Criminal Injuries Compensation Board (CICB)

An attempt by the government to change the way compensation is paid under this scheme was recently overturned by the House of Lords. There may well be changes in the future. Before making any application, you should check the up to date position at your local Citizens' Advice Bureau, law centre or neighbourhood advice centre.

- The Criminal Injuries Compensation Board is run by the state and pays compensation to people of any age who have suffered physical or mental injury as a direct result of a crime of violence, for example assault, wounding, rape or some other sexual offence.

- The following are not covered
  - injuries outside Great Britain, for example on holiday abroad;
  - minor injuries where the award would be less than £1,000, for example cuts and bruises or sprains where there is no scarring, or temporary shock or distress;
  - injuries caused in accidents;
  - injuries caused by attacks by animals, for example a dog, unless the owner set it on you or it was known to be vicious and the owner failed to control it;
  - injuries caused by motor vehicles, unless the driver deliberately ran you down and has disappeared.

- Victims of domestic violence may be able to obtain compensation.

- It is also possible for children and young people who have suffered physical or sexual abuse within the family to receive compensation. However, if at the time of the incident you and the abuser were living in the same household, the award must not benefit them and it must be in your interests to make the award. The abuser must have been prosecuted unless there are good reasons why this could not happen.

- There does not have to have been a prosecution and a conviction of the person who injured you before an award can be made. As a general rule, you must report the incident yourself to the police as soon as possible afterwards, giving a truthful account of the full circumstances and you must co-operate with any prosecution, although the CICB will not insist on these requirements in the case of children and young people.

- You might not receive an award or the award may be reduced if you were responsible for the incident causing the injury, for instance
  - you were playing a dangerous game (an award was refused where an 11 year old and a 12 year old were firing stones from a catapult and one of them lost an eye);

○ you struck the first blow or provoked the other person, or agreed to take part in a fight, even if they went further (for example you wanted a fist fight and they produced an iron bar).

● An application form must be completed.

● If you are under the age of 18, your parent (or guardian) must make the application on your behalf. If you are the subject of a *care order (see Chapter 11, The Children Act 1989, heading (c)(5))* your social worker will make the application.

● The application form should be returned as soon as possible and within 3 years of the incident causing the injury, although the CICB will be sympathetic in the case of children and young people.

● The CICB then investigates the claim, which will include making enquiries of the police, the hospital and your GP etc.

You may be asked to send photographs or to have your injuries looked at by a member of the Board.

● A member of the Board will decide the application and you will be told of the decision. If it is disallowed you will be given reasons.

● The compensation is assessed in the same way as awards of *damages* by the civil courts in personal injury cases *(see heading (b) below)*.

● The adult acting on your behalf will decide whether to accept the award.

● If the adult is not satisfied with the decision, it is possible to ask for a hearing before at least 2 other members of the Board. This must be done within 3 months of the decision.

● Payment of the award may be made immediately to the adult acting on your behalf or, if it is a large award, it may be invested and managed by the CICB until you are 18.

● In fatal cases where a parent dies from criminal injuries, compensation will be assessed in the same way as under the Fatal Accidents Act 1976 *(see heading (d) below)*.

- The CICB does not pay any legal costs. Full legal aid is not available for applications but a solicitor may be able to help you in preparing the application under the Green Form Scheme *(see further Chapter 48, Solicitors and Legal Aid, heading (b))*.

If you need help in making the claim, you should go to your local Citizens' Advice Bureau, law centre or neighbourhood advice centre, or see a solicitor (but keep in mind that you may have to pay for a solicitor).

The address of the CICB is given in Part Three, Where to Go for Information and Help, under heading (J), Victims of Crime. If you need somebody sympathetic to help you through what may be a very difficult and stressful time, details of organisations providing support to victims of crime are also given under that heading.

(b) Awards of damages by the civil courts

(1) How damages are assessed

It will help you to understand this part of the chapter if you first read Chapter 51, Suing and Being Sued.

- This chapter concentrates on the most common situation in which you are likely to *sue* for *damages* which is for personal injuries caused in an accident or if you have been assaulted. (*Damages for faulty goods and services are dealt with in Chapter 29.*)

- It is important to consider whether or not a person is worth *suing*. Even if they were clearly responsible for the accident in which you were injured, if they do not have any money, they are not going to be able to pay any *damages* that may be awarded against them.

- For this reason, the key question is whether the proposed defendant has insurance. If he or she does have insurance, it will usually be the insurance company that has to pay out.

- If you are injured in a road traffic accident and wish to *sue* the driver for *damages*, you must give the driver's insurance company notice of the proceedings in advance or within 7 days of commencing them.

● Quite often, insurance companies are prepared to reach an agreed *settlement* rather than face the heavy costs of unsuccessfully defending a court action.

● Sometimes cases start, but they *settle* before they actually come to trial or at the door of the court.

● Awards of *damages* in personal injury cases are aimed at restoring the person injured, so far as money can do so, to the position they were in immediately before the accident.

● Awards are itemised under different 'heads'. There is usually a once and for all assessment of the plaintiff's losses, both past and future.

● *Special damages* are designed to compensate for financial losses already suffered, for example

    ○ replacing torn clothing;

    ○ fares to and from hospital;

    ○ treatment costs;

    ○ repairing a damaged vehicle;

    ○ hiring an alternative vehicle whilst yours is being repaired;

    ○ past loss of earnings.

● An estimate will also be made of any loss of earnings likely to arise in the future due to the injury, for example because the injury is such that you cannot work at all, or you can no longer do the job that you used to do, for example a professional footballer who sustains whiplash to his neck in a car accident.

● *General damages* are designed to compensate for pain, suffering and loss of enjoyment of life caused by the injury, for example

    ○ you have to have an operation and must remain in hospital for a period of time;

    ○ you suffer permanent damage, for example facial scarring or loss of teeth;

    ○ troubles develop later on, for example a compound fracture to your leg doesn't heal properly and you experience a nagging pain when walking long distances;

○ you can no longer pursue a hobby you used to enjoy, for example you used to do aerobics but a back injury stops you from bending over.

● *General damages* are assessed by the judge. In making the assessment, the judge will read any medical reports and take into account whether there has been a complete recovery and what the position is likely to be in the future.

Your lawyer will show the judge reports of similar cases where awards have been made in the past, to assist him or her to reach a decision as to the correct level of the award in your particular case.

● Deductions will have to be made in respect of any money that has already been paid to you as a direct result of the accident so that you are not compensated twice over. These deductions may include certain pay outs by private insurance companies, the Motor Insurers' Bureau *(see further heading (c) below)* or the CICB *(see heading (a)(2) above)* and also certain welfare benefits.

● *Damages* may be reduced if you were *contributorily negligent*, in other words where the accident was partly your own fault.

● There is also a rule that you must *mitigate your losses*. For example

○ if your car was damaged and has to be repaired, you can hire a car whilst it is in the garage but, in order to recover the full hire costs, the car hired must be of a similar make, model and age to your own, you must have your car repaired as soon as possible and you cannot hire for an unduly long period. For example, the owner of a 10 year old Ford Escort which will take 2 weeks to repair cannot hire a Rolls Royce for 3 months and expect the defendant to pay;

○ you must not make your injuries worse, for example if you have hurt your back and your doctor tells you to rest in bed but instead you go out dancing and you slip a disc. You will get less by way of *general damages* than if you had followed the doctor's advice.

● It can take some time for a case to come to court and, accordingly, any award will usually include interest to allow for inflation.

In cases of severe injuries, where there is an urgent need for money, the court can make an immediate award which will be taken into account when the final award is decided.

(2) What happens to damages?

● The general rule is that the loser pays the winner's legal costs, but the amount that he or she is ordered to pay may be less than your actual legal costs. Accordingly, it is possible that some *damages* may be used to pay part of your costs. This can happen both where you are paying your solicitor privately and also if you are legally aided (because of the operation of the *statutory charge, see further Chapter 48, Solicitors and Legal Aid, heading (b)*).

● Damages, and any costs, should be paid to your solicitor who should pay them over to you *(but see further below)* after any deductions in respect of costs.

● If you are under the age of 18 the proceedings must have been brought through you *next friend (see Chapter 51, Suing and Being Sued, heading (a))* and the *next friend* will consider any offer that is made to *settle* the case.

● If the case does *settle* the court must approve the terms of the *settlement*.

● If you are under the age of 18 any damages that you recover won't be paid out to you or your *next friend*, but will be invested in a special account until you have reached 18.

● The court can make a special direction that you should receive the money immediately, for example if it is a relatively small sum and it would benefit you to have it now.

(c) The Motor Insurers' Bureau (MIB)

● The MIB operates a scheme for compensating people who suffer personal injury as a result of certain road traffic accidents, and also the relatives of those who are killed in similar accidents.

● If you are the victim of an accident caused by a hit and run driver, you can apply direct to the MIB for compensation.

- If the accident was caused by a driver who should have had *third party insurance* but was not actually insured *(the requirement of insurance is dealt with in Chapter 22, Driving, under heading (c))*, the MIB will satisfy any unsatisfied judgement for *damages* obtained in your favour.

This will include any element for loss of, or damage to, your property (apart from the first £175).

You must sue the driver in the normal way.

You must give the MIB notice of the proceedings in advance, or within 7 days of commencing them.

> The address of the MIB is given in Part Three, Where to Go for Information and Help, under heading (U), Accidents.
>
> If you do have an accident you should go to your local Citizens' Advice Bureau, law centre or neighbourhood advice centre, or see a solicitor, without delay.
>
> Details of the Law Society's Accident Line are given in Part Three, Where to Go for Information and Help, under heading (U), Accidents.
>
> You should also read Part Four, Making the Law Work for You, heading (4), which deals with personal injuries.

(d) Claims if one of your parents is killed

- The Fatal Accidents Act 1976 allows a claim for *damages* to be made on behalf of the dependents of a person killed in an accident against the person responsible.

- *Damages* are designed to compensate those people who used to rely on the deceased person to support them financially.

- The court will make one award in respect of all the dependents, for example you, your surviving parent and any brothers or sisters, and then direct how it should be divided up between you.

- If you are under the age of 18 the rule that any *settlement* requires the approval of the court applies. The rules are also the same in relation to what happens to *damages (see further heading (b)(2) above)*.

See also Chapter 3, Accidents and Negligence; Chapter 48, Solicitors and Legal Aid; Chapter 51, Suing and being Sued. Accidents at school are dealt with in Chapter 25, under heading (i); accidents at work are dealt with in Chapter 58, under heading (f).

Chapter 13

It will help you to understand this chapter if you first read Chapter 35, Medical Treatment, headings (a) and (b) which deal with your say in decisions, your consent and confidentiality.

● This is an area of the law that is still changing and developing. Over recent years it has been recognised by the medical profession and by the judges that young people should be able to have a say in medical decisions and treatment affecting their bodies, and to make up their own minds. Where they are considered to have sufficient maturity and intelligence to understand what is involved, their choices will often prevail over what their parents want for them.

● Once a girl is 16 she is entitled to advice about contraceptives and to be prescribed any method of contraception appropriate to her needs without her parents' knowledge and consent (the same applies for boys).

● A girl under the age of 16 cannot lawfully consent to sexual intercourse although she herself will not be committing any criminal offence if she does have sexual intercourse below this age.

- A girl (or a boy) who is under the age of 16 and who is sexually active can receive contraceptive advice and supplies at the doctor's discretion.

- The relevant guidelines advise doctors that before giving contraceptive advice and supplies to a girl who is under the age of 16, they should normally try to obtain her agreement to telling her parents. However, if the girl is not willing to involve her parents, she is likely to have sexual intercourse with or without protection and she is capable of understanding what is proposed, the doctor should not inform her parents and need not have their consent.

- Parents cannot obtain a court order to prevent doctors from giving contraceptive advice and supplies to girls under the age of 16 without their parents' knowledge and consent.

- Anyone can buy condoms over the counter in chemists and some supermarkets and late night shops.

> Wearing a condom helps protect against unwanted pregnancy, and also infection from HIV and other sexually transmitted diseases.
> If you wish to receive contraceptive advice and supplies, see Part Three, Where to Go for Information and Help, under heading (E), Abortion and Contraception.

See also Chapter 1, Abortion; Chapter 38, Parental Responsibility and Decisions About Your Life and Your Upbringing; Chapter 45, Sexual Intercourse.

Chapter 14

Are you bound by them?

● In general terms, a contract is an agreement between 2 people where something of value changes hands in return for the payment of money. An obvious example is buying something from a shop.

● A contract does not need to be in writing in order to be binding.

● Until you have reached the age of 18, with 2 exceptions, the law does not consider you to be capable of making a contract and you are not bound by your side of the contract. If you break it, you cannot be *sued* in a civil court to enforce it, and nor can your parents, unless you entered into the contract on their behalf or one of them is a *guarantor (see below)*.

● You are also not legally responsible for your debts. This does not mean that you can just keep what you have acquired without paying for it – the other person can apply to the court for the return of the goods.

● The 2 exceptions are

○ contracts for necessaries, which include things you actually need, such as food, clothing and accommodation, but not luxury items such as stereos.

in this situation, the contract as a whole must be for your benefit and you are bound to pay a reasonable price for the item;

○ contracts of employment, or apprenticeship, that benefit you in the future, but you will not be bound if the contract is not favourable to you.

● Shopkeepers and others may refuse to enter into contracts with you except if you pay cash in advance or they may insist that one of your parents acts as a *guarantor*, in other words they agree to pay if you do not.

● If you are under the age of 18 and you make a contract with an adult, they are bound by their side of the contact.

See also Chapter 8, Borrowing Money, Getting Credit Cards and Making Hire Purchase Agreements; Chapter 29, Goods and Services; Chapter 51, Suing and Being Sued.

Chapter 15

THE COURTS AND THE LEGAL SYSTEM

(a) Criminal, civil and family law

● There are laws about practically every aspect of people's lives which attempt to regulate how people should lead their lives.

● *Criminal law* is to do with the protection of the public from those who break the law by committing criminal offences, such as murder, rape or theft. The law sets out the behaviour that can amount to a criminal offence and the punishments that can be imposed upon offenders by the courts.

● The technical term for facing criminal proceedings is *prosecution.* If you admit the offence or it is proved against you this is called a *conviction (see further Chapter 16, Criminal Proceedings).*

● *Civil law* is every other area of the law that isn't criminal law.

Civil law has many different branches, including the law of *torts* (*torts* are civil wrongs, such as negligence, nuisance and trespass), contract law, family law and education law.

An important part of civil law is to do with resolving disputes between people.

● The technical term for bringing a civil action is *suing (see further Chapter 51, Suing and Being Sued).*

● The civil courts may order one person to pay compensation to another person called an *award of damages*, for example if you are injured in an accident *(see further Chapter 12, heading (b)).*

● The civil courts may also make orders called *injunctions* to prevent certain types of behaviour, for example assault and trespass.

● Sometimes, the same conduct may be a criminal offence and a *tort*, for example if you are assaulted. Some aspects of civil law may also have criminal consequences, for example a parent who fails to provide a child of compulsory school age with a proper education.

● *Family Law* is a branch of civil law that may frequently concern you because part of family law has to do with matters affecting your life and your upbringing.

● The courts can become involved to sort out problems relating to children and young people in *private law family cases,* for example, where you should live if your parents divorce or separate *(see further Chapter 20, Divorce and Separation)* and in *public law family cases*, for example if it is not considered safe for you to remain at home and the social services department of your local authority applies for a *care order (see further Chapter 10, Care Proceedings; Chapter 52, Supervision Orders).*

(b) The courts

(1) The youth court

● Criminal cases are normally dealt with in your local youth court which is part of the *magistrates' court*, and not by a judge and jury (juries sit in the *Crown Court*, which only hears adult cases, other than particularly serious charges against people under the age of 18).

● Magistrates are ordinary men and women from the local community who are not paid for what they do. They are not legally qualified but they receive special training and they are advised on the law by their *clerk*, who usually sits near them.

- At least 2 magistrates must hear the case and there will normally be 3 of them. Some courts have *stipendiary* magistrates, who are qualified lawyers and are paid. In the youth court *stipendiaries* usually sit with 2 lay magistrates.

- The handling of prosecutions is usually the responsibility of the *Crown Prosecution Service* (CPS).

(2) The family proceedings court

- This is another part of the magistrates' court. Certain magistrates receive additional special training so that they can hear family cases.

- Public law family cases start in the family proceedings court, but if there are difficult issues involved or the case is likely to take some time, it will be transferred to a care centre (*see below*).

(3) The county court

- Civil actions are normally dealt with in your local county court by a judge without a jury.

- County courts hear most cases unless the sum of money claimed is very large or the issues raised are very complicated. In these situations the case will be heard in the High Court.

- Some county courts are *divorce county courts* and *family hearing centres* and they deal with all aspects of private law cases, for example, if your parents divorce or separate, where you will live and who you will see. They also deal with adoption cases (*see further Chapter 4*) and have the power to grant protection to victims of domestic violence (*see further Chapter 21*).

- Some county courts are also *care centres* and they deal with public law family cases involving difficult issues or likely to last more than 3 days.

(4) The High Court

- The High Court hears civil actions where a large sum of money is claimed and/or the issues raised are very complicated.

- The High Court has a *Family Division* which hears the really difficult public and private law family cases and those in which you are making your own application to the court (*see further Chapter 11, The Children Act 1989, heading (d)*) as well as *Wardship* cases (*see further Chapter 56*).

Again, there will be a judge, but no jury.

An appeal made from a decision of a family proceedings court will be dealt with in the High Court.

● The High Court also has a power called *judicial review*. This concerns the way in which public bodies and government departments, including the social services and housing departments of local authorities and local education authorities, exercise their powers and make decisions.

● In applications for *judicial review*, an attempt is made to challenge a particular decision on the basis that it was not properly taken, for example the public body or department did not act in good faith or fairly, or took into account something irrelevant, or ignored something relevant, or approached the decision by way of a fixed policy instead of considering the case on an individual basis.

● The usual rule is that applications for judicial review must be made within 3 months of the decision in question and, generally, will only be heard if all other available methods of challenging the decision have been followed. For example

○ before applying to *judicially review* the social services department of a local authority for failing to provide services for children in need, a complaint should usually be made *(see further Chapter 47)*;

○ decisions of local education authorities in relation to admission to particular state schools, cannot be *judicially reviewed* until after an appeal has been made to the local *education appeal committee (see further Chapter 25, heading (b))*.

● The High Court may make an order *quashing* (in other words overturning) the decision, and/or require the public body or department to make a different decision and/or prohibit it from acting in a particular way.

(5) The Court of Appeal

● The Court of Appeal hears all appeals where there is a right of appeal in criminal and civil cases. There is a right of appeal where there are issues of law or a mixture of issues of law and issues of fact, but not where there are only issues of fact.

There will usually be 3 judges sitting to decide the case.

(6) The House of Lords

● The House of Lords is the final appeal court in all cases.

Ordinarily, the House of Lords will only hear cases in which there is a point of law of general public importance.

There will usually be 5 judges sitting to decide the case.

(c) Tribunals

● Tribunals are similar to courts in that they make decisions but they are less formal in their procedures.

Tribunals have been established to deal with newly developing areas of the law such as employment *(industrial tribunals are dealt with in Chapter 58, Working, under heading (i))*, welfare benefits and education.

They are intended to be cheaper and quicker than courts. Each type of tribunal has its own rules about its composition and the procedures it follows.

● Full legal aid is not available for tribunal hearings, but a solicitor may be able to assist you in preparing the application under the *Green Form Scheme (see further Chapter 48, Solicitors and Legal Aid, heading (b))*.

You can pay privately for your own solicitor to represent you at the hearing or, alternatively, you are allowed to be represented by a worker from a law centre, a trade union official or a friend.

● The *Council on Tribunals* has a general duty to supervise all tribunals, such as industrial tribunals, special educational needs tribunals, social security appeal tribunals and other bodies such as education appeal committees and housing benefit review boards. It can deal with general complaints about their constitution and operation, but has no power to intervene in individual cases.

(d) Ombudsmen

● Ombudsmen are appointed to look into unfair treatment and abuses of power by government departments and various other public bodies to decide whether you have suffered injustice caused by *maladministration*.

● Anybody can complain and it is free. Ombudsmen are completely independent.

● If they find that the complaint is justified, ombudsmen can recommend a solution to the problem and make awards of compensation.

However, you may not find the relevant ombudsman of much assistance to you as the work they do is of limited scope.

Details of the Council on Tribunals and the various ombudsmen are given in Part Three, Where to Go for Information and Help, under heading (V), Consumer Protection.

Chapter 16

The powers of the police and your rights are dealt with in Chapter 40.

(a) Criminal responsibility

- The age of criminal responsibility in this country is 10.

If you are under the age of 10 you are treated as incapable of committing a criminal offence and you cannot be prosecuted.

- A child under the age of 10 who keeps on getting into trouble with the police can be made the subject of a *care order (see Chapter 11, The Children Act 1989, heading (c)(5))* or a *supervision order (see Chapter 11, heading (c)(6))* by a family court, if he or she is suffering, or likely to suffer, 'significant harm' because of being beyond parental control *(see further Chapter 10, Care Proceedings and Chapter 52, Supervision Orders).*

- If you are aged 10 or over, but have not yet reached 14, you can only be convicted of a criminal offence if the prosecution are able to prove that you know right from wrong. It must be shown that you actually appreciated at the time that what you were doing was seriously wrong and not just naughty or mischievous and you can be asked direct questions about your knowledge. Doing the act which is a criminal offence and running away from the police may not be enough.

● Once you are 14 you have full criminal responsibility for your actions in the same way as an adult.

(b) Cautions

● If you are caught doing something you shouldn't be doing and it is of a trivial nature, you will probably receive an unofficial telling off from the police officer on the spot. That will be the end of the matter.

● Even if you have committed a more serious offence, instead of being taken to court, you could receive a formal caution at the police station *(this is not the same thing as the caution that the police must give you on arrest before they interview you (see further Chapter 40, The Police: Their Powers and Your Rights) and on charging you (see further heading (c) below))*.

● You are likely to be offered a caution if the offence is not very serious and you have never been in trouble with the police before. It is widely felt that it does more harm than good for children and young people to enter into the criminal justice system and the hope is that you will have learned your lesson by being cautioned.

● You and your parents (or guardian) will be told to go to the police station where a senior uniformed police officer will give you an official warning to the effect that although the matter will be taken no further on this occasion, you should not do it again and if you do you are likely to have to go to court.

● Unlike a conviction by a court, a caution does not give you a criminal record *(see further Chapter 43, Records and Access to Information, heading (a))*. However, a record will be made of the fact that you have been cautioned and if you commit any further offences, it may be referred to in court and taken into account when sentencing you.

- Before you can be cautioned
  - the police must have enough evidence to prove the case against you; *and*
  - you must admit the offence; *and*
  - you and your parents (or guardian) must agree to your being cautioned.

- If you have a good defence you should not accept a caution. Your position can be a difficult one because if you don't accept the caution, you may be prosecuted and you run the risk of getting a criminal record.

If you are in any doubt, you should get legal advice before agreeing to a caution.

(c) Being prosecuted

(1) Summonses

- For more minor criminal offences and most road traffic offences, which are not arrestable offences *(see Chapter 40, The Police: Their Powers and Your Rights, heading (b))* the police may take out a summons against you.

- You must be warned at the time or within 14 days that you may be prosecuted. A summons will be sent to you in the post at a later stage.

- Many police forces have a *Juvenile Bureau* and, even in respect of more serious criminal offences, the matter may be referred to the Bureau for a decision to be taken about prosecution. If the Bureau decides to prosecute, they will apply for a summons.

- Generally, the police have 6 months from the date of the offence to go before a magistrate or a magistrates' clerk to ask for a summons to be issued.

- A summons is a document requiring you to attend a particular court. It tells you the date, time and name and address of the court you have to attend. The summons contains details of the offence you are accused of having committed.

(2) Charges

● In respect of more serious criminal offences, if you have been arrested and detained at the police station and the custody officer decides that there is sufficient evidence, you will generally be charged.

● The charge will be read out to you and you will be cautioned, in other words told that you need not say anything in reply. The new words of the caution are

'You do not have to say anything. But it may harm your defence if you do not mention now something which you later rely on in court. Anything you do say may be given in evidence.'

● Once you have been charged, normally, you should not be asked any further questions.

● You will receive a charge sheet which tells you the date, time and name and address of the court you have to attend. The charge sheet contains the details of the offence you are accused of having committed.

● Following a charge you should normally be released from the police station and will be given bail to attend a particular court, on a particular date and at a particular time. Bail may be refused in certain circumstances *(see further heading (e) below).*

(3) Which court?

● If you are under the age of 18 the case against you will normally be dealt with in your local youth court *(see further heading (d) below).* It is only in the Crown Court that there is trial by jury. Very serious charges against adults must be dealt with in the Crown Court and fairly minor offences must be dealt with in the magistrates' court. In respect of most offences in between, adults have the right to choose whether to be tried by a judge and jury in the Crown Court or for their case to remain in the magistrates' court. You do not have this choice.

● If you are facing a charge of murder or manslaughter, your case must be dealt with in the Crown Court.

● If you are aged 10 or over and you are charged with a *grave crime* for which an adult may be punished with more than 14 years imprisonment, the youth court can send you to the Crown Court to be tried.

The Crown Court has power to order your long-term detention. The youth court decides whether to deal with the case or send it to the Crown Court *(see further heading (f) below)*.

● If you are jointly charged with somebody aged 18 or over, you will both appear in the adult magistrates' court. If the court and the adult agree that the case should be dealt with in the magistrates' court and you both plead not guilty your trial will be heard there. If you plead guilty or are found guilty, you will be sent to the youth court for sentence unless you are discharged or fined *(see further heading (f) below)*. If the case is one that the court or the adult decides should be heard in the Crown Court, you could be sent there too or sent to the youth court.

● If your 18th birthday occurs after you have been charged, but before you have entered a plea of guilty or not guilty, and if the charge carries with it the right to choose trial by judge and jury in the Crown Court, you can choose to have your case dealt with in this way. Otherwise you will be dealt with in the adult magistrates' court.

(d) What happens in the youth court?

See generally Chapter 15, The Courts and the Legal System, under heading (b)(1).

● The youth court deals with offenders aged 10 to 17 inclusive.

● You must attend court on the date and at the time shown on the summons or charge sheet. If you do not, the court could issue a warrant for your arrest.

● The proceedings are more informal than in an adult court. Nobody wears wigs and gowns, you will be called by your first name and you will be asked if you admit or deny the offence, rather than whether you plead guilty or not guilty. If you give evidence, you make a promise to tell the truth, rather than swearing to tell the truth, and this applies to all other witnesses even if they are adults.

● The youth court is not open to the public. Any newspaper, television or radio report must not give your name, address or the name of your school, or any other information that may identify you, and no picture of you may be published, without the permission of the court.

● If you are under the age of 16, you must be accompanied at all stages by a parent (or guardian) or social worker (if you are being looked after by the local authority, *see generally Chapter 9*). If no suitable adult attends with you, the case is likely to be put off to another day. The adult comes into court with you and sits next to you or behind you.

● When your case is called on, you will be told to stand in front of the magistrates and to stay standing until you are told to sit down.

● You will be asked by the magistrates' *clerk* to confirm your name, address and age, and the charge will be read to you.

● If you are not ready, for example if you have not had an opportunity to see a solicitor, you can ask for the case to be put off to another day. This is called an *adjournment*.

● You will be asked if you admit or deny the offence. Your lawyer will advise you what you should do.

● It is for the prosecution to prove the case against you beyond reasonable doubt. You are innocent until you are proved guilty and, generally, the magistrates are not told about any previous convictions and/or cautions you may have until after the trial.

● If you deny the offence, it is likely that the case will be adjourned to enable the prosecution to bring their witnesses to court.

● At the trial, the prosecution lawyer will begin by briefly telling the magistrates what the case is about and then call the prosecution witnesses to give evidence. Your lawyer will have the opportunity to challenge each of them by *cross-examination*, in other words asking them questions.

● You will have the opportunity to give evidence and state your version of events. You can be cross-examined by the prosecution lawyer. Any witnesses you have will be called to give evidence.

● Your lawyer will then make a speech to the magistrates on your behalf. The prosecution lawyer may reply if there is an argument on a point of law.

● The magistrates will then leave the court to make their decision. When they return you should stay standing until after they have given their decision.

● If the charge is not proved you will be free to leave.

● If the charge is proved, or if you admitted it, the magistrates will sentence you.

● It is up to the court to decide the appropriate punishment you will receive subject to the maximum penalties for the offence laid down by Parliament.

● If you admit the offence there is no need for a trial. The prosecution lawyer will give the magistrates an outline of the details of the offence. At this stage he or she will tell them about any previous findings of guilt called *convictions* and/or cautions you may have and may make applications for costs and *compensation (see further heading (f) below)*.

● Your lawyer will tell the magistrates all about why you committed the offence and anything else that is relevant about you so as to try and persuade the magistrates to give you a light sentence.

● The magistrates will take into account the nature and seriousness of what you did. They will consider any circumstances that make the particular offence more serious, for example if you used a weapon to assault another person or if you stole from your employer, and any circumstances that make it less serious, for example if the other person provoked you into assaulting them or if you stole something from a shop on the spur of the moment.

● If you pleaded guilty early, the magistrates will take this into account and you will receive credit for this, in other words the sentence will be less severe.

● The magistrates will also consider your character and personal circumstances. These include whether you have any previous convictions and/or cautions, how you have responded to previous sentences, your educational or career prospects for the future, whether there are any problems within your family and the likelihood of your offending again.

● You are likely to get a more lenient sentence if it is your first offence, if you admitted it at the earliest opportunity and if you gave assistance to the police, for example to recover a stash of radio/cassette players stolen from cars.

● The magistrates may deal with you then and there but, if they want to know more about you, or if they think that the case is serious enough to justify a community sentence or a custodial sentence *(see further heading (f) below)*, they will adjourn the case for a *pre-sentence report* to be made on you by a social worker if you are under the age of 13 or by a probation officer if you are aged 13 or over.

● A pre-sentence report assists the magistrates to decide the most suitable method of dealing with you and contains full information about the offence and about you. The person making the report will interview you, and may visit your home and speak to members of your family, and may seek a report from your school. They will propose the sentence that they consider to be the most appropriate one for you.

● You may be able to appeal against the *conviction* and/or against any sentence you receive if it is too severe in all the circumstances. Your lawyer will advise you about this.

You should also read Part Four, Making the Law Work for You, heading (5), which deals with criminal proceedings.

(e) Bail

● Bail means not being deprived of your freedom until such time as the case is finally decided.

● Following arrest, if a decision has not been taken whether to charge you, you may be released on bail to return to the police station at a later date once further investigations have been made.

If you fail to do so, you can be arrested.

- Once you have been charged with an offence you must be released on bail to appear in court at a later date unless there are exceptional circumstances *(see further below)*.

- In both of these situations the custody officer may impose conditions on your bail if they are necessary to ensure that you

  - answer to your bail; *or*

  - do no commit an offence while on bail; *or*

  - do not interfere with witnesses or obstruct justice.

- The sorts of conditions that can be imposed include

  - that a parent or another responsible adult stands as *surety*, in other words they agree that if you do not turn up they will have to pay a certain sum of money;

  - that you live and sleep at a particular address;

  - a curfew, in other words you must be indoors between certain hours;

  - that you must not go to a particular place;

  - that you do not have any contact with the victim and/or any witnesses.

- The conditions of your bail will be sent out on your charge sheet.

- You can apply to vary any of these conditions by applying

  - to the original or another custody officer at the same police station; *or*

  - to the youth court.

The conditions can be removed or altered or different conditions imposed.

- Following charge, the custody officer has power to refuse bail in certain situations, for instance

  - if you refuse to give your name and address or give false details; *or*

  - there are reasonable grounds for believing that you will fail to appear at court (for example you do not have a permanent home or have failed to attend in the past); *or*

○ there are reasonable grounds for believing that detention is necessary

– to prevent a further offence (where you have been arrested for an offence for which an adult may be imprisoned); *or*

to prevent injury to another person or loss of or damage to property (where you have been arrested for a non-imprisonable offence); *or*

– to prevent you from interfering with the administration of justice or the investigation of an offence; *or*

– for your own protection; *or*

○ if you are under the age of 17, if there are reasonable grounds for believing that you ought to be detained in your own interests.

● If you have been refused bail and you are under the age of 17, you must not be kept in a cell but should be transferred to local authority accommodation (usually a children's home) except where

○ this is not practical; *or*

○ you have reached the age of 15 and it appears that local authority accommodation would not be adequate to protect the public from serious harm from you (the age is shortly to be reduced to 12).

● You must be brought before the youth court as soon as possible, for example later the same day or first thing the following morning (except if this is a Sunday or public holiday, when it will be the day after).

● Once you have been brought before the youth court you have a right to bail between hearings except if you are charged with murder, attempted murder, manslaughter, rape or attempted rape and you have a previous conviction for such an offence.

● You need not be granted bail if the offence is one which the Crown Court could hear if you were an adult and at the date of the offence you were already on bail for another offence. This does not apply to offences which cannot be heard in the Crown Court such as threatening behaviour or taking a motor vehicle without the owner's consent.

- The court may refuse bail if satisfied that
  - there are substantial grounds for believing that you will
    - fail to appear at court; *or*
    - commit an offence while on bail; *or*
    - interfere with witnesses or obstruct the course of justice; *or*
  - you should be detained for your own welfare.

- You may be granted bail with conditions similar to those that can be imposed by a custody officer.

- If the offence is one which the Crown Court could hear if you were an adult, the prosecution can apply to have your bail taken away or for conditions to be imposed if new information has come to light since you were bailed.

- If you are not granted bail, you should be *remanded*, in other words sent to
  - local authority accommodation (usually a children's home) if you are under the age of 17;
  - a *remand centre* if you are aged 17 or over but have not yet reached 21;
  - boys of 15 or 16 can be sent to a remand centre if
    - they are charged with a violent or sexual offence or an offence for which an adult may be punished with more than 14 years imprisonment; *or*
    - they have a history of running away while remanded to local authority accommodation and committing imprisonable offences;

      and

    - it is necessary to protect the public from serious harm from them.

Under new rules yet to come into force, boys who have reached the age of 12 but are not yet 17 who fulfil these conditions may be remanded to *secure accommodation* provided by the local authority.

- If you are granted bail and fail to turn up in court, a warrant may be issued for your arrest.

You may also be committing a further criminal offence.

(f) Sentencing and penalties

The youth court has the power to impose various sentences depending on the seriousness of the offence and also your age. In the list that follows, if no minimum age is shown you should assume that the sentence can be used on you at any age over 10 (before you are 10 you cannot commit a criminal offence and so it follows that you cannot be sentenced).

(1) Absolute discharge

● Although you have been convicted of the offence, if the court feels that you are only technically guilty and it is such a small matter that it is not necessary to punish you, you can be given an absolute discharge. This means that no penalty is imposed.

(2) Conditional discharge

● For minor matters, where the court feels that you deserve to be given a chance, you can be conditionally discharged. You will not be punished for the offence at the time but, if you commit another offence within a set period of up to 3 years, you will be dealt with for both the original and the later offences.

(3) Binding over

● This is a written promise to keep the peace and be of good behaviour for a set period, usually up to a year although the maximum period is 3 years. If you break your promise you will have to pay a fixed sum of money.

If you are aged 10 or over, but have not yet reached 14, the maximum sum is £250.

If you are aged 14 or over, but have not yet reached 18, the maximum sum is £1,000.

● In any case where you are under the age of 16 and are sentenced for an offence, your parents can be bound over to take proper care of you or to exercise proper control over you so as to prevent you from re-offending for up to 3 years (or until you are 18, if that is sooner).

(4) A fine

● This is an amount of money that you pay to the court.

● If you are aged 10 or over, but have not yet reached 14, the maximum fine is presently £250 unless a lower maximum is laid down for the offence by Parliament.

If you are aged 14 or over, but have not yet reached 18, the maximum fine is presently £1,000, unless a lower maximum is laid down for the offence by Parliament.

● The court fixes the correct level of the fine according to the seriousness of the offence and how much money you have. You may be given time to pay or ordered to pay in instalments.

● If you are under the age of 16 your parents will be ordered to pay your fine unless it would be unreasonable.

● If you are aged 16 or 17 your parents can be ordered to pay your fine.

(5) Compensation orders

● If you cause personal injury or loss of, or damage to, property, you can be ordered to pay compensation of up to £5,000 to the victim of your crime as well as, or instead of, any other sentence.

● The court must always consider making a compensation order although it may not make one if you do not have any money, and your actual ability to pay must be taken into account.

● If you are under the age of 16 your parents will be ordered to pay your compensation unless it would be unreasonable.

● If you are aged 16 or 17 your parents can be ordered to pay your compensation

---

See also Chapter 12, Compensation, heading (a)(1), Victims of crime, Compensation orders through the criminal courts.

---

(6) Community sentences

● These are, or include, one or more community orders, being

○ attendance centre orders;

- ○ supervision orders;

- ○ probation orders;

- ○ community service orders;

- ○ combination orders.

● Before making a community sentence the court must be of the opinion that

- ○ the offence alone, or combined with another associated offence, is serious enough; *and*

- ○ it is the most suitable way of dealing with you.

● If you do not obey the terms of a community sentence you can be brought back to court and dealt with in various ways which include a fine or having the sentence revoked and another sentence imposed, which could be a detention in a young offender institution if you are aged 15 or over *(see further below)*.

(7) Attendance centre order

● You are usually ordered to go to an attendance centre for 2 hours on alternate Saturday afternoons. The idea is that you should give up some of your leisure time. Attendance centres are normally run by the police and you do things like physical exercise or craft work.

● If you are aged 10 or over, but have not yet reached 16, the maximum number of hours is 24.

● If you are aged 16 or over, but have not yet reached 21, the maximum number of hours is 36 .

● If you are aged 14 or over, the minimum number of hours is 12.

● The offence must be punishable with imprisonment in the case of an adult.

● There must be an attendance centre available locally before an order can be made.

(8) Supervision order

● This is an order placing you under the supervision of a local authority social worker for not more than 3 years.

● Your consent is not required before the order can be made.

- The duty of the supervisor is to advise, assist and befriend you.

- You must keep in touch with your supervisor and allow him or her to visit you.

- The order may include requirements that you live with a named person and comply with directions given to you by your supervisor for *intermediate treatment* for up to 90 days. The supervisor can require you to live in a particular place or take part in particular activities, for example attend residential or day training courses.

- The court itself can impose similar requirements upon you, and also prevent you from going out at night or participating in certain activities, such as going to football matches. These requirements can only be made with your parents' consent if you are under the age of 14, or with your consent if you are aged 14 or over.

- If you commit a serious offence during the period of the supervision order and your offending is due to your home circumstances you can be ordered to live in local authority accommodation for up to 6 months.

(9) Probation order

- This is an order placing you under the supervision of a probation officer for between 6 months and 3 years.

- You must be aged 16 or over.

- Your consent is required before the order can be made.

- This must be seen as a suitable way to try and stop you from getting into trouble again.

- Probation is similar to supervision and you must keep in touch with your probation officer and keep any appointments.

- Requirements can be attached to a probation order, for example to live in a probation hostel, to attend a probation centre for up to 60 days, to undergo treatment for drug or alcohol dependency or to receive treatment from a psychologist or psychiatrist.

(10) Community service order

- This is an order that you perform unpaid work in the community for between 40 and 240 hours

- You must be aged 16 or over.

- The offence must be punishable with imprisonment in the case of an adult.

- Your consent is required before the order can be made.

- You must be suitable to do the work. It is not regarded as a soft option.

- The exact number of hours you will work each week and the nature of the work will depend upon what is available locally. It must not interfere with your school, college or job.

(11) Combination order

- If you are sentenced to both probation and community service, the probation must be for 1 to 3 years and the community service must be for 40 to 100 hours.

(12) Custodial sentence

- If you receive a custodial sentence, you will be deprived of your freedom for a certain period.

- You cannot be given a custodial sentence unless you refuse to consent to a community sentence or the court is of the opinion that

  o the offence alone, or combined with another associated offence, is so serious that only such a sentence is justified; *or*

  o the offence is a violent or sexual offence and only such a sentence is adequate to protect the public from serious harm from you.

- You cannot be sent to prison until you are 21 but, if you are aged 15 or over, you can be detained in a young offender institution *(see further below)*.

- You cannot receive a suspended sentence until you are 21.

- If you commit murder, you will be detained during Her Majesty's pleasure, in other words without a time limit.

- The Crown Court has power to order your long-term detention in certain circumstances, for instance

  o if you are aged 10 or over and you are convicted of a grave crime for which an adult may be punished with imprisonment of 14 years of more (for example robbery, rape, possession of a class A drug with intent to supply or burglary of a house or flat), or indecent assault on a woman;

○ if you are aged 14 or over and you are convicted of causing death by dangerous driving or death by careless driving while affected by drink or drugs.

● Only the Crown Court has this power, not the youth court if it deals with you for one of these offences. The only custodial sentence that the youth court can impose is detention in a young offender institution.

(13) Detention in a young offender institution

● You must be aged 15 or over.

● The offence must be punishable with imprisonment in the case of an adult.

● If you are under the age of 18 the minimum period of detention is 2 months.

● The maximum sentence that a youth court can impose is 6 months for 1 offence or 12 months for 2 or more offences.

● The youth court can send certain offenders to the Crown Court for sentence as the Crown Court has power to impose a sentence of detention in a young offender institution of up to 2 years even if the offender is under 18.

● With sentences of 12 months or under, you are automatically entitled to be released after serving half your sentence (this is called 'remission' or 'early release').

(14) Destruction order

● If you are convicted of offences such as possessing controlled drugs or offensive weapons, the court can order these to be destroyed.

(15) Exclusion order

● Exclusion orders are designed to deal with the problem of football hooliganism.

● The court has power to prevent you from attending league and cup football matches if you are convicted of an offence connected with such a match, for example if you were violent or had alcohol with you at a game.

Exclusion orders are dealt with more fully in Chapter 41, Public Order Offences, Football Matches, Trespassers and Raves, under heading (b).

(16) Deferred sentence

● The court can delay sentencing you for up to 6 months.

● You must give your consent to this.

● Sentence will usually be deferred because there's about to be a change in your life, for example you have been offered a job and would be able to pay compensation.

● The court will set out what is expected of you during the period of the deferment and, if you comply, it is highly unlikely that you would be sent to a young offender institution.

(17) Secure training order

● The Criminal Justice and Public Order Act 1994 introduces a new sentence for 12, 13 and 14 year olds. This is a period of detention in a secure training centre followed by a period of the same length under supervision. The total period must be between 6 months and 2 years. The offender must have been convicted of 3 or more offences punishable with imprisonment in the case of an adult while on a supervision order.

● At the time of writing this book secure training orders have yet to become law.

(g) Being a witness in a criminal case

● If you are under the age of 16 a parent (or guardian) must go with you to court.

● If you are under the age of 14 you will give unsworn evidence, in other words you do not have to take an oath to tell the truth. There is no minimum age for giving evidence, but you will be asked if you understand the difference between a truth and a lie.

● The party on whose behalf you have been called will take you through your version of events. This is called *examination-in-chief*. The other party, or parties, will then *cross-examine* you.

- If the case is being heard in the adult magistrates' court or the Crown Court, an order can be made that any newspaper, television or radio report must not give your name, address, or the name of your school, or any other information that may identify you, and no picture of you may be published, without the permission of the court.

The name of the victim of a sexual offence must never be revealed.

- If you are under the age of 18 and you are the victim of a sexual or violent offence, you are specially treated as a witness in order to minimise the stress and anxiety. In particular

    ○ it may be arranged for you to give your evidence from behind a screen so that you do not feel intimidated by seeing the offender,

    ○ there is a rule that you can only be cross-examined by a lawyer, not by the offender;

    ○ the court can direct that the courtroom be cleared while you are giving your evidence, except for those directly concerned with the case and the press.

- If you are under the age of 14 and the victim of a violent offence, or under the age of 17 and the victim of a sexual offence, the court may be able to receive a video recording of your evidence, in other words you will previously have been interviewed by a social worker and a police officer and this interview will be shown in court. You won't have to give your evidence-in-chief in court, but you may still have to attend if the defence wish to cross-examine you.

- If the court has a live television link, you may be able to give your evidence from another room without having to go into court. There will be a camera in that room so that you can be seen by those in the courtroom and you will see the lawyer who is questioning you (or the judge) on a TV screen.

The court may have a special room for witnesses and its own witness service to assist you before, during and after the hearing. You should ask the police about this beforehand.

Take a magazine or book with you to read, as you may have to wait a long time for the case to be called.

If you have an important reason to leave early, tell the usher or other court official so that they can try and arrange for you to give your evidence first.

Don't talk about the case to other witnesses or people waiting outside the courtroom.

After the trial is over, you may be able to get back your travel expenses to and from court, and the cost of any food or drink you bought whilst waiting.

Details of organisations providing support to victims of crime are given in Part Three, Where to Go for Information and Help, under heading (J), Victims of Crime.

Being a victim of a sexual offence is dealt with in Chapter 45, Sexual Intercourse, under heading (c).

Chapter 17

● It is a criminal offence to take a pedal cycle without the owner's consent so you should be careful before 'borrowing' a friend's bike without their permission.

● There are various offences you can commit in relation to bicycles for which you can be fined *(see further Chapter 16, Criminal Proceedings, heading (f)(4))*. These include:

  ○ dangerous cycling on a road, including a cycle lane and a bridleway;

  ○ careless or inconsiderate cycling;

  ○ defective brakes;

  ○ having 2 persons on a bicycle;

  ○ riding a bicycle when unfit through drink or drugs.

● The Highway Code states that you must obey traffic signs and traffic light signals and you must not cycle on the pavement.

At night you must use front and rear lights and a red rear reflector.

It is a good idea to wear light coloured clothing, reflective belts and arm bands and to fit wheel reflectors so that you can be seen easily. It is also in your interests to wear a cycle helmet, although this is not compulsory.

Chapter 18

DISABILITY

(a) General

● The law in this country does not make it unlawful to discriminate against people on the grounds of any disability they may have. Some public bodies, organisations and companies must treat all people equally, others may choose to do so. An attempt to increase the rights of disabled people by new legislation has recently failed but a further attempt is being made.

● It is generally felt desirable that a person who is disabled should be given the opportunity to lead as normal a life as possible within society by being given access to the same facilities and services that the able-bodied have, and by being offered educational, training and employment opportunities appropriate to their needs.

● There are a variety of laws covering disability, but disabled people of all ages often face difficulties in establishing their rights and enforcing them. Some of the main entitlements of disabled children and young people are briefly set out below.

Leaflet HB6, Equipment and Services For Disabled People, should be available at all Benefit Agency Offices. This lists the main forms of help available through the National Health Service (NHS) and local authorities for people with different kinds of disabilities, including those who are deaf or hard of hearing, blind or partially sighted, who have speech and language impairments, or are physically disable including disabled children.

Your local Benefits Agency office will be listed in your local telephone directory under 'Benefits Agency'.

Details of organisations that may be able to provide advice and practical assistance are given in Part Three, Where to Go for Information and Help, under heading (G), Disability. If you are disabled, the best way to find out more about your rights is by contacting them.

(b) Children in need

See generally Chapter 47, Social Services and Children in Need.

● By virtue of the Children Act 1989, the social services department of the local authority have a general duty to safeguard and promote the welfare of all *children in need* within their area, and to help the families of such children to bring them up in their own homes, wherever possible, by providing a suitable range of services.

● A *child in need* is somebody under the age of 18 who is unlikely to achieve or maintain a reasonable standard of health or development, or whose health or development may suffer if he or she does not get the help required. The definition specifically includes disabled children.

● The Act says that you are disabled if you are blind, deaf or dumb, or suffer from mental disorder of any kind, or are substantially and permanently handicapped by illness, injury or congenital deformity.

● Every local authority has a duty to open and maintain a register of disabled children within their area and must make an assessment of their needs.

● Services must be provided that are designed to

○ minimise the effect on disabled children of their disabilities; *and*

○ give such children the opportunity to lead lives which are as normal as possible.

● As well as the normal range of services, special services must be provided, including

  ○ social work visits at home and the provision of advice, information and referrals;

  ○ practical help in the home, for example a home help;

  ○ adaptations in the home for greater convenience and safety;

  ○ special equipment and telephones;

  ○ meals; *and*

  ○ respite care, holidays, outings and associated travel expenses.

● If the local authority fails in these obligations, you have a right to make a complaint. The *Secretary of State for Health* may also declare a local authority in default *(see further Chapter 9, Care Order and Accommodation – Being Looked After by the Local Authority, heading (g))*.

(c) Education

See generally Chapter 25, Education.

● Disabled children have the same entitlement to state education as all other children. If you are so disabled that you cannot go to school, you should be provided with a home tutor.

● If you are incapable of walking to school and wouldn't otherwise be able to attend, even if you do not live more than 3 miles away from your school the LEA may provide you with free transport to and from school by means of special school buses or travel passes.

● Disabled children should be educated wherever possible within a mainstream school rather than in a special school. In some schools, suitable adaptations have been made to the premises to enable disabled children and young people to attend and they may be provided with special aids and equipment to help them get the most out of being at school.

● Just because you are disabled, this does not mean that you have *special educational needs (see further Chapter 25, Education, heading (k))* unless your disability is such that it affects your ability to learn.

● Mainstream schools should provide speech and language therapy and special classes.

(d) Youth training (YT)

See generally Chapter 59, Youth Training.

● YT is a means of acquiring work skills and qualifications. It is open to disabled young people as well as the able-bodied.

● All 16 and 17 year olds have the right to an offer of a YT place if they are not in work or full-time education. If, while you were under the age of 18, you were so disabled or sick that you were unable to go on YT, the right may extend beyond your 18th birthday until you, are 25.

You must continue to be eligible for YT in all other respects.

● YT is only open to people who are considered to be capable of eventually taking up open employment. If your disability is so great that you would have no prospect of obtaining and keeping any job that an able-bodied person would be able to do, you cannot go on YT.

● If you are disabled, the careers officer must make an assessment of your *special training needs*. You are treated as having special training needs if you have any physical or sensory impairment, for example you cannot walk, or are blind, deaf, or cannot speak, and also if you have learning difficulties.

You are entitled to be provided with an individually tailored YT programme in line with any needs that you may have.

● In addition, appropriate facilities and support should be made available to enable you to join and benefit from YT, for example adaptations to premises and equipment and an interpreter service for the deaf.

● All providers of YT must be committed to promoting equal opportunities for all and you must not be discriminated against in relation to YT on the grounds of disability. However, if you are discriminated against because of any disability you may have, this does not give you the right to go to an industrial tribunal.

● If you qualify for disability living allowance you will still receive this while you are on YT *(see further heading (f) below)*.

(e) Employment

See generally Chapter 58, Working.

● Disabled people have the same rights in the work place as able-bodied employees.

● Employers having 20 or more employees are required to employ 3% registered disabled people.

● Jobcentres operate a *Disabled Persons Register.*

Disability employment advisers should be available to give you information and advice about schemes operating in your area for people who have difficulties in finding and keeping work because of disability.

(f) Welfare benefits

It will help you to understand this part of the chapter if you first read Chapter 57, Welfare Benefits.

The telephone numbers of the free Disability Benefits Helpline and the Social Security Rights Advice Line are given in Part Three, Where to Go for Information and Help, under heading (G), Disability.

● Contributory benefits relating to disability, such as incapacity benefit, are outside the scope of this book because it is unlikely if you are under 18 that you will have paid enough national insurance *(see Chapter 54, Tax and National Insurance)* in order to qualify for these.

● If you are disabled you may be entitled to income support (IS) and housing benefit (HB).

● Disabled 16 and 17 year olds are generally entitled to IS if they

○ have left school or college and cannot work or go on YT because of their disability; *or*

○ are still at school or college in full-time education.

● The rules governing HB are the same as for able-bodied people.

● The rules governing council tax benefit are the same as for able-bodied people.

Apart from this, the amount of council tax that would otherwise have to be paid, may be reduced if a person with a physical disability lives in the property.

● If you have a disability you may qualify for free NHS prescriptions, dental treatment, eye test and glasses. *The general rules regarding eligibility are set out in Chapter 35, Medical Treatment, under heading (d).*

You may also be able to get help with NHS hospital travel costs, free NHS hospital appliances and free NHS hearing aids.

● Disabled children and young people may also qualify for certain non-contributory benefits on the grounds of their disability. These include severe disablement allowance, disability living allowance and disability working allowance.

● Severe disablement allowance (SDA) is a non-contributory, non-means-tested benefit and therefore it is not affected by your savings, earnings or other income, or by how much money your parents have.

● SDA is available for people aged 16 or over who do not qualify for incapacity benefit, and who have not been able to work for at least 28 weeks because of illness or disability, or who work under medical supervision and have a low income.

You may be able to get SDA if you are under the age of 19 and still at school, or college, in special education, or if you have less than 21 hours a week of supervised study.

The rate of payment from April 1995 onwards for those under 40 is £47.30 per week.

Once you receive SDA, you may also be entitled to top-up IS payments.

> Many young people miss out on SDA. If you think that you may be entitled, you should take advice without delay because, while you are under the age of 20, no disability test applies.

● Disability living allowance (DLA) is a non-contributory, non-means-tested benefit and therefore it is not affected by your savings, earnings or other income, or by how much money your parents have.

DLA does not count as income for IS or HB purposes.

DLA is paid to people who need help with their personal care and/or with getting around, because they are ill or disabled.

There are 2 elements

○ care needs, for example you need help with washing, dressing or using the toilet or, if you are aged 16 or over, with preparing a cooked main meal; *and*

○ mobility needs, for example if you cannot walk, have difficulties walking or need somebody to walk with you when outdoors.

DLA is paid at various rates according to the extent of your disability. The rate from April 1995 onwards are

Care needs	higher rate	£46.70 pw
	middle rate	£31.20 pw
	lower rate	£12.40 pw
Mobility needs	higher rate	£32.65 pw
	lower rate	£12.40 pw

You must normally have needed help for at least 3 months and be likely to need it for at least a further 6 months.

● Disability working allowance (DWA) is a means-tested benefit for people aged 16 or over who work at least 16 hours per week but have an illness or disability that limits their earning capacity.

You (and any partner) must not have savings of more than £16,000 (savings between £3,000 and £16,000 will affect the amount you get).

The amount you get depends on whether you have a partner, how many children you have living with you, and their ages, and how much money you (and any partner) have coming in each week.

● If you have been severely disabled as a result of vaccination against diphtheria, tetanus, whooping cough, tuberculosis, polio, measles, mumps or rubella you may be able to get a one-off lump sum payment, currently £30,000. This is called *vaccine damage*.

● If you are the victim of crime and you become disabled you may be able to make an application to the Criminal Injuries Compensation Board *(see further Chapter 12, Compensation, heading (a)(2))*.

● If you become disabled through an accident at work you may be able to get industrial injuries disablement benefit and/or industrial injury compensation. *You should discuss this with your trade union representative or go to your local Citizens' Advice Bureau, law centre or neighbourhood advice centre.*

Chapter 19

What discrimination is and enforcing your rights

● It is unlawful to treat a person less favourably than others on grounds of their

○ colour, race, ethnic or national origin or nationality; *or*

○ sex or marital status.

● It is not actually unlawful to discriminate against people on other grounds including their youth and any disability they may have.

● Discrimination is a civil wrong and if it involves threats or assault, it may also be a criminal offence *(see Chapter 15, The Courts and the Legal System, heading (a))*.

● The areas where you are most likely to meet unlawful discrimination are

○ at school; *or*

○ at work; *or*

○ in the provision of accommodation, goods and services.

● Discrimination can be *direct*, for example if a landlord refuses to show a flat to any black people, or *indirect*, for example if a job in which height is irrelevant is advertised 'Only people over 6 feet tall need apply' (this discriminates because not many women are over 6 feet).

● There is no lower age limit for making complaints about being discriminated against.

> If you believe that you have been the victim of unlawful discrimination, you should contact your local Citizens' Advice Bureau, law centre or neighbourhood advice centre.
> You can also contact the Commission for Racial Equality (CRE) or the Equal Opportunities Commission (EOC). Their addresses are given in Part Three, Where to Go for Information and Help, under heading (Q), Discrimination.

The CRE and the EOC will give you free information and practical and legal advice. They may be able to make an investigation and take steps to stop discriminatory practices.

● You should ask your adviser to help you draft a race or sex *discrimination questionnaire* to send to the person who you feel has discriminated against you. This asks them to give the reason why they treated you in the way that they did. Their answers can be used in evidence.

● If you are discriminated against at work you may be able to go to an *industrial tribunal* for compensation *(see further Chapter 58, Working, heading (i))*.

There is a time limit of 3 months from the date of the discriminatory act.

● In other cases you may be able to sue for *damages* in the county court *(see Chapter 15, The Courts and the Legal System, heading (b)(3)) and see further Chapter 51, Suing and Being Sued, heading (a) and Chapter 12, Compensation, heading (b), Chapter 48, Solicitors and Legal Aid)*.

You must bring your claim within 6 months.

● The sums awarded can contain an element for your injured feelings.

● If your case raises an important issue of law, the CRE or the EOC may take it up on your behalf.

Discrimination at school is dealt with in Chapter 25, under heading (j), and discrimination and sexual harassment at work are dealt with in Chapter 58, under headings (g) and (h).

Chapter 20

DIVORCE AND SEPARATION

It is an unfortunate fact that sometimes parents split up and stop living together. If they and you are able to agree which parent you should live with and the arrangements for seeing the other parent, there is no need for the court to become involved.

(a) What happens in court?

● If there is a dispute the court can make any *section 8 order*, in other words a *residence order (see Chapter 11, heading (c)(1))*, a *contact order (see Chapter 11, heading (c)(2))*, a *specific issue order (see Chapter 11, heading (c)(3))* or a *prohibited steps order (see Chapter 11, heading (c)(4))*.

● These orders can be made in favour of either or both of your parents when they no longer live together.

● In all these cases there are certain principles that the court must apply. *(These are set out in Chapter 11, under heading (b).)* There are certain other general principles that the court tends to apply but it depends upon the circumstances of each individual case.

- These principles include
  - as regards *contact orders*, you have a right to keep in touch with the parent with whom you are not living. Some form of contact will be ordered unless there are strong reasons to suggest that it would not be in your best interests.
  - as regards *residence orders*, in most situations brothers and sisters should be brought up together.

    There is no rule that a teenage girl should be with her mother and a teenage boy should be with his father.

    You should have your base with one parent, rather than moving backwards and forwards between their homes unless this is what you all want.

- Generally, from the age of 12 upwards, greater attention will be given to your views. The older you are, and the greater understanding you have of your situation, the more likely it is that the court will listen to what you want and follow your wishes and feelings; there was a recent court case of a 13 year old boy and an 11 year old girl who did not want to see their father because of his strong religious beliefs and the court said that it would be wrong to force them.

- You are not expected to attend court to act as a witness for either of your parents and the majority of cases go ahead without your needing to be there.

(b) Your say in where you will live and who you will see

- The court has a duty to find out your wishes and feelings but is not bound to follow them.

  If there is a dispute about residence or contact, the court will probably appoint a *court welfare officer*. He or she is an independent probation officer who will be requested to prepare a report on matters relating to your welfare.

- The court welfare officer will interview your parents and any other important people in your life, and seek information about you from your school, doctor and social services. He or she should make an appointment to see you, either at home or at their office. This is your opportunity to express your wishes and feelings.

> It is very important that you tell the court welfare officer what you want, not what you think will please your parents. If you don't know what you want, you should say so. You don't have to talk to the court welfare officer if you don't want to.

● Occasionally, particularly in the case of older teenagers, you may have to go to court to see the judge at his or her request. If you feel particularly strongly about something you can ask to see the judge and tell him or her exactly what you want.

● The judge will see you privately in his or her room. The judge has a duty to give your parents an outline of what you said but not every little detail.

● It is up to the judge whether or not to see you. Not all judges like talking to children and young people and would rather leave it to the court welfare officer.

● In exceptional circumstances, for example if you have very strong views, you can apply to be made a separate party to existing proceedings already going on between your parents.

● Normally, you require a *guardian ad litem* in order to make such an application. The role of the *guardian ad litem* is to safeguard your interests. In most cases the *Official Solicitor to the Supreme Court* acts as your *guardian ad litem*, but any suitable and willing adult can be a *guardian ad litem. This is not the same person as the guardian ad litem in civil proceedings: That kind of guardian ad litem is dealt with in Chapter 51, Suing and Being Sued, under heading (b).*

● If you wish to participate directly without a *guardian ad litem*, you can do this with *leave* (that is, permission) of the court.

● Alternatively, you do not need a *guardian ad litem* if your solicitor considers that you have sufficient understanding to be capable of giving *instructions* in relation to the proceedings, and has accepted those instructions from you. Being able to give instructions means telling your solicitor what you want, deciding which parts of the evidence you challenge, making decisions as matters arise, giving evidence yourself and being cross-examined.

- The court has the final power to decide the question of your understanding.

- If, during the course of the proceedings, you and the *guardian ad litem* disagree about what is in your best interests, you can apply to the court for their removal so that you continue being represented only by your solicitor. The court must grant you leave if you have sufficient understanding to participate as a party in the proceedings without a *guardian ad litem*.

(c) 'Divorcing' your parents

- Cases about children divorcing their parents have hit the headlines recently. Legally, you cannot actually divorce your parents but it may be possible for a court to allow you to live elsewhere.

- If you have a very poor relationship with your parents, are very unhappy at home and wish to live with another adult family member or friend, that person can apply for a *residence order (see Chapter 11, The Children Act 1989, heading (c)(1))* in their favour.

- You may be able to make your own application in your own right, but you require *leave* (that is, permission) of the court to make the application and the court must be satisfied that you have sufficient understanding to make the application.

> Before you launch into an application, you should try if possible to discuss the problem with your parents to see whether you can sort it out, or you could approach a sympathetic adult family member or friend to act as a go-between. Court proceedings are stressful and often cause a great deal of bitterness. There are also trained mediators and conciliators who work with families to try and help them to resolve their problems without going to court. Details of organisations that may be able to assist in overcoming a conflict within the family are given in Part Three, Where to Go for Information and Help, under heading (D), Family and Personal (Support and Counselling Services).

If you feel that you have no choice but to make the application, the procedure for doing this is dealt with in Chapter 11, The Children Act 1989, under heading (d).

See also Chapter 11, the Children Act 1989; Chapter 26, Emigrating, Going to Live Abroad and Holidays; Chapter 33, Leaving Home and Running Away; Chapter 36, Names; Chapter 48, Solicitors and Legal Aid; Chapter 56, Wardship.

(d) Maintenance, financial arrangements and the Child Support Agency (CSA)

(1) Financial orders made by the court

● The court has power in divorce and separation cases to make a wide range of financial orders in respect of dependent children who are under the age of 18.

● It is outside the scope of this book to discuss these in any detail but, essentially, the court can make orders about such matters as

○ who should own the home where you live;

○ the payment to you directly, or to the other parent on your behalf, of lump sums;

○ who should pay the fees, if you go to a private school;

○ the financial provision to be made to the parent with whom you live.

● The court's main concern will be to keep a roof over your head until you finish full-time education.

● At 16 in certain circumstances, notably if you are still in full-time education, you can bring your own application against a parent for maintenance and/or a lump sum.

(2) The Child Support Agency (CSA)

● Maintenance for children used to be paid through the court but this is no longer always the position.

● The government has recently created the CSA which operates a new system for the assessment and collection of maintenance for children. The date on which the system will come fully into force has now been delayed indefinitely so existing court orders for maintenance may continue.

● Child support maintenance is the amount of money paid by the absent parent to the parent with whom you live as a contribution to your upkeep. The CSA applies a mathematical formula to work out how much should be paid, taking into account each parent's income and essential outgoings, and subject to certain limits.

● Applications can be made to the CSA in respect of all children who are under the age of 16, and those who are aged 16 or over but have not yet reached 19 and are still in full-time secondary education and are not, and never have been, married.

● You cannot apply for child support maintenance yourself in your own right (you can in Scotland!).

● The court can still make orders for extra maintenance, for example for meeting the expenses caused by any disability, and items such as private school fees.

Chapter 21

Obtaining protection in the county court by an injunction

The law is going to change in about the Autumn of 1995 so as to make injunctions available to a wider range of people. You will need to check the position with a solicitor.

● If your parents are married, or unmarried and living together, and one parent is violent towards the other parent and/or violent towards you, that other parent can apply for an injunction in the county court *(see Chapter 15, The Courts and the Legal System, heading (b)(3))* under the Domestic Violence and Matrimonial Proceedings Act 1976 (the DVMPA) to protect themselves and/or to protect you against the violent parent.

● Let us assume that the violent parent is your father (or step-father). The court can grant an injunction containing one or more of the following terms

   ○ restraining him from using violence towards your mother, and from threatening, molesting, harassing or pestering her;

○ restraining him from using violence towards you, and from threatening, molesting, harassing or pestering you;

These are called *non-molestation injunctions.*

○ excluding him from the family home or a part of it, or the area surrounding the family home.

This is called an *ouster injunction.*

If your father is proved to have broken any of the terms of an injunction, he can be sent to prison for up to 2 years or punished in some other way (it is unlikely that he would be sent to prison on the first occasion).

● If your father has assaulted your mother and/or you causing actual bodily harm, for example punching which results in bruising, and he is considered likely to do it again, the judge can attach a *power of arrest* to the injunction. This enables your father to be arrested immediately by the police for any breach of the injunction and to be brought before a judge within 24 hours to be dealt with.

● Injunctions will not be made simply because it would be in your best interests.

● *Ouster injunctions* are reserved for the more serious cases where there is no other way to protect your mother and/or you. They tend to last for a limited time, usually 3 months.

● You cannot use the DVMPA to make an application in your own right.

● The position is more complicated if your parents are not married and not living together or if, say, your mother's ex-boyfriend, who is not your father, is being violent, because the DVMPA does not apply. Your mother can *sue* in assault (and in trespass if the home is in her sole name) for injunctions to protect herself. If you are the victim and you are under the age of 18, you may be able to bring a similar claim in assault through your mother acting as your *next friend (see further, Chapter 51, heading (a)(1)).*

● A problem that sometimes arises is violence and harassment following the breakdown of a relationship. For example

○ you finished with your boyfriend and he has taken to standing outside your house shouting abuse and telephoning you repeatedly in the middle of the night. The county court has power to grant injunctions in assault and/or nuisance to protect you against this kind of behaviour, and to stop your ex-boyfriend from communicating with you if it is harming your health.

If you are under the age of 18, you may be able to bring a claim through one of your parents acting as your *next friend*.

● If you are under the age of 18 and you are the one behaving in this way, an action can be commenced against you. One of your parents will have to act as your *guardian ad litem (see further Chapter 51, Suing and Being Sued, heading (b))*. The courts are reluctant to grant injunctions against teenagers who are still at school.

● If there is an injunction in force against you which you break and you are under the age of 17, you cannot be punished by being deprived of your freedom.

● If you are aged 17 or over, but have not yet reached 21, and you break the terms of an injunction, you cannot be sent to prison, but you may be detained in a young offender institution if no other method of dealing with you is appropriate.

Detention in these circumstances does not carry with it any right to early release *(see Chapter 16, Criminal Proceedings, heading (f)(13))*.

Many police forces now have special domestic violence units to deal with these kinds of situations and you will find the police to be far more sympathetic than was once the case. These units can offer practical help and advice.

Details of various organisations offering practical, emergency help and emotional support to the victims of domestic violence are given in Part Three, Where to Go for Information and Help, under heading (I), Victims of Domestic Violence and also under heading (J), Victims of Crime.

See also *Chapter 2, Abuse and Child Protection Procedures; Chapter 42, Punishment and Discipline; Chapter 51, Suing and Being Sued. The position if a violent parent is prosecuted and you have to attend court as a witness is dealt with in Chapter 16, under heading (g). Compensation if you are injured is dealt with in Chapter 12, under headings (a) and (b).*

Chapter 22

DRIVING

The laws about driving motor vehicles apply when you drive on a public road or in any other public place (for example a car park), but not if you drive on private land (for example if you live on a farm). There are many different rules and requirements. It is possible to commit a large number of different road traffic offences.

(a) When and where you can drive and licences

● If you are under the age of 16 you can only ride a bicycle *(cycling is dealt with in Chapter 17).*

● If you are aged 16 or over you can drive an invalid carriage, a moped, a mowing machine and a pedestrian controlled vehicle. You can also drive a motor car if you receive disability living allowance at the higher rate *(see Chapter 18, Disability, heading (f)).*

● If you are aged 17 or over you can drive a manual or automatic motor car, a motorcycle, a scooter, a small van (for goods or passengers with up to 9 seats), a minibus and a tractor.

However, you must not ride a motorcycle with an engine capacity of less than 50cc (including a moped and a scooter) on the motorway at any age.

● If you are aged 18 or over you can drive a small lorry and an ambulance for a health authority.

● If you are aged 21 or over you can drive a large lorry, a bus and a coach.

● Before you drive you must have obtained the necessary licence. *Application forms are available at post offices.*

● At first, you will get a *provisional licence* and you will be a learner driver *(see further heading (b) below)*. You will need to take and pass a test in order to get a full licence.

● If you drive under the minimum age or without the correct licence you will be committing the road traffic offence of driving otherwise than in accordance with a licence.

● You may not be able to get a licence, for example if you have had an epileptic attack within the last 2 years or you are unable to read a number plate 5 car lengths away in daylight while wearing glasses.

(b) Learner drivers

● You must display L plates that can be seen clearly at the front and back of the vehicle.

● Learners must not drive on the motorway.

● As regards a *car*

  ○ you must have a provisional licence;

  ○ you cannot drive on your own until you have taken and passed a test; *and*

  ○ you must be supervised by somebody who is at least 21 and has held a full licence for that type of car (manual or automatic) for at least 3 years and still holds it.

● As regards a *motorcycle*

○ if you are learning to ride a motorcycle, moped or scooter you must take basic training with an approved training body before you go on the road. Once you have completed the training, they will issue you with a certificate and you must take a test and apply for a full licence within 2 years;

○ you can ride on the road with a provisional licence but, until you have taken and passed your test, you must not

– carry a pillion passenger; *or*

– pull a trailer; *or*

– ride a motorcycle with an engine capacity of more than 125cc.

> If somebody offers to teach you to drive make sure that they have insurance (see further heading (c)(1) below). If you are being charged for lessons, the driving instructor should be registered with the Department of Transport and you should ask to see their certificate. It is in your interests to go to a reputable driving school even though this may be more expensive.

(c) Some general rules about driving

(1) Documents and insurance

● As well as a valid licence, as long as your vehicle is parked on the road even if it is not being used, you must have

○ a current *tax disc* which must be displayed on the vehicle; *and*

○ valid *third party insurance* (that is, to compensate anyone else who suffers damage or personal injury as a result of your negligent driving.

The responsibility is on you to make sure that you have insurance.

> If, for example you drive a friend's car, you should not take their word that you are covered by their policy. You should check their insurance certificate yourself.

● It is no defence that you made a mistake and genuinely thought that you were insured. It is also an offence to allow your vehicle to be used by somebody who is not insured.

● If you apply for insurance, the information that you give to the insurance company must be accurate otherwise your insurance may be invalid. It is a criminal offence to knowlingly make a false statement in order to obtain insurance or cheaper insurance, for example lying about how long you have been driving.

● You must have a current *MOT certificate* – if your vehicle is over 3 years old, it must be taken to a garage once a year for a full test to ensure that it is roadworthy and a certificate will be issued.

● If you are stopped by the police for any reason, you can be asked to show your licence, insurance certificate and any MOT certificate.

You don't have to carry them with you, but you will be given 7 days to take them to your nearest police station.

Some police officers will insist on a proper insurance certificate and will not accept a cover note.

(2) Your vehicle

● All parts of your vehicle, for example the brakes, lights and tyres must be kept in good condition and working order.

This is your responsibility and it is no defence, for example, to say that you did not realise that your lights were not working.

● The condition of your vehicle must not be a danger to other road users, for example if you have an accident, you must not leave it unrepaired with jagged metal sticking out.

● Any load must be properly secured and not stick out dangerously.

● In a *car*

  ○ you must not carry too many passengers;

  ○ you and your front seat passenger must wear seat belts; *and*

  ○ if rear seatbelts are fitted, rear seat passengers must wear them.

● On a *motorcycle*

  ○ you must not carry more than one passenger; *and*

○ you must wear an approved safety helmet (unless you are a Sikh and wear a turban).

(3) Accidents

● If you are involved in an accident, whether or not it is your fault, which causes injury to somebody other than you or damage to a vehicle other than yours, or to any animal or roadside property (for example a nearby wall or tree), you must

○ stop and give your name and address (and the name and address of the owner of the vehicle if it belongs to somebody else) and the registration number of the vehicle to any other person who asks for them.Where there are 2 or more drivers involved, they must all swop these details;

○ if you drive away without stopping, you will be committing an offence;

○ if there is nobody else around, you must still wait a reasonable time just in case somebody comes along;

○ if nobody does come along (for example you hit a parked car in the middle of the night), you must report the accident to the police within 24 hours;

○ if another person is injured in the accident, you must show them your insurance certificate. If you do not have this on you, you must report the accident at a police station within 24 hours and produce the insurance certificate at the same time.

(4) Speeding

● You must keep within the speed limits that is to say

○ 30 mph in a built up area unless another speed limit is shown;

○ 60 mph on a single carriageway;

○ 70 mph on a dual carriageway or motorway.

It is an absolute offence to break the speed limit and it is no defence that you were not causing any danger or did not realise how fast you were going.

(5) Careless driving

You must drive with due care and attention and with proper consideration for other road users. If your driving is below the standard to be expected from a 'reasonable driver' in all the circumstances, you will be committing an offence. This includes any error of judgement, for example pulling out of a side road without looking or driving too close to the vehicle in front so that you cannot pull up in time if they brake suddenly.

(6) Drink driving

● You must not drive if you are unfit through drink or drugs or with excess alcohol.

> Although you are allowed to drink a certain amount of alcohol, it is better not to have anything to drink when you are driving because it affects your ability to drive safely.

● A police officer in uniform can require you to take a roadside breath test if he or she reasonably suspects you to have alcohol in your body or to have committed a moving traffic offence. The request will be proper even if it is made once you are on private land provided the police officer is making an investigation in good faith. The police are not supposed to do random tests, but the reality is that they will usually be able to justify asking you to take a test.

● If you refuse to take the test, or the test is positive, you are likely to be arrested and taken to the police station and asked to provide a sample of breath on a Lion Intoximeter machine.

You must blow twice and the machine will produce a printout.

The lower reading is the basis of the decision whether you will be prosecuted.

● The legal limit is 35 microgrammes of alcohol in 100 millilitres of breath.

● If the lower reading is less than 40, you are unlikely to prosecuted.

If it is less than 50, you are entitled to have a sample of blood or urine analysed.

The limits are 80 milligrammes of alcohol in 100 millilitres of blood and 107 milligrammes of alcohol in 100 millilitres of urine.

The police decide which sort of sample it will be. It is not for you to make the choice.

● If the Lion Intoximeter is not working, or for some medical reason you cannot provide a sample of breath, you will be requested to provide a sample of blood or urine.

The police decide which it will be. It is not for you to make the choice.

● Unless you have a reasonable excuse, you must not fail to provide a specimen. You need to have a medical reason, for example if you are asthmatic and incapable of blowing into the Lion Intoximeter.

If, for example, you are asked to give a sample of blood and you are genuinely terrified of needles, this may be a reasonable excuse. In a recent court case a genuine phobia of catching AIDS was accepted as a reasonable excuse.

● The penalties for refusing to provide a specimen and for drink driving are the same – you will have to go to court and you will automatically be disqualified for at least a year unless there are *special reasons* and you will probably be fined *(see further heading (d) below)*.

(7) 'Borrowing' your parent's car

● You should never do this without their permission because you could be committing the criminal offence of taking a motor vehicle without the owner's consent.

● You could be disqualified and your parents' insurance certificate will not cover you.

(d) Motoring offences and penalties

(1) Disqualification

● If you are convicted of offences like driving with excess alcohol or while unfit through drink or drugs, refusing to provide a specimen and dangerous driving, normally, the court must disqualify you for at least a year.

- Disqualification means that you will lose your licence and must not drive for the period of the disqualification.

If you do, you will be committing the criminal offence of driving while disqualified which is regarded seriously by the courts.

A disqualified driver cannot have valid insurance.

- For these offences, the court has no choice but to disqualify you unless there are what is called *special reasons*. These are very rare.

Examples of special reasons in drink driving cases are

- ○ if you thought you were drinking orange juice but your friends were lacing your drinks with vodka and you were unaware of this;

- ○ if you moved your car a very short distance because there was no choice, for example an ambulance could not pass.

It is not a special reason that you were mistaken about the amount of alcohol you had had to drink.

- For other offences that carry penalty points *(see below)* the court may decide to disqualify you for a period, usually up to 6 months.

It is common for people who do more than 100 miles per hour on the motorway (the limit is 70 mph) to be disqualified for about a month.

- You can be disqualified even though you do not yet hold a licence and, once you do get it, the fact you have been disqualified will appear on your licence for 10 years from the date of the disqualification.

This is likely to make insurance more expensive and may present a problem if you wish to hire a car or apply for a driving job.

- You must be present in court before you can be disqualified.

(2) Penalty points

- For some offences, penalty points must be endorsed on your licence. These are called *endorsable* offences.

Again, you do not have to have a licence before penalty points can be counted against you and they will remain on your licence for 10 years.

● Points remain current for 3 years and on each occasion you commit a road traffic offence, they are added on. Once you reach 12 points you must be disqualified for at least 6 months unless it would cause you exceptional hardship, for example you are the only breadwinner in your family and you work as a delivery driver for a small firm that could not keep you on if you were disqualified.

● The number of penalty points that must be endorsed may be fixed or variable according to the particular offence and the seriousness. For example

Offence	Points
careless or inconsiderate driving	3 to 9
failing to stop after an accident, or to report an accident	5 to 10
driving without insurance	6 to 8
driving while disqualified	6
driving otherwise than in accordance with a licence	3 to 6
speeding	3 to 6
going through a red traffic light	3
dangerous condition (including too many passengers)	3
defective brakes	3

(3) Fines

See generally Chapter 16, Criminal Proceeding, heading (f)(4).

● All road traffic offences carry a financial penalty and this is the most likely way of dealing with you together with any penalty points and/or disqualification.

● Some offences only carry a financial penalty. For example

   ○ driving without an MOT certificate;

   ○ not wearing a seat belt;

   ○ stopping on a clearway.

- The maximum fine for most road traffic offences is £1,000 but, if you are aged between 10 and 13, you cannot be fined more than £250.

- Some road traffic offences carry imprisonment in the case of an adult which means that you could be detained in a young offender institution for up to 6 months, but this is extremely rare. Examples of road traffic offences that are imprisonable are

  o driving with excess alcohol or while unfit through drink or drugs;

  o refusing to provide a specimen;

  o dangerous driving;

  o failing to stop after an accident;

  o driving while disqualified.

(e) Fixed penalties and summonses

- Fixed penalties are available for more minor road traffic offences, for example parking offences (which do not carry penalty points) or going through a red traffic light.

- If you commit one of these offences, a police officer may give you a fixed penalty ticket.

- Where the offence is *endorsable (see heading (d)(2) above)*, you must give the licence to the police officer then and there or take it to the nearest police station within 7 days. You have 28 days to pay the fine.

- Fixed penalties avoid the time and expense of going to court.

  The fine will be a set amount which is likely to be lower than the court would impose – it is presently £40 for endorsable offences like going through a red traffic light, speeding and driving otherwise than in accordance with a licence.

- The number of penalty points may also be fewer. For example fixed penalties carry 3 points for speeding and for driving otherwise than in accordance with a licence, whereas the court can impose 3 to 6 points for these offences.

● If you do not accept the fixed penalty you can request a court hearing.

● In cases where fixed penalties do not apply, you will normally get a summons through the post telling you when and where to got to court.

You should read this carefully.

● The summons sets out the offence which you are said to have committed and may contain a brief outline of the facts upon which the prosecution rely.

● For many offences you can plead guilty by post without having to attend court. The summons will tell you whether you can do this.

This procedure does not apply for offences carrying automatic disqualification such as driving with excess alcohol *(see heading (d)(1) above)*.

● If you wish to plead guilty by post, you need to complete the form on the back of the summons, sign it and send it back to the court. You must enclose your licence.

● If you wish to plead not guilty, the usual procedure is to write to the court and ask for a date to be fixed for the hearing.

● Legal aid is not generally available for road traffic offences.

Road traffic offences can be proved in your absence so it is important that you do not ignore any summons and that you attend on the date of the trial.
You must always take or send your driving licence to court.

Chapter 23

● The Misuse of Drugs Act 1971 makes it a criminal offence to be in possession of *controlled* (that is, illegal) drugs for your own personal use.

● Possession means having control over the drugs. Therefore, if you leave drugs in your bedroom while you go out, you are still in possession of them. However, seeing somebody else taking drugs, say, at a party, does not amount to possession.

● You must know that what you are in possession of is, in fact, a controlled drug.

● More serious criminal offences are committed if you possess controlled drugs with intent to supply them to somebody else or if you supply or offer to supply them to somebody else.

● It is worth pointing out that the term 'supply' simply means handing over possession and includes giving drugs away or sharing them with friends as well as selling them for money or dealing. For example

    ○ if you have a cannabis joint which you pass around at a party, you could be guilty of supply;

○ if somebody else asks you to look after their stash of drugs and to hand them back later, you could be guilty of supply;

○ if a group of friends put their money together, and one of them buys drugs on behalf of the rest, he or she could be guilty of supply.

● The Misuse of Drugs Act divides drugs into categories and imposes penalties according to how dangerous they are considered to be. For example

Class	Drugs included	Maximum period of imprisonment for an adult	
		Possession	Supply
A	heroin, cocaine, crack, LSD, ecstasy	7 years	life
B	cannabis, marijuana, amphetamines, barbiturates	5 years	14 years
C	tranquillisers (like valium) sedatives, painkillers	2 years (these can be possessed legally with a prescription)	5 years

Anabolic steroids are not controlled drugs at present, but the law is likely to change in the near future.

● If you are taking controlled drugs, your parents do not have to report you to the police.

● However, your parents can commit a criminal offence if they

○ permit the smoking of cannabis in their home (but, strangely, not, for example injecting heroin, snorting cocaine or taking ecstasy); or

○ know or turn a blind eye to the fact that their child is using their home for the supply of controlled drugs (remember this includes sharing) and do nothing to stop it; or

○ knowingly permit the growing of cannabis plants in the house or garden.

● If you bring controlled drugs into your home which your parents find, the law does not oblige them to hand the drugs over to the police but, if they do not do this, they must destroy them immediately, for example by flushing them down the toilet.

● If the police have reasonable grounds to suspect that you are in possession of a controlled drug, they can search you, and detain you in order to search you, and search your vehicle.

They can seize anything they find that appears to be evidence of a drug offence.

You may be committing a criminal offence if you intentionally obstruct them, for example by swallowing the drugs or by throwing them away.

● Such searches can take place in private as well as public places.

● Your school has no right to insist that you undergo a drug test and you cannot be tested against your will. If you do agree to a drug test, you will usually be asked to provide a sample of urine.

Be warned, if you take controlled drugs or give them to somebody else (whether or not for profit) not only are you putting your health at risk, you could end up with a criminal record. You may think 'Its only a bit of dope', but the law sees it differently.

If you have a problem with drugs see Part Three, Where to Go for Information and Help, under the heading (L), Drugs.

See also Chapter 40, The Police: Their Powers and Your Rights.

Chapter 24

● This can be done at any age. It is up to the shop, and they may not be prepared to do it unless you are accompanied by a parent.

Shops that pierce ears, noses and any other parts of the body should be registered with the local authority. You should check that the needles are sterilised and fresh needles are used for each customer, otherwise you risk infection from HIV.

Chapter 25

This is a complicated area of the law. A large number of rules exist to ensure that you receive an education because without one you may miss many opportunities in life. If you are under the age of 16, you cannot reject education. If you fail to go to school or misbehave in school there are various ways in which you can be punished.

(a) Compulsory attendance at school and your right to receive education

● You must receive education while you are of *compulsory school age*.

● You are of compulsory school age from the first term after your 5th birthday until around the time you are 16.

  ○ if your 16th birthday is between 1 September and 31 January you can leave school at the end of the spring term (you will be 16);

  ○ if your 16th birthday is between 1 February and 31 August you can leave school on the Friday before the last Monday in May (you may still be 15).

● Your parents have a legal duty to educate you properly and they must ensure that you receive proper full-time education suitable to your age, ability, aptitude and any special educational needs you may have, by regular attendance at school or otherwise.

● Your parents can send you to a state school or a private school (being an independent fee-charging school). They don't have to send you to school at all so long as they make arrangements that are satisfactory to your *local education authority* (LEA), for example they can teach you at home themselves or organise a home tutor for you.

● If your parents do not provide you with a proper education in certain circumstances they may be committing a criminal offence.

● You are allowed days off for religious festivals and also for holidays during term-time provided that the school gives its permission.

(b) Free education, transport and school meals

You will find your local education authority listed in your local telephone directory under 'Education Authorities' or the name of your local authority.

● Free state schools are run by LEAs and an LEA has a duty to provide sufficient suitable schools in its area.

● Grant-maintained schools are also free but are self-governing and independent of the LEA.

● You also have a right to full-time education until your 19th birthday *(see further heading (c) below)*.

● You alone cannot decide which state school to go to. If your parents wish you to go to a particular state school, their preference should normally be followed by the LEA.

● However, their right to choose is not absolute. They may be refused, for example because the school is

   ○ full up; *or*

   ○ not in the area where you live; *or*

○ a Church school and you are not for instance a Christian.

● If admission is refused to a particular state school, your parents have a right of appeal to an *education appeal committee*, but you do not have that right.

● If there is a good reason why you cannot go to school, the LEA must still provide you with an education. For instance

○ if you are in hospital for more than a brief period. Some hospitals do have their own special schools but, if not, the LEA must arrange for teachers to come and visit you;

○ if you are disabled *(see further Chapter 18, Disability, heading (c))* or have a genuine phobia of school or are pregnant, you may be entitled to receive home tuition or there may be a special unit you can attend in your area;

○ if you are excluded from school *(see further heading (g) below)* the LEA's duty still applies.

● The *Department for Education* has produced the 1994 updated *Parent's Charter – Our Children's Education*, which has been sent to every household in England and is aimed at improving standards in schools.

(1) Charges

● State education is free and, while you are still of compulsory school age, you and your parents cannot be made to pay for activities in school hours that are part of the *National Curriculum (see further heading (d) below)*, for example swimming and music lessons.

A charge can be made for individual music tuition and extra trips outside school hours, for example skiing holidays. However, you should not be charged for field trips that are part of your geography class (except that you may have to pay for your food and accommodation while on the trip).

(2) Free transport

● The LEA has a duty to provide you with free transport to and from school by means of special school buses or travel passes if your school is over 3 miles walking distance from your home, measured by the nearest available route.

● This only applies if you are at a school which the LEA decided you should attend, and not if your parents chose the school even though there is actually a school within 3 miles that would be suitable.

(3) School meals

● The LEA is entitled to charge you for school meals.

● If your parents are on income support or you are entitled to income support in your own right *(see Chapter 57, Welfare, Benefits, heading (b))* you are entitled to free school meals.

● If you bring in your own packed lunch you must be provided with somewhere comfortable to eat it.

(c) Staying on after school leaving age

● The LEA has a duty to provide suitable education for those aged 16 or over, but who have not yet reached 19, and who wish to receive full-time secondary education.

● This can be provided at a school, sixth form college, city technology college or further education college.

● If your school does not offer the subjects you want to study you should be given a place elsewhere.

● Even if you are unable to remain at school because of bad examination results, the LEA should provide you with an appropriate course somewhere else.

● State schools, sixth form colleges and city technology colleges are free.

● Fees may be charged for further education colleges, although you may be able to get a *grant* from the LEA.

● You may qualify for an *educational maintenance allowance* from the LEA if your parents have a low income.

These are all matters that vary from LEA to LEA. If you want to find out more, it is a good idea to ask your school or college to put you in touch with an education welfare officer.

(d) Your say in educational matters and what you learn

● Once you have reached the age of 16, your parents cannot force you to stay on at school against your will.

● It would be equally difficult to stay on at school if your parents insisted that you should leave. If there is an adult family member or friend with whom you could live and who would be prepared to allow you to carry on going to school, they could apply for a *residence order (see Chapter 11, The Children Act 1989, heading (c)(1))* in their favour.

● If your parents disagree with one another or if you disagree with your parents about the choice of school, an application can be made for a *specific issue order (see Chapter 11, The Children Act 1989, heading (c)(3))*. If it is you who makes the application, you must have *leave* (that is, permission) of the court. To obtain leave you must satisfy the court that you have sufficient understanding to make the proposed application.

● This is an area in which your say is important and the court is unlikely to force you to go somewhere where you would be miserable and your ability to learn would be affected. For instance, in a recent court case, a 14 year old boy was allowed to leave boarding school and attend a local day school because he wished to spend more time with his father.

(1) The National Curriculum

● This applies in all state schools but is not compulsory in private schools.

● It sets out the subjects you must study and the basic minimum education you must receive.

● The 'core' subjects are English, maths and science.

● The 'foundation' subjects are technology, history, geography, a modern foreign language, music, art and physical education.

● The National Curriculum also provides for religious instruction at the primary and secondary school stages, and sex education at the secondary school stage *(see further below)*.

● The Government has introduced certain changes to the National Curriculum with effect from September 1995, in particular, allowing schools greater freedom to decide how they will teach particular subjects and more hours to teach non-curriculum subjects, and making history and geography no longer compulsory at 14.

● Teachers in state and private schools are allowed to express their own political, moral, social and economic views when giving lessons, provided these do not break the law or affect other people's rights and are not discriminatory *(see further Chapter 19, Discrimination)* or offensive.

● You and your parents cannot stop a teacher from teaching you in a particular way. However, representations can be made to the head teacher, school governors and the LEA if you or your parents are unhappy about the way in which you are being taught.

● The Local Government Ombudsman cannot investigate internal school matters such as the curriculum and discipline.

(2) Religious assembly and instruction

● You can be excused from religious assembly by your parents. You are also entitled to days off for your own religious festivals.

● Religious instruction is compulsory in state schools but you can be excused from it by your parents.

(3) Sex education

● State secondary schools must provide sex education (including teaching about HIV, AIDS and other sexually transmitted diseases).

● Guidelines suggest that all sex education must be provided in such a manner as to encourage young people to have regard to moral considerations and the value of family life.

● Your parents can withdraw you from all, or part, of sex education lessons.

(e) Truancy and education supervision orders

● If your parents send you off to school in the morning but you do not actually go in or do not stay in school, in certain circumstances, your parents may be committing a criminal offence.

● The fact that you are not going regularly to the school at which you are a registered pupil is not of itself the basis for a *care order (see Chapter 11, The Children Act 1989, heading (c)(5))*. However, you could be made the subject of a *care order* if you are suffering, or are likely to suffer, 'significant harm' because of being beyond parental control *(see further Chapter 10, Care Proceedings)*, for example if instead of going to school you're spending the day hanging round the local shopping centre and getting into trouble with the police.

● If you are truanting, an *education welfare officer (EWO)* will make an investigation and will visit you and your parents at home.

● If you are of compulsory school age and you are not being properly educated, which includes not attending regularly at a school at which you are a registered pupil, the LEA may apply to the family proceedings court for an *education supervision order*.

● Such an order will not be made if you are away from school because of sickness or for an unavoidable reason but the fact that, for example, your mother is ill and you are expected to stay at home and look after the rest of the family is no justification.

● If an *education supervision* order is made, the court will appoint an EWO to be your supervisor. The EWO will visit you regularly to give advice to you and your parents and help you to try and sort out your problems about school, for example if you're not going to school because of bullying.

● The EWO can give directions to you and your parents stating what should be done to make sure that you are properly educated.

● The EWO must first listen to your wishes and feelings and those of your parents and take them into account.

● If you do not comply with an *education supervision order*, your parents could be committing a criminal offence and it could result in a *care order*.

● An *education supervision* order lasts 1 year and can be extended up to 3 years. It ends when you are no longer of compulsory school age or if you are made the subject of a *care order*.

Bullying in schools has become a widespread problem and various organisations have been set up to try and overcome it. Their details are given in Part Three, Where to go for Information and Help, under heading (C), Youth Services; the relevant entries are marked (E).

(f) Punishment and discipline

(1) Discipline

● The head teacher is entitled to lay down rules about the standards of behaviour expected from you and any punishment you may receive if you break these rules. The rules should be made known to you.

● You can be sent home for the day, for example if you are disruptive or are not wearing school uniform (or also if you have an infectious disease).

● It depends entirely on your school whether you have to wear a school uniform. (The LEA may provide cash or vouchers towards the cost of school uniform or sports kit.)

● If you break the rules about discipline you can have your privileges withdrawn or be held in detention. However

  ○ you must not be held in detention for an unduly long time;

  ○ the whole class should not be held in detention because the idea is to punish the wrongdoer;

  ○ your parents should be told, and their agreement obtained; *and*

  ○ you should not be put at risk, for example if you would miss the last bus home.

● A teacher can confiscate something dangerous, for example a knife, or something you shouldn't have, for example cigarettes if you are under the age of 16, but your teachers should not search you against your will, and the item should be given to your parents at the end of the day.

(2) Corporal punishment

● This covers not just caning but any form of assault, including slapping, hitting with a ruler or a plimsoll, shaking, pulling hair, throwing chalk or books and any other form of rough handling.

- Corporal punishment by teachers has been unlawful in state schools since 1987 and must not be used. This rule applies equally to grant-maintained schools, special schools (these are schools catering for children with special educational needs, *see further heading (k) below)* and also to pupils who have assisted places at private schools.

- There is an exception where it is necessary to stop someone from getting hurt or to prevent damage from being done to any property. Even then, only reasonable force may be used.

- Teachers in private schools can use corporal punishment, provided it is reasonable and not excessive. If the corporal punishment is not unduly severe, it does not amount to a breach of the European Convention on Human Rights *(see further Chapter 55)*.

- It is not a criminal offence to use corporal punishment in state schools but if any teacher, whether at a state or a private school, goes beyond what is moderate and reasonable, he or she may be guilty of assault, which is both a criminal offence and a *tort (see Chapter 15, The Courts and the Legal System, heading (a))*.

- If unlawful corporal punishment is used against you you may have a civil claim for assault for which you can *sue* for *damages* in the civil courts *(see further Chapter 51, Suing and Being Sued, heading (a); Chapter 12, Compensation, heading (b); and Chapter 48, Solicitors and Legal Aid)*.

- Your claim for *damages* will be against the LEA if you go to a state school, or the school governors in the case of a private or a grant-maintained school. You could claim against the teacher who assaulted you, but they are unlikely to have the money to pay any *damages*, whereas the LEA and the school itself will have insurance.

(g) Exclusion and expulsion from school

- If you commit a serious breach of discipline, for example smoking cannabis, hitting a teacher or bullying other pupils, you can be excluded from school temporarily or permanently. If it is permanent this is called expulsion.

- If there is an expulsion from a private school it is difficult to challenge the decision.

- At a *state school*

  ○ you can be excluded for a fixed period or periods of up to 15 days in any term. You cannot be excluded indefinitely although you can be expelled;

  ○ it is a decision for the head teacher who must without delay inform your parents, giving the period of the exclusion and the reasons;

  ○ your parents have a right to make representations to the school governors and the LEA but, unless you are aged 18 or over, you cannot do so;

  ○ if you are excluded for more than 5 days in 1 term, which includes expulsion, or you lose the opportunity to take a public examination, the head teacher must without delay inform the school governors and the LEA;

  ○ your parents have the right to make representations to the school governors and the LEA. They have the power to order the head teacher to reinstate you, if appropriate;

  ○ your parents have a right of appeal to an *education appeal committee* against a decision not to reinstate you where you have been expelled (but there is no right of appeal against a temporary exclusion);

  ○ the committee can overturn the expulsion and direct your reinstatement or uphold the decision to expel you;

  ○ unless you are aged 18 or over you have no right of appeal or to be present or heard.

- If you are expelled from school whether it is a state school or a private school, and you are still of compulsory school age, you must still receive an education and the LEA must provide another school or a special unit or a home tutor.

(h) Reports and records

● A written report on your progress should be sent to your parents at least once every year.

● State schools (including grant-maintained and special schools) keep a record of your attendance, behaviour, academic achievements, other skills and abilities and general progress in school. This is updated every year and includes information from teachers, EWOs, educational psychologists (if you've seen one) and other education support staff.

● A written request for a copy can be made to the governing body of the school whether the record is kept on a computer or manually. Whether or not you are entitled to see a copy depends on your age, for instance

○ if you are under the age of 16 your parents can seek a copy but you have no right to see it;

○ if you are aged 16 or over, but have not yet reached 18; both you and your parents are entitled to receive a copy;

○ if you are aged 18 or over only you are entitled to receive a copy.

● There may be a small fee payable. The copy should be received within 15 working days of receipt of the request.

● The obligation to disclose information only refers to the period from 1 September 1989. Information can be withheld on various grounds, including

○ where disclosure is likely to cause serious harm to your physical or mental health or emotional condition, or that of somebody else; *or*

○ it is relevant to the question of whether you are at risk of abuse; *or*

○ it is a reference given by a teacher in response to a request from a potential employer, a university, another school or any other place of education or training.

● When you leave a state school to go on to further education, training or work, you will receive a report called a *National Record of*

Achievement which gives a summary of your achievements in school and is designed to help you plan for the future.

● If you move schools or become a student at any further or higher educational establishment, your records may be transferred to that school or other establishment at its request.

(i) Safety at school

● Both state and private schools owe a duty to ensure that you are reasonably safe and members of staff must not be negligent.

● If you are injured because the school premises are dangerous or equipment provided by the school is defective or you are not properly supervised by your teacher, you may be able to *sue* for *damages* for negligence in the civil courts. (*See further Chapter 3, Accidents and Negligence; Chapter 51, Suing and Being Sued, heading (a); Chapter 12, Compensation, heading (b); and Chapter 48, Solicitors and Legal Aid.*)

● Your claim for *damages* will be against the LEA if you go to a state school, or the school governors in the case of a private or a grant-maintained school. You could claim against an individual teacher if they were at fault, but they are unlikely to have the money to pay any *damages*, whereas the LEA and the school itself will have insurance.

If you do have an accident you should go to your local Citizens' Advice Bureau, law centre or neighbourhood advice centre, or see a solicitor without delay.

Details of the Law Society's Accident Line are given in Part Three, Where to Go for Information and Help, under heading (U), Accidents.

You should also read Part Four, Making the Law Work for You, heading (4) which deals with personal injuries.

(j) Discrimination at school

See generally Chapter 19, Discrimination.

● At both state and private schools, you must not be treated less favourably on grounds of your colour, race, ethnic or national origin or nationality or your sex.

● It is permissible to have single sex schools or schools just for pupils who follow a particular religion. However, it is unlawful to further discriminate so that, for example, a Catholic school for girls must not refuse to take a Catholic girl because she is black.

● Mixed schools and colleges must not discriminate in admissions or in the range of subjects available, for example a girl must be allowed to study design and technology and these classes cannot be limited to boys.

● School uniform rules must not discriminate, for example it is unlawful to forbid a Sikh boy to wear a turban and girls at mixed schools should be able to wear trousers.

● If you are subjected to racial or sexual harassment, for example a teacher picks on you because you are black or you always get lower marks even though your work is as good as that of white pupils, this is a form of discrimination.

● If you are the victim of unlawful discrimination at school, you can make a complaint to the *Secretary of State for Education* but, if you are at a state school, you must first complain to the LEA and the school governors. Those at state schools can also complain to the *Local Government Ombudsman (see Chapter 15, heading (d)).*

(k) Special educational needs

● If you are under the age of 19, and have *special educational needs* which signifies learning difficulties such as dyslexia or a speech impediment, you have the right to an education which meets those needs. You should be educated within an ordinary school rather than at a special school wherever possible and your LEA must provide you with extra help in order to achieve this.

● The LEA must make an assessment of what your needs are and provide for these appropriately. This may involve making a *statement*.

● In making the assessment and producing any *statement*, the opinions of your teachers and doctor will be taken into account. You may have to see an educational psychologist and/or have a medical examination.

● Your parents have a right to give their views. If they do not agree with the suggested provision, or the LEA does not intend to make any provision, they have a right to appeal to a *special educational needs tribunal.*

● You have no right of your own to be involved in decisions regarding special needs and *statementing*, but the LEA should listen to what you have to say.

If you claim that the LEA has failed in any of its duties, a letter should be sent to the *Chief Education Officer* giving full details. If no satisfactory response is received

- the matter may be taken to the *Secretary of State for Education;*

- a complaint may be made to the *Local Government Ombudsman (see Chapter 15, The Courts and the Legal System, heading (d));*

- you should consider telling a local councillor or Member of Parliament and asking them to help you;

- it may also be possible to bring an application in the High Court for *judicial review (see Chapter 15, The Courts and the Legal System, heading (b)(4)).*

The addresses of the Department for Education and the Local Government Ombudsman for different parts of the country are given in Part Three, Where to Go of Information and Help, under heading (S), Education, and (V), Consumer protection.

This is a specialist area of the law which most solicitors do not handle. You should first seek the advice of the Childrens' Legal Centre or the Advisory Centre for Education. Their details are also in Part Three, under heading (A), Legal and General, and (S), Education.

Details of other organisations that may be able to assist in relation to educational matters and special needs can also be found under heading (S), Education, in Part Three.

The rights of disabled children and young people in relation to educational matters are dealt with in Chapter 18, Disability, under heading (c).

Chapter 26

EMIGRATING, GOING TO LIVE ABROAD AND HOLIDAYS

● If you are under the age of 16 and both your parents decide that they wish to live in another country permanently, but you don't want to go with them, you will probably have to go, unless they arrange for you to stay with an adult family member or friend or to be accommodated by the local authority *(see further Chapter 9, Care Orders and Accommodation – Being Looked After by the Local Authority, heading (b))*.

● If you cannot reach an agreement with your parents, you may be able to apply to the court for a *residence order (see Chapter 11, The Children Act 1989, heading (c)(1))*, a *specific issue order (see Chapter 11, heading (c)(3))*, or a *prohibited steps order (see Chapter 11, heading (c)(4))*.

● You must have *leave* (that is, permission) of the court to make the application. To obtain leave you must satisfy the court that you have sufficient understanding to make the application *(the procedure for making your own application to the court is dealt with in Chapter 11, heading (d))*.

- It is unlikely that the court would force your parents to stay in this country if they have made plans to make a fresh start elsewhere. If you are approaching 16 and you can show that there will be disruption to your schooling and/or to your own plans for the future, and there is an adult family member or friend who is willing to look after you, the court could make a *residence order* in their favour *(see Chapter 11, heading (c)(1))*.

- If your father does not have *parental responsibility* for you *(see Chapter 38, Parental Responsibility and Decisions About Your Life and Your Upbringing)* and you are not the subject of a *residence order* or a *care order (see Chapter 11, heading (c)(5))*, your mother can take you abroad for whatever period of time she wishes without the need for your father's consent or to make any application to the court for leave.

- If your father does have *parental responsibility*, your mother requires his consent or leave of the court (and the other way round if it is your father who wishes to take you abroad).

- If you are the subject of a *residence order*, the parent, or person in whose favour the order was made, can take you out of the United Kingdom for up to 1 month, that is, for short holidays abroad, but if they wish to go for any longer they must have the written consent of every person who has *parental responsibility* for you, or the leave of the court.

- In the absence of the necessary consent or leave the person who takes you out of the country will be committing a criminal offence.

- The court can deal with these kinds of disputes by making a *specific issue order* on the application of the parent wishing to take you, or a *prohibited steps order* on the application of the parent wishing to prevent your removal from this country.

- The outcome of the case depends on all the circumstances. In emigration cases, judges are placing increasing emphasis on the views of the children and young people concerned. The court is unlikely to prevent the emigration if the plans of the parent who wishes to take you are properly thought out and if the emigration will provide you with better opportunities for the future and you will still have a chance to see the other parent at regular intervals.

On the other hand, in a recent court case leave was refused to the mother of 2 boys, aged 10 and 11, who enjoyed seeing their father and wanted to see more of him, liked their school and didn't want to leave England.

The details of organisations assisting in the recovery of abducted children are given in Part Three, Where to Go for Information and Help, under heading (W), Other Useful Contacts.

See also Chapter 9, Care Orders and Accommodation – Being Looked After by the Local Authority; Chapter 11, The Children Act 1989; Chapter 20, Divorce and Separation; Chapter 33, Leaving Home and Running Away; Chapter 38, Parental Responsibility and Decisions About Your Life and Your Upbringing; Chapter 48, Solicitors and Legal Aid. The position regarding removal from this country if you are the subject of a care order is dealt with in Chapter 9, Care Orders and Accommodation – Being Looked After by the Local Authority, under heading (e).

Chapter 27

Some rules about taking part in performances

(1) Public performances

● If you are under the age of 16 you cannot take part in any public performance, for example acting, dancing, singing or playing music, for more than 3 days in any 6 month period, without a licence from the local authority, where

  ○ there is a charge to see the performance;

  ○ it takes place in licensed premises or a club;

  ○ it is going to be filmed or recorded for broadcasting, for example TV, cinema or radio.

● You need a licence even if the performance does not involve you taking any time off school.

● The local authority must be satisfied that you are fit to do the performance, there are proper arrangements for your welfare and your education will not suffer.

● If you are under the age of 13 it must be shown that the part can only be taken by a child of your age.

- It is not necessary to have a licence for a school production, for example an end of term play or concert where you do not receive any payment.

(2) Dangerous performances

- If you are under the age of 16 you cannot take part in any dangerous performances, including acrobatic and contortionist performances.

- If you are under the age of 12 you cannot be trained to take part in dangerous performances.

- If you are aged 12 or over, but under the age of 16, a licence must be obtained from the local authority before you can receive such training.

(3) Performing abroad

- If you are under the age of 16, and wish to go abroad to play or perform for profit, you must have a licence from the magistrates' court.

(4) Hypnotic shows

- It is a criminal offence for a person to give a public exhibition, demonstration or performance of hypnotism on a person under the age of 18, whether or not there is a charge to see the show.

Chapter 28

FIREWORKS

● Fireworks must not be sold to any child or young person who appears to be under the age of 16.

● Fireworks must not be discharged in a street or public place.

● It is a criminal offence to possess a smoke bomb, fireworks or distress flare at a league or cup football match and when entering or trying to enter the ground.

Chapter 29

(a) Faulty goods – your rights and remedies

● Buying and selling goods involves making a contract *(see further Chapter 14)* which the law will enforce.

● The Sale of Goods Act 1979 (SGA) exists to protect customers. It always applies when the seller sells goods in the course of business, whether the goods are new or second hand, whether you buy them in a sale or at a discounted price, and whether you buy them from a shop, a market stall or a mail order catalogue.

● The SGA sets out certain terms which apply to every business seller and cannot be excluded even if the seller tells you otherwise.

● With purely private sales, for example if you buy a car from a friend or in reply to a classified ad in the local paper from a private individual rather than from a dealer, only the two terms described in sub-paragraphs 1 and 2 below apply. In purely private sales, the SGA provides no remedy if the goods are defective.

● The terms are

1   The seller has a right to sell the goods.

You can only sell what is yours. If you buy stolen goods you don't actually own them even if you paid a reasonable price and didn't know they were stolen. If the true owner comes along, he or she is entitled to have the goods back and you are entitled to get your money back from the seller.

> You should be careful if, say, you are offered a brand new radio/cassette player for £25 which you know is worth a great deal more. You could be committing the criminal offence of dishonestly handling stolen goods.

2   Goods must correspond with their description.

For example, a plastic jacket must not have a sign on it saying 'genuine leather'.

3   The goods must be of *satisfactory quality* and *reasonably fit for the purpose for which they are bought.*

This means that the goods must be free from defects and do what they are supposed to do, for example a pair of wellington boots must not let in the rain.

○   *Satisfactory quality* relates to the actual condition of the goods and their age, appearance, description and price are relevant. You would not expect the same performance from a 10 year old car with over 100,000 miles on the clock as you would from a brand new car. This term does not apply where the seller has pointed out any defects before the contract was made, or where the buyer has actually examined the goods before purchasing them and he or she should have noticed the defects.

> You must inspect an item thoroughly. You are actually better off not looking at it at all than just checking it over quickly.

○   *Goods must be reasonably fit for their purpose.* The buyer must make it known to the seller the purpose for which the goods are required. This will usually be fairly obvious. For instance, if you ask for a CD player you are entitled to expect to be able to listen to CDs on it. If you actually want it for cassettes, you did not ask the sales assistant whether it was suitable for use in this way and you jam up the mechanism, the seller will not be at fault.

● If you receive a manufacturer's guarantee (most electrical equipment carries a 12 month guarantee), this does not alter the fact that your contract is with the person who sold you the goods. The guarantee is additional to any remedies you have against the actual seller.

Where there is a manufacturer's guarantee, do not allow yourself to be fobbed off by the seller. It is up to you whether you take action against the manufacturer under the guarantee, the seller under the SGA or both.

● If an item develops a fault after you've had it for a little while, it depends on its nature and age whether you have any remedy under the SGA. For instance, provided that you treat it carefully, you would expect to be able to drive a brand new car without any problems for quite some time, but an old banger is a different proposition!

● The remedies provided for under the SGA are a *refund* (that is, getting back the amount you paid) and/or *damages,* and not repairs. If you are happy with having your item repaired, you can agree to this but you are entitled to refuse and insist on a refund as long as you act quickly *(see further below)*. If you agree to the seller attempting to repair the item, you will not lose your remedies.

● You cannot insist on an exchange. If a reputable shop offers an exchange, this could be a sensible solution.

● The seller cannot insist that you have the item repaired, accept an exchange or take a credit note.

● The goods must actually be faulty. If you break an item yourself through rough handling, or change your mind and decide you don't want it, you have no rights or remedies. If you had the opportunity, say, to try on clothes in a shop and didn't bother, and when you get home you realise they don't fit or suit you you are stuck with them unless the shop is prepared to give you a refund or an exchange as a gesture of goodwill.

- *You must act quickly once you have discovered a defect.* If you continue to use the item after you have discovered the defect you may lose your right to a refund. You must make it plain that you are rejecting the item, preferably by taking it back immediately. If you delay you may have to accept repairs because your only claim will be in *damages* for the cost of repairing the fault.

- The *damages* to which you are entitled are

  - the cost of having the item repaired by a reputable repairer, where a refund is not appropriate (because for instance you have had the item for some time before it became defective or because you delayed taking it back after it became defective); *or*

  - if it cannot be repaired, the difference in value between what you paid for the item and its value in its defective state;

  - compensation for any consequential losses. For instance, if you buy an iron which overheats due to a wiring problem and you burn a hole in your best silk shirt, you are entitled to the cost of another similar shirt.

- If you suffer personal injuries through defective goods you have a claim against the manufacturer and/or wholesaler, as well as the actual seller.

(b) Services

- Where a person provides services in the course of business, there is a term that he or she will carry out the work with *reasonable care and skill*.

- You are entitled to have the job done properly and to a reasonable standard.

- If this does not happen, you are entitled to withhold payment and claim *damages,* that is, compensation for any consequential losses. For example

  if you go to the hairdressers for a perm and you end up with a burnt scalp and your hair looks a frizzy mess

  - you should not pay;

○ you are entitled to the cost of a visit to another hairdressers to put it right;

○ you are entitled to general damages for your personal injuries and for the disappointment caused to you.

● If, say, you take something in for repairs or dry cleaning, you must always make it plain when you want it back. Otherwise, the law only provides for the work to be completed within a 'reasonable time'. For example, if you want your dress dry cleaned for a wedding the next day, unless you pay for express service, normally, this would not be a reasonable time.

● It is in your interests to agree the *price* in advance where this is possible, or to ask for a written estimate or quotation. If you do not do this, you are bound to pay a 'reasonable price', which could actually be a great deal more than you anticipated.

● Those who provide services, for example travel agents and dry cleaners, may belong to associations which lay down codes of practice for their members. Such codes have no legal standing, but the association may be able to assist you if you are dissatisfied with the service you received.

Details of organisations and bodies that exist to protect the interests of consumers are given in Part Three, Where to Go for Information and Help, under heading (V), Consumer Protection.

All local authorities have a trading standards department. Trading standards officers investigate complaints about false descriptions, prices, weights and measures, safety of products, consumer credit and other things like cigarette sales to children.

Your trading standards department will be listed in your local telephone directory under the name of your local authority.

See also Chapter 3, Accidents and Negligence; Chapter 12, Compensation, heading (b), Awards of damages by the civil courts; Chapter 14, Contracts; Chapter 48, Solicitors and Legal Aid; Chapter 51, Suing and Being Sued. You should also read Part Four, Making the Law Work for You, heading (3), which deals with faulty goods.

Chapter 30

Who brings you up if your parents die?

● A guardian is somebody who is appointed to look after a child or young person until they reach 18 if their parents die.

● 2 or more people can be appointed to act as guardians jointly, but a guardian must be an individual rather than, for example, a local authority or the NSPCC.

● A guardian will have *parental responsibility* for you *(see Chapter 38, Parental Responsibility and Decisions About Your Life and Your Upbringing)*. Therefore a guardian is able to make all the major decisions such as where you will live and go to school. A guardian can arrange getting a passport for you. If you are arrested, the police must inform your guardian and, if you face a criminal charge, your guardian must accompany you to the youth court.

● If your parents are, or have been, married or your father has *parental responsibility* for you *(see Chapter 38)* either or both of your parents can appoint a guardian for you.

● If your parents are unmarried and your father doesn't have *parental responsibility*, only your mother can appoint a guardian for you. This means that even if you live with your father he will not automatically have a right to look after you on your mother's death.

● The appointment can be made in a will, or by a special deed of appointment, or in writing so long as the document is dated and signed. A family court also has power to appoint guardians.

● Parents can choose anyone they like to be your guardian. An unmarried mother can appoint a father without *parental responsibility*.

● Where both parents have *parental responsibility* for you, the appointment by the parent who dies will not take effect until after the surviving parent dies. There is an exception where the appointment is made by a parent in whose favour there is a *residence order (see Chapter 11, heading (c)(1) and see further below)*.

● The court will make the appointment if both parents had *parental responsibility* for you and they both die without appointing a guardian, or if your father doesn't have *parental responsibility* and your mother dies without appointing a guardian. The court will generally appoint a member of your family who is willing to be your guardian.

● You can apply to the court to bring to an end the appointment of the guardian.

You must have *leave* (that is, permission) of the court.

If there is nobody else with *parental responsibility* for you, another guardian will have to be appointed in their place.

These rules are quite complicated and some examples may make things clearer.

Your parents were unmarried and lived together, your father doesn't have parental responsibility, your mother dies without appointing a guardian

    ○ the court will usually appoint your father to be your guardian or make a *residence order* in his favour.

Your parents were unmarried, your father doesn't have parental responsibility, your mother dies having appointed your aunt to be your guardian

- the appointment of your aunt takes effect immediately although your father is able to apply for a *residence order* so that he can look after you. If he succeeds, he will share *parental responsibility* with your aunt.

Your parents were unmarried, your father doesn't have parental responsibility, your mother dies without appointing a guardian, you don't see your father very often, you are very close to your aunt who can offer you a home

- the court could appoint your aunt to be your guardian as well as your father and they will act jointly.

Your parents were married, your mother dies, having appointed her sister (your aunt) to be your guardian

- the appointment will not take effect until after your father dies. He can appoint his brother (your uncle) to be your guardian. On your father's death, your aunt and uncle will be your guardians, acting jointly.

  (The position is the same if your parents were unmarried and your father has *parental responsibility*.)

Your parents were married but separated or divorced, you lived with your mother before she died and she has appointed your aunt to be your guardian

- if your mother didn't have a *residence order*, your father can look after you;

- if your mother had a *residence order*, your father and your aunt will share *parental responsibility*. If they can't agree where you should live, the court will have to decide which of them should have a *residence order*.

See also Chapter 32, Inheritance and Wills; Chapter 38, Parental Responsibility and Decisions About Your Life and Your Upbringing.

Chapter 31

HOUSING AND HOMELESSNESS

(a) Your rights if you have nowhere to live

There are 2 separate sets of rules under which the social services department and the housing department of the local authority may owe duties to children and young people who are homeless.

You may be able to apply to either or both departments depending on your circumstances. The 2 departments are supposed to co-operate with one another so that you do not end up being sent backwards and forwards between them.

This is a complicated area of the law and what follows is intended only to be a general outline.

To find out more about your rights and for practical assistance, you should contact one of the organisations listed in Part Three, Where to Go for Information and Help under heading (R), Housing and Homelessness.

You will find the details of the social services office covering your area in your local telephone directory under the name of your local authority; the listing will usually be 'Social Services, Children and Families'.

You will find the details for your local housing department or neighbourhood housing office in your local telephone directory under the name of your local authority.

Most local authorities have homeless persons units and housing advice centres or housing aid centres which may be able to find you a home or a hostel place and help you with housing benefit. Housing advice and aid centres also give advice to people who are having problems with their landlords. Look in your local telephone directory under the name of your local authority to find the details.

(1) Duties owed by the social services department of the local authority

The duties of the social services department to provide accommodation for children in need are dealt with in full in Chapter 9, under heading (b).

● If you are under the age of 18, and there is nobody who can look after you and you have nowhere to live, the social services department have a duty to provide you with accommodation.

● If you are aged 16 or 17 they have a duty to provide you with accommodation if your welfare is likely to be seriously prejudiced if no accommodation is provided. This means that if you are unhappy at home and decide to leave, you have nowhere to go and are on the streets and you ask to be received into accommodation, the social services department must provide you with accommodation. In this situation your parents cannot prevent you from being received into accommodation or remove you against your will.

This is not necessarily the position as far as housing departments are concerned because you may be intentionally homeless (see further heading (2) below).

● The accommodation provided by the social services department usually means a foster home or a children's home rather than a permanent home of your own, although this may be provided if you are aged 16 or 17. The social services department, in order to fulfil its duties, may request the help of the housing department which must comply with the request insofar as it is able to do so in line with its own duties. The social services department may also approach voluntary organisations, housing associations and private landlords.

● If you wish to challenge a decision regarding the provision of accommodation you can use the complaints procedure *(see Chapter 9, Care Orders and Accommodation – Being Looked After by the Local Authority, heading (g))* or you may be able to make an application for judicial review *(see Chapter 15, The Courts and the Legal System, heading (b)(4))*.

If you do feel that a decision is wrong, you should contact one of the organisations listed in Part Three, Where to Go for Information and Help under heading (R), Housing and Homelessness or go to your local law centre or see a solicitor without delay.

(2) Duties owed by the housing department of the local authority

● The exercise of their duties by housing departments to house homeless people has resulted in many applications for *judicial review* in recent times and there is a great deal of case law on the subject.

● The basic rule under the Housing Act 1985 is that every local authority has a duty to ensure that accommodation is made available to every person who is

○ homeless;

○ in priority need; *and*

○ did not make themselves intentionally homeless.

● All 3 conditions must be satisfied for the housing department to be obliged to provide you with a permanent home of your own, usually a council flat or house. In reality if you go the housing department they may well require the social services department to exercise their duties to accommodate you. However, if you are aged 16 or 17 and you do satisfy all the conditions, the housing department may accept that they have a duty to house you.

● You are homeless if you have no accommodation in this country available for you to live in or are threatened with homelessness within 28 days. For a young person this might mean that you cannot live at home with your parents because, for example

- you are an orphan; *or*

- you've quarrelled with your parents and they've thrown you out; *or*

- you are forced to leave in order to avoid sexual or physical abuse or domestic violence.

● A priority need for accommodation arises if, for example

- you are vulnerable, that is, you cannot fend for yourself because of any mental illness, handicap or physical disability you may have and/or any other special reason, but just because you are a young person does not make you vulnerable;

- you are pregnant;

- you have a child living with you; *or*

- you have lost your home through an emergency, for example because of fire or flood.

● You will make yourself intentionally homeless if you give up or deliberately do anything which causes you to lose accommodation which is available to you and which it is reasonable for you to continue to occupy.

● Therefore you will not satisfy this condition if you don't get on with your parents and it is your choice to leave home, but you may satisfy it if, for example you leave because you are being sexually or physically abused.

● If you appear to be homeless and in priority need you are entitled to be given temporary accommodation, for example in a hostel or a bed and breakfast hotel, while the housing department makes further enquiries.

● If, for example

- you are homeless and in priority need, but you deliberately made yourself homeless; *or*

- you are unintentionally homeless, but not in priority need

the housing department have a duty to provide you with advice and assistance. This generally consists of a list of local housing associations and accommodation agencies.

● Where you are in priority need, but deliberately made yourself homeless, there is a further duty to provide you with somewhere temporary to stay for a fixed period, usually 28 days, while you try and sort yourself out.

● Where you qualify for a permanent home, the housing department is not bound to provide it immediately if there is nothing available. In practice, this means that you could remain in temporary accommodation for some time.

● If you qualify you are entitled to be offered somewhere suitable, taking into account your personal circumstances and needs, and it might even be in another area. However, accommodation would not be suitable if, for example

  ○ it is near to where your parents live and you are under threat of violence from them;

  ○ you have difficulty walking and it is a flat located on the top floor and there's no lift;

  ○ it is a long way from your work or college and you wouldn't be able to get there; *or*

  ○ it is unfit for human habitation (but the fact that it is cramped or in a poor decorative state doesn't make it unsuitable).

● Generally, you only get one offer and, if you unreasonably refuse this, the housing department no longer have a duty towards you. *It is therefore important that you make them fully aware of all your needs and requirements. If you are offered somewhere that isn't very nice, you probably have no option but to take it.*

● You are entitled to be notified in writing of all decisions taken by the housing department and for full reasons to be given.

● Challenges to any decision can be made by means of *judicial review (see Chapter 15, The Courts and the Legal System, heading (b)(4)).*

If you do feel that a decision is wrong, you should contact one of the organisations listed in Part Three, Where to Go for Information and Help under heading (R), Housing and Homelessness or go to your local law centre or see a solicitor without delay. You should take with you the written reasons supplied by the housing department.

See further Chapter 33, Leaving Home and Running Away.

(b) Tenants, licensees and squatters

(1) Tenants

● Even though you may pay rent to a landlord for a bedsit, flat or house, in law, you cannot become the tenant until you have reached the age of 18.

● A tenant has the right to occupy the property to the exclusion of other people, including the landlord, until the tenancy comes to an end or the court makes an order for possession.

● As a general rule, tenants have greater rights than licensees, for example about repairs and being able to remain in occupation once the tenancy has ended.

(2) Licensees

● You can be granted a licence to live somewhere at any age. You do not have to be 18. Licences can be granted, for example, by private licensors (landlords), housing associations and the council.

● A licence is a personal permission. Further examples of the sorts of situations in which you have the status of a licensee include

   ○ if you live at home, you have a licence from your parents to occupy your bedroom and to share the rest of the property with other family members also living there;

   ○ if you are a lodger in somebody else's home where, for example, meals and laundry are provided and your room is cleaned for you, you have a licence to be there;

   ○ if you have a room in a hostel or bed and breakfast hotel or in student or other similar shared premises, you are a licensee.

● A licence can be brought to an end by the licensor giving the licensee a reasonable period of notice. If you pay rent and do not share any part of the property with the licensor you must receive a written *notice to quit* allowing you a minimum of 4 weeks in which to leave.

Furthermore you cannot be evicted without a proper application being made to the county court *(see Chapter 15, The Courts and the Legal System, heading (b)(3))* for a *possession order.*

● If the licensor evicts you, for example he or she changes the locks, the licensor could be committing a criminal offence.

In addition, you may be able to make an application in the county court *(see Chapter 15, The Courts and the Legal System, heading (b)(3))* for an injunction to enable you to re-enter the property and/or to *sue* for *damages* for *unlawful eviction (see further Chapter 51, Suing and Being Sued).*

● You also have a right not to be harassed and not to be put under pressure to leave. Harassment is any act which stops you living safely and peacefully in your home and may occur if, for example

○ you are assaulted or subjected to abuse or threats;

○ builders are sent in at unsociable hours;

○ the gas or electricity is turned off.

This kind of conduct may amount to a criminal offence as well as giving rise to a claim for an injunction to prevent it from continuing and/or a claim for *damages.*

If you are unlawfully evicted or harassed you should go to the police without delay and to your local housing advice centre or housing aid centre and ask to talk to the tenancy relations officer or harassment officer whose job it is to deal with complaints or go to your local Citizens' Advice Bureau, law centre or see a solicitor.

● If you have a licence from a private licensor or a housing association, you do not have the right that certain tenants have to remain in occupation once the tenancy has ended.

● If you have a licence from the council of a flat or a house (but not of a room in a hostel or bed and breakfast hotel or in student or other similar shared premises) you may have this right provided that you occupy the property as your only or principal home.

(3) Squatters

● If you move into a property without any permission you will be a *trespasser*, also called a squatter. You will have no right to remain there.

● You could also be committing a criminal offence if you refuse to leave when requested to do so by the rightful occupier.

● At present, it is necessary to apply to the county court for a *possession order* against a squatter and there is a special, speedy procedure for doing this.

You must be given notice of the proceedings. This is normally done by pinning a *summons* to the front door.

If you deny that you are a squatter and wish to try and persuade the judge not to make a *possession order,* or to give you some more time before you have to leave, you have the right to go to court on the date given in the summons and be heard.

If you do not leave after a *possession order* has been made, it is likely that the court *bailiffs* will be sent in to evict you. It is also a criminal offence to resist or obstruct a bailiff in the course of an eviction.

● However, under new laws that have yet to come into force, the rightful occupier or somebody acting on his or her behalf (for example, a private security guard) can use reasonable force to enter and evict squatters provided that they have a statement signed by the rightful occupier and witnessed by a magistrate verifying their right of occupation.

● The procedure for obtaining a *possession order* is also going to change so that the rightful occupier will be able to go to court without giving the squatters any notice, and be immediately granted an *interim possession order*. Once a *possession order* has been obtained the squatters must leave within 24 hours of being informed, and they must not return, or they will be committing a criminal offence.

See further Chapter 41, Public Order Offences, heading (c), Trespassers. The rules relating to the payment of housing benefit in respect of rent are dealt with in Chapter 57, heading (c).

Chapter 32

● You cannot make a will until you are 18 although there is an exception if you are in the armed forces.

(a) Receiving gifts under a will

● You can have personal possessions (for example jewellery or ornaments) or money left to you in a will.

The will may state that you cannot actually receive the money until you reach a certain age, or get married, but any income produced by that money may be used before then for your maintenance or education.

● Until you have reached the age of 18 you cannot own property (that is, land or a house) in your own right. Property can be left to you in trust until you are an adult. This means that it is looked after on your behalf by an adult named in the will until you are old enough to have it transferred into your name. Meanwhile if the will says so, you may be able to live there.

(b) What happens if a parent dies without making a will or leaves you out of their will?

● If a person does not make a will and they die, this is called *intestacy*. There are special rules about what happens to an intestate's money, property and personal possessions (called their *estate*).

● These rules provide that

    ○ the surviving husband or wife is entitled to

    – all the dead parent's personal possessions;

    – the first £125,000 of the rest of their estate; *and*

    – any income produced by half of the rest of their estate for their lifetime.

    – if the family home is jointly owned, it will pass automatically to the surviving husband or wife

    (if the family home was rented in the name of the parent who dies, it will normally be inherited automatically by the surviving husband or wife);

    ○ the children are entitled to

    – half of the rest of the dead parent's estate, after the first £125,000, to be divided in equal shares; *and*

    – the whole of the other half after the death of the surviving husband or wife to be divided in equal shares. If the children are still under 18, it will be held on trust until they reach 18, or marry, but any income produced may be used before then for their maintenance or education;

    ○ if there is no surviving husband, or wife, the whole of the estate goes to the children.

● If a parent who dies does make a will but leaves you out of it, or does not provide adequately for your maintenance, the Inheritance (Provision for Family and Dependents) Act 1975 enables an application to be made to the court for 'reasonable' financial provision from the estate.

- Such an application can be made by
  - the surviving husband or wife;
  - any child (including an adopted child, *see further Chapter 4, Adoption*) of the dead parent. The child can be any age but adult children are generally expected to look after themselves;
  - any other person who was being maintained by the dead parent immediately before his or her death.

- The court has wide powers to award maintenance and/or lump sums and to make orders about the family home.

- The court will make whatever order it considers appropriate taking into account all the circumstances of the case including the incomes and needs of everyone involved and whether you are still receiving education or training.

- The effect of these rules is not simply that if you are left out of the will you may be able to get something but also, if everything is left to you, somebody else may be able to challenge this and receive all or part of what you would otherwise have received.

See also Chapter 30, Guardians.

Chapter 33

● Once you have reached the age of 18 you can leave home and you do not need the permission of your parents.

● If, while you are under the age of 18, the reason you are very unhappy at home and no longer wish to live there is that you are being abused in some way, the social services department of your local authority, once they have been made aware of this, must make an investigation and take whatever steps they consider necessary to protect you (*see generally Chapter 2, Abuse and Child Protection Procedures*).

● At 16 or 17 you can leave home with your parents' consent or if you are married (their consent is also required for you to get married, *see further Chapter 34, Marriage*).

● If you do leave home at 16 or 17 without your parents' consent they could attempt to prevent this by applying to the High Court (*see Chapter 15, The Courts and the Legal System, heading (b)(4)*) to make you a Ward of Court (*see further Chapter 56, Wardship*). They might also report you to the police as missing.

In practice, if you are aged 16 or over and have found somewhere to live, a job or a college place and are in no danger, it is unlikely that the police would be willing to become involved. It is also unlikely that the High Court would force you to return home against your will.

● If you are aged 16 or 17 the social services department have a duty to provide you with accommodation if your welfare is likely to be seriously prejudiced if no accommodation is provided. This means that if you are unhappy at home and decide to leave, you have nowhere else to go and are on the streets, and you ask to be received into accommodation, the social services department must provide you with accommodation.

● In addition, if you are aged 16 or 17, the social services may provide you with accommodation if you ask to be received into accommodation and they consider that it would be in your best interests.

● In either case, your parents cannot prevent you from being received into accommodation or remove you against your will.

● If you are under the age of 16 your parents can prevent you from being received into accommodation if they object and can offer you a home. Even if they agreed to begin with, they can change their minds and remove you against your will.

The only way that you could continue to be looked after by the local authority instead of remaining with your parents is if the grounds exist to apply for a *care order (see further Chapter 11, The Children Act 1989, heading (c)(5); care proceedings are dealt with in Chapter 10).*

● If you are under the age of 16 and are very unhappy at home and wish to live elsewhere, but your parents do not agree, a court order must be obtained. You or the adult family member or friend with whom you are proposing to live, can apply to the court for a *residence order (see Chapter 11, The Children Act 1989, heading (c)(1))* in their favour. If you make the application, you require *leave* (that is, permission) of the court to make the application. Before granting you leave, the court must be satisfied that you have sufficient understanding to make the application. *(See further Chapter 11, The Children Act 1989, heading (d). 'Divorcing' your parents is dealt with in Chapter 20, Divorce and Separation, under heading (c).)*

● If you are under the age of 16 and you run away, you may find it very hard to survive as you are not legally allowed to work full-time *(see Chapter 58, Working, heading (a))*. You cannot get income support *(see Chapter 57, Welfare Benefits, heading (b))* and you may not be able to afford rented accommodation.

● Many young people who run away from home end up sleeping rough and drifting into criminal activities, drugs and prostitution. It is also a criminal offence to beg in a public place and, in certain circumstances, being on the streets may amount to the criminal offence of obstructing the highway.

● If you are under the age of 18 and the police find you, and they have reasonable cause to believe that you would otherwise be likely to suffer 'significant harm', they can remove you to suitable accommodation and keep you there for a period of up to 72 hours. This is known as being taken into *police protection. (See further Chapter 2, Abuse and Child Protection Procedures, heading (d).)*

● The police must immediately inform the social services department of your local authority.

● If you appear capable of understanding, the police must immediately tell you about the steps that have been taken, give you the reasons, and inform you about any further steps that may be taken.

They must also find out your wishes and feelings.

● You might be placed with temporary foster parents or in a children's home. If you request it, this address can be kept secret from your parents, although the police must inform your parents, all those with *parental responsibility* for you *(see Chapter 38, Parental Responsibility and Decisions About Your Life and Your Upbringing)* and anyone with whom you were living immediately before being taken into police protection, that you are in police protection, and the reason for this.

● It may be that the social services department of your local authority consider that you will require further protection once the 72 hours is over. In these circumstances an application will be made to the family proceedings court *(see Chapter 15, heading (b)(2))* for an *emergency protection order (EPO))*.

● *EPOs are explained in Chapter 2, under heading (e).* At the end of the EPO, and provided that you are under the age of 17 the local authority must decide whether there are grounds to apply for a *care order (see Chapter 11, The Children Act 1989, heading (c)(5)* or a *supervision order (Chapter 11, heading (c)(6)).*

● Given that you may actually be making things worse for yourself by running away, it is a decision that you should consider very carefully. If you are extremely unhappy at home, you should try to talk about this to a sympathetic adult whom you trust, for example your teacher or doctor (or social worker if you have one) to try and find an alternative solution.

If you feel too embarrassed and upset to do this and would rather talk to somebody who doesn't know you and your family, Childline and the NSPCC run free, confidential telephone helplines with experienced counsellors available 24 hours a day to discuss your problems. Their telephone numbers are given in Part Three, Where to Go for Information and Help, under heading (B), Children and Young People in Danger or Distress.

There are also many different organisations providing counselling and mediation for young people and their families to help them overcome their problems, and their details are given in Part Three, Where to Go for Information and Help, under headings (C), Youth Services, and (D), Family and Personal (Support and Counselling Services).

● If you really do feel that you have no choice but to run away, think carefully about where you are going to go and try and sort out your accommodation before you leave. You should take suitable clothing, some money and some form of identification such as your birth certificate or passport.

● If you have nobody who can help you, the town or city where you go may have temporary *night shelters, refuges or hostels* which may be prepared to take you in until you find somewhere more permanent.

● Squatting *can be very dangerous* and, if you move into a property without any permission, you will have no right to remain there.

You may also be committing a criminal offence if you refuse to leave when requested to do so by the rightful occupier.

Squatting is further dealt with in Chapter 31, Housing and Homelessness, heading (b)(3) and Chapter 41, Public Order Offences, heading (c), Trespassers.

There are various organisations that can tell you more about your rights and provide practical assistance. Their details are given in Part Three, Where to Go for Information and Help under heading (R), Housing and Homelessness.

You will find the details of the social services office covering your area in your local telephone directory under the name of your local authority. The listing will usually be 'Social Services, Children and Families'.

Most local authorities have homeless persons units and housing advice centres or housing aid centres which may be able to give emergency advice and assistance. Look in your local telephone directory under the name of your local authority to find the details.

See further Chapter 2, Abuse and Child Protection Procedures; Chapter 11, The Children Act 1989; Chapter 31, Housing and Homelessness; Running away from care is dealt with in Chapter 9, Care Orders and Accommodation – Being Looked After by the Local Authority, under heading (f).

Chapter 34

● In this country you cannot get married until you have reached the age of 16.

● A marriage in which either of the parties is under the age of 16 is not a valid marriage, in other words it is not recognised by the law.

This is so if you live in this country even if you get married in a country which allows you to marry at a younger age.

● If you are aged 18 or over you can decide for yourself to get married and there is no need for your parents' permission.

● If you are aged 16 or over, but have not yet reached 18, you must have the written consent of your parents and every person who has *parental responsibility* for you *(see Chapter 38, Parental Responsibility and Decisions About Your Life and Your Upbringing).* If you are the subject of a care order, you must also have the written consent of the local authority.

● If you forge the necessary consent or lie about your age the marriage is still valid but you will be committing a criminal offence.

● If consent cannot be given, for example because one of your parents has disappeared and cannot be traced, the *Registrar of Marriages* can give special consent.

● If consent is refused you can apply to a family court for permission. You will need to show that your parents, or others with *parental responsibility* for you, are being unreasonable.

● There are certain people whom you cannot validly marry, including

    ○ your mother or father;

    ○ your sister or brother;

    ○ your half-sister or half-brother;

    ○ your aunt or uncle;

    ○ your grandmother or grandfather

      (whether they are members of your natural family or your adoptive family, but members of step-families can marry one another, and first cousins can marry one another);

    ○ somebody who is already married;

    ○ somebody of the same sex as you.

See also Chapter 38, Parental Responsibility and Decisions About Your Life and Your Upbringing; Chapter 56, Wardship.

Chapter 35

(a) Your say in decisions and your consent

● The law provides that at 16 you can consent in your own right to any surgical, medical and dental treatment. This includes any examination, blood and other tests, and having an anaesthetic.

● The requirement of consent arises in all cases, including those involving adults, because otherwise there would be an assault which is both a criminal offence and a tort (*see Chapter 15, The Courts and the Legal System, heading (a)*).

● Consent is not necessary in an emergency, for example if you are rushed to casualty having been knocked unconscious in a road traffic accident and you might die if an operation is not carried out immediately.

● If for example your parents are Jehovah's Witnesses and do not believe you should have a blood transfusion, the High Court (*see Chapter 15, The Courts and the Legal System, heading (b)(4)*) has power to override their objections if your life is in danger.

● This is an area of the law in which there have been a large number of court cases over the last few years and the law is still changing and developing. Following the decision of the House of Lords in Mrs Gillick's case, it has been recognised that young people should be able to have a say in medical decisions and treatment affecting their bodies and to make up their own minds. The greater their understanding of the issues involved, the more important their say.

● Somebody under the age of 16 who is *competent* can independently seek medical advice and give valid consent to medical treatment without the need for consent from their parents as well.

● *Competency* signifies the ability to fully understand the choices and consequences including the nature and purpose of any medical treatment and to weigh up the risks and benefits and any side-effects.

● It is for the doctor (or dentist or health worker) to form an opinion as to whether you are capable of understanding what is involved. This depends to an extent on your maturity and intelligence, the state of your physical and mental health and the seriousness of the medical treatment proposed.

● It seems that the courts are more willing to allow somebody under the age of 16 to have the final say when it comes to consenting to medical treatment as opposed to refusing to consent to medical treatment. In the latter situation, the young person's refusal may be overridden if that would be in their best interests and provided that there is parental consent or the court authorises it. In a recent case of a girl of 15½ whose condition required monthly blood transfusions and daily injections and who decided to refuse further transfusions, the court authorised her doctor to treat her, if necessary by force, because she was not considered to be *competent*.

● This appears to apply even if you are aged 16 or over, but have not yet reached 18, as in another recent case where the court ordered the admission of a 16 year old girl suffering from anorexia nervosa, to a unit specialising in the treatment of eating disorders even though it was against her wishes.

● The position would seem to be that there is no absolute right to decide not to receive medical treatment and the court will not agree to a refusal where this would lead to death or severe permanent injury.

- Applications to the court in relation to medical treatment may be made by you, your parents, anyone with *parental responsibility* for you (*see Chapter 38, Parental Responsibility and Decisions About Your Life and Your Upbringing*), your doctors or the social services department of your local authority. Such applications should generally be made in the High Court by means of an application for a *specific issue order* (*see Chapter 11, The Children Act 1989, heading (c)(3)*).

- A *Ward of Court* must have the consent of the High Court to any non-routine or major medical treatment until they are 18 regardless of whether they are *competent*. One of the ways in which your parents can seek to override your wishes regarding medical treatment, if you are over the age of 16 but have not yet reached 18, is to bring wardship proceedings (*see Chapter 56, Wardship*).

- Your consent is required to an HIV test and blood taken from you for one purpose cannot also be analysed for HIV without you knowing.

- If it appears that a person under the age of 18 might be HIV positive, and a test is felt to be in their best interests, a High Court judge has the power to authorise this.

(b) Confidentiality

- The duty of confidentiality owed by a doctor to a person who is under the age of 16 is as great as that owed to somebody aged 16 or over, and any information that your doctor learns from you or about you should not be passed on to any other person.

- However, there is no absolute right to complete confidentiality and, if your health is at serious risk, your doctor may wish to involve your parents.

- If you have been sexually or physically abused within your family, and you tell your doctor, he or she must inform the social services department of your local authority having first tried to obtain your agreement to doing this.

- The results of an HIV test should never be passed on to anyone else without your consent where the test is undertaken at a special clinic or hospital. However, if your local GP does the test and you are found to be HIV positive, he or she could tell your family or partner even if you object.

See also Chapter 1, Abortion; Chapter 2, Abuse and Child Protection Procedures; Chapter 11, The Children Act 1989, heading (d), Making your own application to the court; Chapter 13, Contraception; Chapter 38, Parental Responsibility and Decisions About Your Life and Your Upbringing; Chapter 56, Wardship. Your rights to access to your medical records is dealt with in Chapter 43, Records and Access to Information, under heading (c), Access to information held about you by the officials.

(c) The Patients' Charter

● The Patients' Charter applies to all parts of the National Health Service (NHS).

● It provides that everyone is entitled to be registered with a family doctor. If you are not registered, your local *family health services authority* (FHSA) must find you a doctor within 2 days.

● You are entitled to change your doctor at any time and you do not have to have a special reason. However, there may be a practical problem in that a doctor is entitled to refuse to take you on as a patient if you live too far away or if he or she already has enough patients. Your FHSA must help you to find a new doctor.

● You are entitled to receive emergency care at any time.

● Information must be published by the FHSA about local medical services.

● The FHSA must investigate any complaints about doctors, dentists, opticians and pharmacists in their area, and respond to your comments and suggestions about services. Complaints should be made within 13 weeks.

● You should receive an *NHS medical card* with your NHS number on it. You should keep this in a safe place and always take it with you when you go to the surgery, otherwise you may have to pay. You should state your NHS number if you are writing to the FHSA.

You will find the address and telephone number of your FHSA on your medical card, or look in your local telephone directory under the name of your local health authority.

(d) Free National Health Service (NHS) prescriptions, dental treatment, eye tests and glasses

● The NHS generally provides free health care for everybody, but there are certain items including prescriptions, dental treatment (including check ups) eye tests and glasses, that you do have to pay for unless you fall into a special category.

You will find the relevant leaflets about them in doctors' and dentists' surgeries, in opticians and at your local Benefits Agency Office.

● The rules about these special categories vary slightly.

● Generally, in order to qualify automatically for free prescriptions, dental treatment, eye tests and vouchers to help you meet the cost of glasses or contact lenses because your sight has changed, you must be

○ under the age of 16 (under the age of 18 in respect of dental treatment); *or*

○ aged 16 or over, but under 19 and still in full-time education; *or*

○ receiving income support or family credit, or the partner of somebody who receives either of these benefits; *or*

○ (in respect of prescriptions and dental treatment) pregnant or have had a baby within the last 12 months; *or*

○ (in respect of prescriptions) suffering permanently from a serious medical condition, such as diabetes or epilepsy; *or*

○ (in respect of eye tests and glasses) registered blind or partially sighted, or diabetic or a glaucoma patient.

● If you are aged 16 or over and you and any partner have a low enough income (it is your income that counts and not that of your parents even if you live with them) you may not have to pay for prescriptions, dental treatment, eye tests and glasses or you may only have to pay a reduced charge. You will need to fill out an application form in order to receive an *exemption certificate*.

Details of organisations and bodies dealing with matters relating to health are given in Part Three, Where to Go for Information and Help, under heading (F), Health.

See also Chapter 18, Disability; Chapter 57, Welfare Benefits.

Chapter 36

(a) Can you change your name?

● There is a legal duty to register a child's birth within 42 days of the birth and to give the name by which it is intended the child will be known.

● A parent can change the name given on registration or add new names within 12 months of birth. After that, the name on your birth certificate can never be altered.

● Whatever first name or names and surname are shown on your birth certificate, you and your parents don't have to use all or any of those names.

● Legally, your name is the name by which you are generally called and no legal formalities are required to change it.

● If you wish to be known by a different name, all you have to do is to use it every day and to ask your family, friends and teachers to call you by that name *(but see below for the position if you are the subject of a residence order or a care order)*.

● You cannot change your name in order to mislead or defraud other people.

● If your parents disagree with your choice of a different name, you may be able to apply to the court for a *specific issue order (see Chapter 11, The Children Act 1989, heading (c)(3))*. You require *leave* (that is, permission) of the court to make the application. To obtain leave you must satisfy the court that you have sufficient understanding to make the proposed application *(the procedure for making application to the court is dealt with in Chapter 11, under heading (d))*.

● Situations can arise in which you may be required to provide official proof that you have abandoned one name and intend, instead, to be known by another name, for example applying for a new passport or driving licence. It is advisable to obtain written evidence.

● This can be done by means of a *statutory declaration*, or by executing a deed of change of name called a *deed poll* (you will usually need to see a solicitor to prepare the necessary paperwork).

● A *statutory declaration* is a signed statement sworn in front of a solicitor.

There is no lower age limit for making a statutory declaration.

● A *deed poll* is a formal deed, which will be accepted for all official purposes.

You can apply to file this in the High Court *(see Chapter 15, The Courts and the Legal System, heading (b)(4))* as a permanent record (this is called enrolling).

You must be aged 16 or over to enrol a *deed poll* on your own behalf.

(b) Can your parents change your name?

● Provided you are not the subject of a *residence order* or a *care order (see further below)* either or both of your parents can change your first name or names and surname simply by calling you by that name and notifying your school, doctor and dentist. For example

Your parents are married, but separated or divorced, you live with your mother and there is no residence order in force

    ○ your mother can change your surname from your father's surname to the surname she had before she got married.

Your mother is unmarried or widowed, you live with her and she gets married

○ your mother can change your surname to your step-father's surname.

● If there is a dispute about a change of name, the parent wishing to make the change can apply to the court for a *specific issue order (see Chapter 11, The Children Act 1989, heading (c)(3))* or the parent opposing the change can apply for a *prohibited steps order (see Chapter 11, heading (c)(4))*.

● If you disagree with the change, you may be able to apply to the court for a *prohibited steps order*. You require *leave* (that is, permission) of the court. To obtain *leave* you must satisfy the court that you have sufficient understanding to make the proposed application.

● If there is in force a *residence order (see Chapter 11, The Children Act 1989, heading (c)(1))* or a *care order (see Chapter 11, heading (c)(5))*, no person may cause you to be known by a new surname without either the written consent of every person who has *parental responsibility* for you *(see Chapter 38, Parental Responsibility and Decisions About Your Life and Your Upbringing)* or leave of the court.

Your written consent is not required.

For example

Your parents are divorced and you live with your mother who has a residence order in her favour and she remarries

○ your mother cannot call you by your step-father's surname and you cannot use that surname except with your father's agreement in writing or *leave* of the court.

You are in care and living with long-term foster parents

○ they cannot call you by their surname and you cannot use that surname except with the agreement in writing of your parents and the local authority or *leave* of the court.

● If the court is asked to permit a child or young person's name to be changed, the court will look at all the circumstances of the case. Judges tend to vary in their approach, some stress the significance of the child knowing his or her own identity and maintaining the link with the natural father's family, whereas others concentrate on the embarrassment and confusion caused to a child by having a different surname from the rest of the family. Your name is a matter of importance and your wishes regarding the change will play a part in the decision, as well as the strength of your attachment to your stepfather, or foster parents, and whether your natural father plays an active part in your life.

● If you are adopted, your adoptive parents can change your name. It is usual for them to include the new name in their application for an *adoption order*. The change will be made at the time of the *adoption order* and the details will be entered on the *Adoption Contact Register (see further Chapter 4, Adoption)*.

● Parents can enrol a *deed poll* for their child who is under the age of 18, but a deed poll cannot be enrolled for a young person aged 16 or over without their consent. The parents must show that the change of name is for the benefit of the child or young person and all those with *parental responsibility* must give their written consent.

See also Chapter 4, Adoption; Chapter 11, The Children Act 1989; Chapter 20, Divorce and Separation; Chapter 38, Parental Responsibility and Decisions About Your Life and Your Upbringing; Chapter 48, Solicitors and Legal Aid. The position regarding changing your name if you are the subject of a care order is dealt with in Chapter 9, under heading (e).

Chapter 37

● Nationality means citizenship. If you are a British citizen, you have a right to live and work anywhere in the United Kingdom (England, Wales, Scotland and Northern Ireland).

● If you were born in the United Kingdom before 1 January 1983, you are a British citizen by birth regardless of your parents' nationality.

● If you were born in the United Kingdom on or after 1 January 1983, you are a British citizen by birth

  ○ if your mother is a British citizen or she has settled here, whether or not your parents are married; *or*

  ○ if your father is a British citizen or he has settled here, and your parents are married.

● If you have stayed in the United Kingdom for 10 years since birth without being absent for more than 90 days in any one year, you can apply to be a British citizen.

● If you were born outside the United Kingdom, you are a British citizen by birth

○   if your mother is a British citizen; *or*

○   if your father is a British citizen and your parents are married.

● In special circumstances there is a discretion for the *Home Office* to register children as British citizens.

● If you are not a British citizen by birth and are legally adopted in the United Kingdom by a British citizen, you will automatically become a British citizen from the moment you are adopted.

● It may be possible to have dual nationality if the laws of both countries allow this. If they don't, and you are eligible to be a citizen of two countries, at some stage you will have to choose which of the nationalities to actually take. Britain allows dual nationality but, for example, America, doesn't, so you will have to decide whether to be British or American. You may lose your right to American nationality if you apply for a British passport.

You should check with the authorities of the other country before applying for a British passport.

This is a complicated area of the law which most solicitors don't handle. If you have a problem, you will need to take specialist advice. You should begin by contacting your local Citizens' Advice Bureau and they should refer you to the nearest organisation dealing with immigration issues. The address of the Home Office and details of organisations giving specialist advice are given in Part Three, Where to Go for Information and Help, under heading (W), Other Useful Contacts.

See also Chapter 4, Adoption; Chapter 39, Passports.

Chapter 38

(a) What parental responsibility means

● The Children Act 1989 defines *parental responsibility* as

'all the rights, duties, powers, responsibilities and authority which by law a parent of a child has in relation to the child and his property'.

● This involves looking after you and making decisions about you. For example, decisions about

○ where you will live;

○ where you will go to school;

○ your name;

○ the religion you will follow;

○ what punishment and discipline you should receive;

○ whether you should have medical treatment;

○ whether you should be allowed to leave home or get married if you are aged 16 or over, but are under 18.

- Until you are an adult somebody will usually have *parental responsibility* for you.

  Parental responsibility ends naturally when you reach the age of 18.

(b) Who has parental responsibility?

- Your mother always has *parental responsibility* for you. She can only lose it if she dies or if you are adopted. She may share it with other people.

- Your father also has *parental responsibility* for you if your parents are married. This continues after divorce or separation even if you no longer live with your father.

- If your parents are unmarried, your father does not automatically have *parental responsibility* for you even if his name is on your birth certificate and you are living with him. An unmarried father can only obtain it if

  ○ your mother is prepared to enter into a formal agreement with him which is registered in the High Court; *or*

  ○ he applies to a family court which makes a *parental responsibility order* in his favour; *or*

  ○ he is granted a *residence order* in his favour *(see Chapter 11, The Children Act 1989, heading (c)(1))*.

- If an unmarried father does obtain *parental responsibility* for you in any of these ways, it can only be lost by a court order, death or adoption.

- If you are adopted, your adoptive parents have *parental responsibility* for you and your natural parents lose it *(see further Chapter 4, Adoption)*.

- If you are the subject of a *residence order* in favour of an adult family member or friend, they have *parental responsibility* for you while the *residence order* remains in force. They will share it with your mother (and your father, if he has it).

- If your parents are dead and you have a guardian, your guardian has *parental responsibility* for you *(see further Chapter 30, Guardians)*.

● If you are the subject of a *care order (see Chapter 11, The Children Act 1989, heading (c)(5))*, the local authority has *parental responsibility* for you while the *care order* remains in force. They will share it with your mother (and your father, if he has it). However, the local authority does not have *parental responsibility* for you if you are being *accommodated (see further Chapter 9, Care Orders and Accommodation – Being Looked After by the Local Authority)*.

● A step-parent does not automatically have *parental responsibility* for you but can obtain it if they are granted a *residence order* in their favour *(see further Chapter 50, Step-parents)*.

● Your parents can arrange for somebody else to look after you, for example a relative, if they are ill or going abroad without you. This does not give that person *parental responsibility* for you but they can do whatever is reasonable for the purpose of safeguarding or promoting your welfare.

(c) Your say

● Over recent years it has been recognised by Parliament and the courts that young people should be able to have a say in decisions about their life and their upbringing. The Children Act 1989 *(see further Chapter 11)* gives effect to this by giving you the right to be heard in cases concerning you.

● As you get older you will be more capable of making your own decisions and no court will force you to do something against your will unless what you want is plainly not in your best interests.

● Therefore, if you have sufficient maturity and intelligence to understand the issues involved, the court will be more influenced by your views and what your parents, or others with *parental responsibility* for you, want may have to give way to what you want.

● If you cannot reach an agreement with them, you have the right to seek *leave* (that is, permission) of the court to make your own application for any *section 8 order*, being a *residence order (see Chapter 11, The Children Act 1989, heading (c)(1))*, a *contact order (see Chapter 11, heading (c)(2))*, a *specific issue order (see Chapter 11, heading (c)(3))* or a *prohibited steps order (see Chapter 11, heading (c)(4))*.

● To obtain *leave* you must satisfy the court that you have sufficient understanding to make the proposed application *(see further Chapter 11, The Children Act 1989, heading (d))*.

● The court will not get involved in minor disputes such as how late you should be allowed to stay out or whether you should be allowed to go on holiday with a friend.

See also Chapter 1, Abortion; Chapter 4, Adoption; Chapter 9, Care Orders and Accommodation – Being Looked After by the Local Authority; Chapter 11, The Children Act 1989; Chapter 13, Contraception; Chapter 20, Divorce and Separation; Chapter 25, Education, heading (d), Your say in educational matters and what you learn; Chapter 26, Emigrating, Going to Live Abroad and Holidays; Chapter 30, Guardians; Chapter 33, Leaving Home and Running Away; Chapter 34, Marriage; Chapter 35, Medical Treatment, heading (a), Your say in decisions and your consent; Chapter 36, Names; Chapter 39, Passports; Chapter 42, Punishment and Discipline; Chapter 44, Religion; Chapter 50, Stepparents; Chapter 56, Wardship.

Chapter 39

This chapter deals with the rules relating to British passports only.

● If you are a British citizen *(see Chapter 37, Nationality)* and you are under the age of 16

○ if your parents are married or divorced, either parent can apply to add you to their passport;

○ if your parents are unmarried and your father does not have parental responsibility for you *(see Chapter 38, Parental Responsibility and Decisions About Your Life and Your Upbringing)*, your mother can apply to add you to her passport;

○ anyone who has *parental responsibility* for you can apply to add you to their passport.

You cannot travel abroad without the person in whose passport you are included.

● A child under the age of 5 will not be issued with a separate passport unless there are exceptional circumstances.

- If you are aged between 5 and 16, and you are travelling abroad without a parent, you can be issued with your own passport in your own name.

Somebody with *parental responsibility* for you will have to make the application on your behalf.

The passport will normally last for only 5 years.

- At 16 you will be deleted from your parent's passport, and you must have your own passport in order to travel abroad.

You still require the written consent of somebody with *parental responsibility* for you before a passport will be issued to you unless you are married or in the armed forces.

- At 18 you can apply in your own right for your own passport.

- Special forms for applying for passports can be obtained from post offices or a passport office.

Make sure that you pick up the correct form for your particular situation. It is always a good idea to allow at least 3 months when making applications in relation to passports.

The addresses of the passport offices for different parts of the country are given in Part Three, Where to Go for Information and Help, under heading (W), Other Useful Contacts.

Chapter 40

See generally Chapter 16, Criminal Proceedings.

● The Police and Criminal Evidence Act 1984 (PACE) and the Codes of Practice made under PACE set out how people are to be treated by the police and the powers that the police have.

● If the police obtain evidence against you by breaking these rules and you are *prosecuted* for a criminal offence, it is a matter for the court to decide whether, in all the circumstances, it would be unfair for the prosecution to be allowed to use that evidence at the trial.

● It used to be the position in this country that you had a complete right to remain silent when interviewed by the police in order to obtain evidence against you. This is no longer so and if you have a defence to a charge which you later rely on at the trial, you are expected to tell the police about this when they interview you. If you don't, the court can take this into account in deciding whether you are guilty.

● However, if the police force you to make a confession by oppression (which includes degrading treatment and the use or threat

197

of violence) or as a result of something said or done which makes it unreliable (for example being told that if you own up you won't be prosecuted or you'll get *bail (see Chapter 16, Criminal Proceedings, heading (e))*, the court must not allow the prosecution to use that confession against you at the trial.

● If the police do break these rules and you are not prosecuted, or there is a trial and the charge against you is not proved, you may have a civil claim *(see further Chapter 15, The Courts and the Legal System, heading (a))* against the police, for example for assault, false imprisonment, trespass or malicious prosecution, for which you may be able to *sue* for *damages (see further Chapter 51, Suing and Being Sued, heading (a); Chapter 12, Compensation, heading (b); Chapter 48, Solicitors and Legal Aid)*.

● There is also a special procedure for making official complaints about individual police officers who have acted in bad faith. Such complaints should be investigated by the *Police Complaints Authority (you should ask about this at your local Citizens' Advice Bureau or the police station)*.

This is a complicated area of the law and what follows is intended only to be a general outline.

(a) Being stopped in the street, searched and questioned

(1) Being stopped

● The police have a general power to stop you and ask you your name and address, where you have been and where you are going, without actually detaining you. This is most likely to happen late at night if you are out on your own or with a crowd of young people.

● You do not have to answer but, if you are not doing anything wrong, it is in your interests to give brief and polite replies to any questions. If you run away or are rude, you could end up getting into trouble – *it is a criminal offence to wilfully obstruct a constable in the execution of his duty.*

● In order to actually detain you so as to search you and ask you questions, the police must have 'reasonable grounds for suspicion'.

This cannot be based on the mere fact that you are a teenager or on your racial origins or the way you are dressed. The police must have seen you doing something wrong or there must be something about your behaviour to alert them (for example you are looking around you nervously or trying to hide something) or they must have received a tip-off.

(2) Being searched

● The police do not have a general power to stop and search you in the hope of finding something of interest to them.

● They must have reasonable grounds for suspecting that they will find stolen articles, or *prohibited articles* which are

   ○ offensive weapons, that is, something made or adapted for causing injury (for example a flick knife or a broken bottle), or something you have with you with the intention of causing injury (for example a kitchen knife); *or*

   ○ somethings you have with you for burglary, theft, taking a motor vehicle without the owner's consent or deception (for example a crowbar, a set of keys or somebody else's credit card).

● They can make a search if you are in any public place or anywhere to which the public have access whether or not for payment (for example the street, a car park, a shopping centre, a cinema or a disco).

● They can search you, anything you are carrying, and your vehicle, for example your car or motorcycle, whether or not you are in or on it and anything in or on your vehicle.

● They can detain you and/or your vehicle for the purpose of the search and seize any stolen or prohibited articles they find.

● They cannot search you if you are in a house, flat or garden unless they have reasonable grounds for believing that you don't live there and don't have permission to be there (for example if they started chasing you down the street and you jumped over a fence into somebody else's garden).

● They do have the power to search you and your vehicle anywhere if they have reasonable grounds to suspect you have a controlled drug in your possession *(see further Chapter 23, Drugs).*

- They can search you if you are at a league or cup football match or on a coach or train travelling to or from such a match and they have reasonable grounds to suspect that you have alcohol with you.

- Before carrying out the search the police can ask your name and address and can question you about your behaviour. If you give a satisfactory explanation, no search may take place.

- You are entitled to be told
  - the name of the police officer and the police station he or she is from. If the police officer is not in uniform, he or she must show you their warrant card;
  - why you are being searched; *and*
  - what is being looked for.

- Your consent to the search should be sought first. If you are not willing to co-operate, the police are entitled to use reasonable force. If you resist, you could be committing the offence of obstruction.

- Searches of your mouth are no longer treated as intimate searches so if you put something in your mouth to hide it, you can be forced to open your mouth.

- If the search takes place in public, the police can only check your outer clothing and can only remove items such as your coat, jacket or gloves.

- If they wish to make a more thorough search (for example by removing a T-shirt or crash helmet), they must take you out of public view, for example to a police van or the manager's office in a department store. Such a search must be carried out by a police officer of the same sex as you and not in the presence of anyone of the opposite sex. *There are further powers of search following arrest and in relation to strip and intimate searches which are dealt with under headings (b) and (e) below.*

- A new power has recently been introduced which enables a superintendent to authorise the stopping and searching of people and vehicles in a particular area over a 24 hour period where there is reasonable belief that incidents involving serious violence may take place in that area and it is necessary to do so to stop their occurrence.

This gives any officer in uniform power to

○ stop pedestrians and search for offensive weapons and dangerous instruments (that is, something sharply pointed or with a blade); *and*

○ stop any vehicle and search the vehicle, its driver and any passenger for such items.

The officer is not required to have any grounds for suspecting that the person or vehicle is carrying such items.

● In all cases the police must make a proper written record giving full details of the search unless the circumstances make it impossible, for example a large group is being searched in connection with a violent disturbance. You are entitled to a copy of this record if you request it within one year, and you must be advised of this.

● The record should include

○ the reason for the search and what was being looked for;

○ the date, time and place the search was made;

○ its results;

○ a note of any injury or damage to property caused by it;

○ the identity of the officer making it.

(3) Being questioned and interviewed

● If the police reasonably suspect you of an offence, you must be *cautioned* before being asked any questions about your involvement or suspected involvement in it. This is defined as an *interview*.

● The words of the *caution* are

'You do not have to say anything. But it may harm your defence if you do not mention when questioned something which you later rely on in court. Anything you do say may be given in evidence.'

However, it will still usually be a good idea not to answer any questions until you have received legal advice *(see further heading (d) below)*.

● You need not be cautioned if you are being asked for your name and address and before being searched. If the police do find stolen or prohibited articles during a search, you should be cautioned before being interviewed about them.

● If you are under the age of 17 the police should not interview you except in the presence of an *appropriate adult (see further heading (d) below)*.

● They should not interview you at school or college unless it is unavoidable and they must have the agreement of your head teacher.

● Wherever you are interviewed (whether on the street, at home, in the police station or in any other place), the police officer must, at that time or shortly afterwards, make an accurate record of what you say, including when and where the interview took place, the time it began and ended, any breaks in the interview and the names of all those present.

● The record must be made on a special form or in the officer's pocket-book and it must be shown to you to read. You should be invited to sign it if it is correct, or to mark those parts that you disagree with. The appropriate adult must also be given this opportunity. *This is an important right. You should read through the record very carefully and only sign it if you do agree, so as to avoid the police saying later on that you admitted something which you actually deny.*

(b) Arrests

● If you have committed a road traffic offence or a minor criminal offence (for example not paying your fare on public transport) and the police are satisfied without needing to make any further investigations that you are guilty, they will take your name and address and you may subsequently receive a *summons (see further Chapter 16, Criminal Proceedings, heading (c))*.

● If you are suspected of a more serious criminal offence and the police wish to make further investigations, it is likely that they will arrest you.

● The police do not have a general power to arrest you.

● They can arrest you with a warrant, which is a written authority from a magistrate, but they can also arrest you without a warrant in certain circumstances.

● The main circumstances are that they have reasonable grounds for suspecting you of having committed, or being in the act of committing, or being about to commit, an *arrestable offence*. Arrestable offences include

  ○ all *serious* offences such as murder, rape, robbery, burglary, theft and assault and offences in relation to controlled drugs;

  ○ other less serious offences such as violent disorder, causing criminal damage, indecent assault, taking a motor vehicle without the owner's consent, driving while disqualified and going equipped for burglary, theft or cheat.

● There are further powers of arrest for

  ○ affray and threatening behaviour and also disorderly conduct if you carry on after having been warned to stop *(see generally Chapter 41, Public Order Offences)*;

  ○ drink driving;

  ○ having alcohol with you at league or cup football match or on a coach or train travelling to or from such a match.

● You can be arrested if you are actually breaching the peace or acting in such a way that a breach of the peace is likely to occur.

● You can be arrested for non-arrestable offences, such as indecent exposure, carrying a bladed or sharply pointed article (for example a pen knife with a blade of more than 3 inches in length) and not paying your fare on public transport, if

  ○ you refuse to give your name and address, or give false details; *or*

  ○ you do not have a permanent address so that you can be *summoned*; *or*

  ○ in order to prevent you from

  – causing injury to yourself or others; *or*

  – causing loss of or damage to any property; *or*

  – committing an offence against public decency; *or*

  – obstructing the highway.

- The police must tell you clearly that you are under arrest and must make clear the reason why you are being arrested (even if this is obvious).

- You must be *cautioned* again *(see heading (a)(3) above)*.

- You should be taken to the police station as soon as practicable after arrest.

- The police are allowed to use reasonable force to restrain you and take you to the police station. They can apply handcuffs if it is necessary.

- You should not be arrested at school or college unless it is unavoidable.

- Upon arrest, the police can search you if they have reasonable grounds for believing that

  ○ you may be a danger to yourself or others; *or*

  ○ you may have anything hidden on you which could be used to assist you to escape or might be evidence of an offence.

- They also have the power to enter and search any premises where you were when you were arrested, or immediately beforehand, to look for evidence relating to the offence for which you were arrested.

- You should not be interviewed following an arrest until after you have arrived at the police station unless the delay would lead to

  ○ interference with or harm to any evidence; *or*

  ○ interference with or physical harm to other people; *or*

  ○ the alerting of other suspects who have not yet been arrested; *or*

  ○ the recovery of property being hindered.

  These are the only situations in which a person under the age of 17 may be interviewed without an *appropriate adult* being present.

(c) Detention at the police station

- On arrival at the police station, you will be brought before the *custody officer* who is responsible for supervising your detention.

● He or she will open a *custody record* in which everything that happens while you are at the police station should be listed. You are entitled to a copy if you request it within a year. The *appropriate adult* and a solicitor (if you request one) are entitled to see the custody record on arrival at the police station *(see further section (d) below)*.

● You must be informed of your rights. At any stage while you are detained, you have the right

   ○ to have someone informed of your arrest; *and*

   ○ to consult privately with a solicitor (and you must be told that independent legal advice is available free of charge from the duty solicitor); *and*

   ○ to consult the PACE Codes of Practice.

You must be given written notice of your rights including the *caution*.

You should be asked to sign the *custody record* to show that you have received the necessary notice.

● The *custody officer* decides whether there is sufficient evidence to charge you and whether you should be charged. If so, you must be charged immediately. If you are under the age of 17 you should not be charged until the *appropriate adult* has arrived *(see further heading (d) below)*.

● The *custody officer* may decide that, rather than charging you, it would be more appropriate for you to receive a formal *caution (see further Chapter 16, Criminal Proceedings, heading (b))*.

● If there is insufficient evidence you may be released without being charged and that will be the end of the matter. Alternatively, the *custody officer* will authorise your detention to secure or preserve evidence relating to the offence for which you are under arrest and/or to obtain such evidence by interviewing you.

● You must be told the grounds for your detention, and they must be recorded in the *custody record*.

● You can be held for up to 24 hours without being charged.

A superintendent can authorise detention in respect of *serious arrestable offences* for up to 36 hours.

If the police wish to hold you for any longer they must apply to a magistrate who can authorise detention for further periods up to a maximum of 96 hours.

● Following these periods, you must be charged or released if there is still insufficient evidence. If further investigations are still required you may be released on bail to attend the police station at a later date *(see further Chapter 16, heading (e))*.

● An inspector must review your detention after 6 hours and then once every 9 hours.

● There is a general right to have 1 friend or relative or other person told of your arrest at the public expense.

You may only receive visits if the custody officer allows it.

● You are normally entitled to writing materials and to speak on the telephone for a reasonable time to one person.

● You have various rights relating to the conditions under which you are detained. The main ones are

   ○   to receive medical attention whenever it seems necessary;

   ○   if you are under the age of 17 you should not be placed in a police cell unless no other secure accommodation is available and the *custody officer* considers that it is not practicable to supervise you if you are not placed in a cell;

   ○   you must not be placed in a cell with a detained adult;

   ○   the room or cell where you are placed must be clean and adequately heated, ventilated and lit;

   ○   blankets, mattresses and pillows must be clean;

   ○   you must be given access to toilet and washing facilities;

   ○   you must receive 2 light meals and 1 main meal in any period of 24 hours and drinks at and between meal times;

   ○   in any 24 hour period you must be allowed at least 8 hours continuous rest, free from questioning or interruption;

   ○   you must be visited once an hour.

(d) The appropriate adult, legal advice and interviews

(1) The appropriate adult

● If you are under the age of 17 the custody officer must, as soon as it is reasonably practicable, inform the person responsible for your welfare that you have been arrested, why and where you are being held. That person is called the *appropriate adult* and they must be asked to come to the police station to be with you.

● The *appropriate adult* will be a parent (or guardian) or other person with *parental responsibility* for you *(see Chapter 38, Parental Responsibility and Decisions About Your Life and Your Upbringing)* and may be your social worker if you are being looked after by the local authority *(see Chapter 9, Care Orders and Accommodation – Being Looked After by the Local Authority).*

● A social worker may be asked to act as the *appropriate adult* if for example

   ○ your parent (or guardian) is the victim of the offence, or a witness; *or*

   ○ you do not get on with your parent (or guardian) and you object to their presence; *or*

   ○ your parent (or guardian) is not able or willing to act as the *appropriate adult.*

If you know another responsible adult whom you trust, you can ask for them to act as the *appropriate adult.*

A solicitor cannot act as the *appropriate adult.*

● The *appropriate adult* has an important role to play in advising and assisting you and observing that the procedures are carried out properly and fairly.

● If the *appropriate adult* was not at the police station when you were informed of your rights, this information must be given again when he or she arrives.

● You and the *appropriate adult* must be advised as to their role and that they are not expected to act simply as an observer and that you can consult privately with the *appropriate adult* at any time.

(2) Legal advice

● The police must not say or do anything to dissuade you from obtaining legal advice.

● If you do not wish to have legal advice, this must be noted on the *custody record*.

● The right to legal advice can only be delayed if you have been arrested for a *serious arrestable offence* and a superintendent has reasonable grounds for believing that the exercise by you of your right to legal advice will lead to

○ interference with or harm to any evidence*; *or*

○ interference with or physical harm to other people*; *or*

○ the alerting of other suspects who have not yet been arrested*; *or*

○ the recovery of property being hindered*.

● You have a right to consult and communicate privately with a solicitor whether in person or by telephone. *It is in your interests to do this in order to protect your position and the very fact of your requesting a solicitor goes some way to ensuring fair play.*

● If you do not know a solicitor, you should be told about the *Duty Solicitor Scheme* and that there is a legal representative on call 24 hours a day to give free legal advice. The duty solicitor is independent of the police and will be a person from a local firm specialising in criminal law.

● Once you have asked to see a solicitor, you cannot normally be interviewed without him or her being present except if you have been arrested for a *serious arrestable offence* and the conditions marked * above apply, or if a superintendent has reasonable grounds for believing that

○ delay will involve immediate risk of harm to people or serious loss of, or damage to, property; *or*

○ awaiting their arrival would cause unreasonable delay to the process of investigation.

● *This is an important right.* If you make a confession having been improperly denied access to a solicitor, it is very likely that the confession will be excluded if the case goes to court.

● The solicitor should advise you about the law that applies in your case and whether it is likely to be in your interests to answer the questions that may be put to you. The solicitor should also intervene

  ○ to prevent the police from asking you any improper or unfair questions;

  ○ if you are becoming confused; *or*

  ○ if you have forgotten to mention something you wanted to tell the police.

(3) Interviews at the police station

● If you are under the age of 17 you must not be *interviewed* nor asked to make or sign a written statement without the *appropriate adult* being present (and a solicitor, if you have requested one, except if the conditions marked * above apply).

● You must be allowed to sit down and you have a general right to at least 8 hours undisturbed rest in any 24 hour period. You are generally entitled to a break from interviewing at meal times plus short breaks for refreshments every 2 hours.

● You must be reminded of the *caution (see heading (a) above)* before you are interviewed and you must be told the names of the interviewing officers.

● If you agree to being interviewed without a solicitor, your agreement must be recorded in writing or on a tape and you must be reminded that you are entitled to free legal advice.

● An accurate record of the interview must be made giving the place of the interview, the time it begins and ends, any breaks in the interview and the names of all those present.

● These days, interviews are generally tape recorded and there are special rules about the sealing of the master tape and providing you with your own copy and any transcript.

(e) Strip and intimate searches, body samples, fingerprints and photographs

● The *custody officer* is responsible for listing any personal possessions you have on you at the police station. He or she can take and retain anything that relates to the offence or anything that you might have acquired for an unlawful or a harmful purpose.

Everything else taken from you must be kept in a safe place and be returned to you once you are released from the police station.

● It is up to the *custody officer* to decide how extensive a search should be made.

If necessary, reasonable force can be used.

(1) Strip searches

● Strip searches involve the removal of more than your outer clothing.

A strip search may only take place if the *custody officer* reasonably considers that it is necessary to remove something which you would not be allowed to keep and you might have hidden.

● It must be carried out by an officer of the same sex as you in an area where you cannot be seen and not in the presence of anyone of the opposite sex.

● If you are under the age of 17 a strip search should only take place in the presence of the *appropriate adult* except if

○ it is urgent, and there is a risk of serious harm; *or*

○ you and the *appropriate adult* agree otherwise.

(2) Intimate searches

● Intimate searches involve examining the ears, nose or anus (or a girl's vagina). Searches of a person's mouth are excluded from these rules.

● An intimate search may only take place if a superintendent has reasonable grounds for believing that you have concealed

○ an article which could cause physical injury to you or to others; *or*

○ class A drugs which you intended to supply to another person *(see further Chapter 23, Drugs).*

It must be the only practicable means of removing the item.

● The reasons for the intimate search must be explained to you before it takes place.

● Generally, intimate searches should only be performed by a doctor or nurse at a hospital or surgery.

● In urgent cases an intimate search for an article that could cause physical injury can be made at the police station by an officer of the same sex as you and not in the presence of anyone of the opposite sex.

If you are under the age of 17 it should take place only in the presence of an *appropriate adult* of the same sex as you unless you and the *appropriate adult* agree otherwise.

(3) Body samples

● Body samples are taken in order to be analysed and may be used as evidence.

● Before a body sample is taken, you must be informed that it may be checked against other samples and information from other samples held by the police as records, or obtained from an investigation of an offence.

● Where consent is required this must be given in writing

○ by your parent (or guardian) if you are aged 10 or over, but have not yet reached 14;

○ by you and your parent (or guardian) if you are aged 14 or over, but have not yet reached 17;

○ by you if you are aged 17 or over.

● If clothing needs to be removed, no person of the opposite sex must be present. If you are under the age of 17 this must only be done in the presence of the *appropriate adult* unless you and the *appropriate adult* agree otherwise.

Intimate samples

● Examples of intimate samples are blood, semen, urine, pubic hair and swabs taken from the ears, nose, anus (and a girl's vagina) and dental impressions.

● An intimate sample can only be taken if

○ a superintendent has reasonable grounds to believe that it will prove or disprove your involvement in a *recordable offence* (that is, broadly, one for which an adult could be punished with imprisonment) and he or she authorises it; *and*

○ there is consent.

● Before you are asked to provide an intimate sample, you must be warned that if you refuse without good cause this may harm your case if it comes to trial. If you are not legally represented, you must be reminded of your entitlement to free legal advice.

● All intimate samples other than urine should only be taken by a doctor, nurse or dentist.

Non-intimate samples

● Examples of non-intimate samples are hair from your head, fingernail scrapings, saliva, swabs taken from the mouth and any other part of body (except the ears, nose, anus or a girl's vagina) and footprints.

● Non-intimate samples can only be taken if consent is given.

● Non-intimate samples can be taken without consent, using reasonable force if necessary, if

○ a superintendent has reasonable grounds to believe that it will prove or disprove your involvement in a *recordable offence* and has authorised it; *or*

○ you are charged with a *recordable offence.*

(4) Fingerprints (including palm prints)

● The police may take your fingerprints if consent is given but they do not have a general right to take your fingerprints simply because you have been arrested.

● If you are aged 10 or over, but have not yet reached 14, your parent (or guardian) must give their written consent.

If you are aged 14 or over, but have not yet reached 17, your written consent is required as well.

If you are aged 17 or over only your written consent is required.

● Fingerprints can be taken without consent, using reasonable force if necessary, if

- a superintendent has reasonable grounds for suspecting that they will prove or disprove your involvement in a criminal offence and has authorised it; *or*

- you are charged with a *recordable offence*;

- you must be informed beforehand that your fingerprints may be checked against other fingerprints held by the police as records, or obtained from an investigation of an offence and that if a *conviction* or *caution* does not result they will be destroyed. A *caution* in this context means a formal caution given at the police station (*see further Chapter 16, Criminal Proceedings, heading (b)*) rather than the *caution* you must be given before being interviewed.

(5) Photographs

● The police may take your photograph if consent is given but they do not have a general right to take your photograph simply because you have been arrested.

● If you are aged 10 or over, but have not yet reached 14, your parent (or guardian) must give their written consent.

If you are aged 14 or over, but have not yet reached 17, your written consent is required as well.

If you are aged 17 or over only your written consent is required.

● Your photograph can be taken without your consent if

- you were arrested at the same time as others and it is necessary to establish who was arrested, when and where, for example in a crowd at a football match; *or*

- you are charged with a *recordable offence*; *or*

- it is authorised by a superintendent where there are reasonable grounds to suspect your involvement in a criminal offence in which there is identification evidence.

Force may not be used for this purpose.

● You must be informed that if you significantly alter your appearance after the photograph is taken this may be given in evidence if the case comes to trial and that, if a *conviction* or *caution* does not result, the photograph and any negatives will be destroyed.

See further Chapter 43, heading (b) for the position regarding the keeping of fingerprints, samples and photographs as permanent records.

(f) Identity parades

● You have the right to request an identity parade if you think that you have been wrongly identified by a witness.

● The police may ask you to take part in an identity parade, but you cannot be forced to do so against your will.

● If you are aged 10 or over, but have not yet reached 14, your parent (or guardian) must give their written consent before you take part.

If you are aged 14 or over, but have not yet reached 17, your written consent is required as well.

If you are aged 17 or over only your written consent is required.

● You must be given a reasonable opportunity to have a solicitor or a friend present. Your solicitor will advise you whether it is in your interests to take part in an identity parade.

● There are a large number of rules governing the conduct of identity parades.

The most important ones are

○ the witness should not be allowed to see you before or after the parade;

○ if there is more than 1 witness, they should not be able to communicate with one another and should each make their identification separately;

○ at least 8 other people of similar age, height and general appearance to you must also take part;

○ you can select your own position in the line;

○ the witness is not entitled to hear you talking unless you give your consent.

● There are special forms for making a record concerning the parade and you are entitled to a copy if you request this within a reasonable time.

- If you refuse to take part in an identity parade, the police may arrange for the witness to see you in another situation in which you could be identified, for example in a shopping centre or at an underground station.

(g) Searches of your home

- The police do not have a general power to enter and search your home as part of their investigations unless they have your consent (preferably in writing) if you are the occupier, or the consent of your parents if you live with them.

- Before seeking consent the police must state the purpose of the proposed search and inform you (and/or your parents) that you are not obliged to consent, and that anything seized may be produced in evidence in court.

Consent can be withdrawn at any time.

- In certain circumstances the police can obtain a *search warrant* which is a written authority from a magistrate to enter and search particular premises for particular items relating to a *serious arrestable offence (see heading (b) above).*

- A search warrant must be used within one calendar month from the date of its issue. It permits entry on one occasion only.

- The police can enter and search premises without consent or a warrant in certain circumstances. The main ones are to

  ○ arrest a person for an arrestable offence;

  ○ recapture an escaped prisoner;

  ○ save life or limb;

  ○ prevent serious damage to property; *and*

  ○ deal with or prevent a breach of the peace.

- They also have the power to enter and search any premises where you were when you were arrested, or immediately beforehand, in order to look for evidence relating to the offence for which you were arrested.

- In addition, if you have been arrested for an *arrestable offence*, an inspector can authorise the search of premises occupied by you where there are reasonable grounds for suspecting that there is evidence on the premises relating to that offence or some other connected or similar offence.

● In cases where the police do not have consent you are entitled to be told

    ○ the name of the police officer and the police station he or she is from. If the police officer is not in uniform, he or she must show you their warrant card;

    ○ why the premises are being searched; *and*

    ○ what it is that they are looking for.

● If the police have a search warrant, this must be produced to you and you must be supplied with a copy.

● If necessary, the police can enter by reasonable force but they must not cause any unnecessary disturbance.

● You can request that a neighbour or friend is present to witness the search.

This must be allowed unless the officer in charge has reasonable grounds for believing that it would seriously hinder the investigation.

● Before any search takes place, you are entitled to receive a written *Notice of Powers and Rights.* This explains the rules about how searches should be conducted, that you may be able to get compensation for any damage caused in entering and searching the premises and gives the address to which an application for compensation should be directed.

● Although the police are not allowed to make a general search of the premises for the purpose of finding something of interest to them, once they are lawfully on the premises they can seize anything which they have reasonable grounds for believing is evidence of any offence or was obtained as a result of criminal activity, and it is necessary to seize it in order to prevent it from being concealed, damaged, altered or destroyed.

● Even if the search was unlawful any evidence seized can normally be used in court.

- The police must make a proper written record giving full details of the search.

- The record should include

    o the address of the premises searched;

    o the date, time and length of the search;

    o the names of the officers who made it;

    o a list of the items seized and the reason for their seizure;

    o whether force was used and, if so, why;

    o details of any damage caused during the search and the circumstances in which it was caused.

Chapter 41

The Public Order Act 1986 and the Criminal Justice and Public Order Act 1994 create various criminal offences which are aimed at controlling certain types of behaviour. It is beyond the scope of this book to consider these offences in any detail but the main ones are described in outline in this chapter. Where there is a reference to 'violence', this means violence towards both people and property and includes throwing any form of missile at or towards another person even if it misses.

(a) Public order offences

(1) Riot

● Riot is committed where 12 or more people present together use or threaten unlawful violence for a common purpose and their behaviour is such that if a person of 'reasonable firmness' were present they would fear for their personal safety.

(2) Violent disorder

● Violent disorder is committed where 3 or more people present together use or threaten unlawful violence and their behaviour is such that if a person of 'reasonable firmness' were present they would fear for their personal safety.

● It can be committed in private as well as public places and may include fights between gangs outside pubs and discos.

(3) Affray

● Affray is committed where a person uses or threatens unlawful violence towards another and his or her behaviour is such that if a person of 'reasonable firmness' were present they would fear for their personal safety.

● The threat must consist of more than just words alone.

● It can be committed in private as well as public places and may include fights between individuals outside pubs and discos.

(4) Threatening behaviour

● This offence is committed where a person

    ○ uses towards another person threatening, abusive or insulting words or behaviour; *or*

    ○ distributes or displays to another person any writing, sign or poster which is threatening, abusive or insulting with intent to

    – cause that person to fear immediate unlawful violence; *or*

    – provoke the immediate use of unlawful violence by that person.

● It can be committed in private as well as public places, except that no offence is committed if the person behaving in this way and the other person are both inside a house or flat at the time.

(5) Disorderly conduct

● This offence is committed where a person

    ○ uses towards another person threatening, abusive or insulting words or behaviour, or disorderly behaviour;

○ displays to another person, any writing, sign or poster which is threatening, abusive or insulting

within the hearing or sight of a person likely to be caused harassment, alarm or distress.

● It can be committed in private as well as public places, except that no offence is committed if the person behaving in this way and the other person are both inside a house or flat at the time.

● It is a defence to show that

○ you were inside a house or flat and had no reason to believe that;

– anyone was within hearing or sight who could be caused harassment, alarm or distress; *or*

– you could be seen or heard by somebody outside; *or*

○ your conduct was reasonable.

● The aim of this offence is to stop gangs of young people being rowdy in the streets late at night and upsetting local residents.

(6) Racial hatred

● It is an offence to with the intention of stirring up racial hatred

○ use threatening, abusive or insulting words or behaviour; *or*

○ display, publish or distribute any written material which is threatening, abusive or insulting; *or*

○ perform any play in public which involves threatening, abusive or insulting words or behaviour; *or*

○ distribute, show or play any film, video or sound recording.

(7) Intentional harassment

● This is a new offence which is committed if with intent to cause and does cause another person harassment, alarm or distress a person

○ uses towards another person threatening, abusive or insulting words or behaviour, or disorderly behaviour; *or*

○ displays any writing, sign or poster which is threatening, abusive or insulting.

- It can be committed in private as well as public places, except that no offence is committed if the person behaving in this way and the other person are both inside a house or flat at the time.

- It is a defence to show that

  ○ you were inside a house or flat and had no reason to believe that you could be seen or heard by somebody outside; *or*

  ○ your conduct was reasonable.

- The aim of this offence is to stop people from being repeatedly harassed, particularly on racial grounds.

(8) Demonstrations and marches

- Children and young people have a right to take part in peaceful protests provided that these comply with directions imposed by the senior police officer present, for example as to the route taken.

- A chief officer of police can apply to the council to ban public processions.

(b) Football matches

- If you are attending any league or cup football match, it is criminal offence to

  ○ throw anything at or towards the pitch or other spectators; *or*

  ○ take part in any racist or indecent chanting; *or*

  ○ go onto the pitch without permission during the match and within 2 hours before the start and 1 hour after the finish.

- It is also a criminal offence to possess a smoke bomb, fireworks or distress flare at a league or cup football match and when entering or trying to enter the ground *(see further Chapter 28, Fireworks).*

- It is also a criminal offence if you are attending any league or cup football match to

  ○ be drunk; *or*

  ○ have alcohol with you; *or*

  ○ have with you a bottle, can or other container for drink capable of causing injury to a person struck by it in areas of the ground open to the public or while entering or trying to enter the ground, during the match and within 2 hours before and 1 hour after the finish.

● The court has power to make an *exclusion order* which prohibits you from attending league and cup football matches if you are convicted of a criminal offence in connection with such a match. This includes

○ any offence (including any of the above offences, any public order offence, assault and criminal damage) committed during the match or while you were entering or leaving or trying to enter or leave the ground within 2 hours before the start and 1 hour after the finish;

○ an offence of disorderly conduct, racial hatred or involving the use or threat of violence to another person or property which was committed on a journey to or from a match; *and*

○ having alcohol with you or being drunk while in a coach or train on a journey to or from a match.

● An *exclusion order* cannot be a sentence on its own and must be additional to another sentence.

It must be for a minimum of 3 months and can last for an indefinite period. After 1 year you can apply to have the *exclusion order* lifted.

● The court can order you to go to a police station within 7 days and have your photograph taken.

● If you disobey an *exclusion order*, you will be committing a further offence.

(c) Trespassers

● If 2 or more people are trespassing on land intending to reside there for any period and the occupier has asked them to leave, and

○ they have damaged the land (including writing graffiti or leaving litter); *or*

○ they have used threatening, abusive or insulting words or behaviour towards the occupier; *or*

○   they have between them brought 6 or more vehicles on to the land

the senior police officer present can direct them to leave and to remove any vehicles or property.

●   If they fail to do so or return within 3 months, they will be committing a criminal offence.

●   This offence is mainly aimed at squatters, hippy communities and new age travellers.

●   Disruptive trespassers can commit the offence of *aggravated trespass* if they are on land in the open air and their purpose is to intimidate, obstruct or disrupt other people engaging in lawful activity.

●   The senior police officer present can direct them to leave and, if they fail to do so or return within 3 months, they will be committing an offence.

●   These offences are mainly aimed at hunt saboteurs and sit-ins at environmental sites against proposed new motorways.

●   A superintendent can apply to the council to ban a *trespassory assembly* which is to be held on land without the permission of the occupier and which may result in serious disruption to the life of the community, or significant damage may be done to land, or a building or monument on it of historical, architectural, archeological or scientific importance.

●   Events such as the summer solstice at Stonehenge may be caught by this provision.

(d) Raves

●   It is not an offence to go to a rave.

●   Superintendents have powers to direct the removal of people waiting for, attending or preparing for, a rave.

●   A rave is defined as a gathering in the open air of 100 or more people at which loud music is played during the night which is likely to cause serious distress to local residents. Once the necessary direction has been given, the police may order the following to leave any land and to take their equipment and vehicles with them

- o 2 or more people preparing to hold a rave;

- o 10 or more people waiting for a rave to begin;

- o 10 or more people attending a rave which is in progress.

- Failure to leave will result in an offence.

- A constable in uniform also has the power to stop any person whom he or she reasonably believes is on their way to a rave and direct them to go elsewhere provided that the person is within 5 miles of the site of the rave.

- Failure to obey will result in a criminal offence.

- These rules do not apply to raves which are held indoors.

See also Chapter 16, Criminal Proceedings; Chapter 40, The Police: Their Powers and Your Rights. Squatters are dealt with further in Chapter 31, under heading (b)(3).

Chapter 42

PUNISHMENT AND DISCIPLINE

● Your parents and all those who have care of you have the power to lawfully correct you. They are entitled to set reasonable boundaries on your behaviour and to attempt to maintain them.

(a) At home

● The punishment you receive should be moderate and reasonable. It must be in proportion to what you have done wrong and be imposed for breaking a fair rule, for example if you have not completed your homework, it may be reasonable to withdraw your pocket money but it would not be reasonable to beat you with a stick.

● Your parents are entitled to use *corporal punishment* such as smacking or slapping but this must be justified. The force used must be reasonable and not excessive bearing in mind your age, understanding, height and build. Punching a child or young person or hitting them about the head are unlikely ever to be considered reasonable.

● The law will not generally interfere in matters of parental punishment and discipline as these are regarded as issues to be regulated within the family. However, there is an exception if a parent goes too far and causes you injuries or you are at risk of harm.

● If the punishment you receive amounts to physical or emotional abuse or ill-treatment, the social services department of your local authority may take whatever steps are necessary to protect you *(see further Chapter 2, Abuse and Child Protection Procedures).*

● You can be made the subject of *care order (see Chapter 11, The Children Act 1989, heading (c)(5))* or a *supervision order (see Chapter 11, heading (c)(6))* by a family court if you are suffering or are likely to suffer 'significant harm' because your parents are punishing you excessively *(see further Chapter 10, Care Proceedings, and Chapter 52, Supervision Orders).*

● It may be possible to obtain an injunction for your personal protection against a physically abusive parent *(see further Chapter 21, Domestic Violence and Harassment).*

● If you are under the age of 16 a parent who assaults, ill-treats, neglects or abandons you so as to cause you unnecessary suffering or injury to your physical or mental health may be committing a criminal offence.

● If the excessive punishment amounts to an assault, whatever your age, this may be a criminal offence.

● The police may wish to investigate the assault and it is likely that they will ask you to agree to a full medical examination in a hospital.
They may also ask you to agree to being interviewed.

If you agree, you will be asked questions by a specially trained police officer and social worker and the interview will probably be videoed.

There are guidelines about how you should be asked question so as to try to make it less upsetting for you.

● If the parent is prosecuted, you may have to give evidence at the trial *(see further Chapter 16, Criminal Proceedings, heading (g)).*

If he or she is convicted, an order for compensation may be made by the criminal courts or you may be able to apply to the Criminal Injuries Compensation Board for compensation *(see further Chapter 12, Compensation, heading (a)).*

● Assault is also a *tort*, and it may be possible to *sue* the parent for damages in the civil courts *(see further Chapter 51, Suing and Being Sued, heading (a); Chapter 12, Compensation, heading (b); Chapter 48, Solicitors and Legal Aid).*

● Corporal punishment is prohibited in all residential homes for children and local authority foster placements. *The position regarding punishment and discipline if you are being looked after by the local authority is dealt with in Chapter 9, Care Orders and Accommodation – Being Looked After by the Local Authority, under headings (c)(3) and (f).*

(b) At school

The discipline that you can be given in school and the range of punishments including exclusion and the ban on corporal punishment in state schools, are dealt with in Chapter 25, Education, under headings (f) and (g).

Chapter 43

(a) Criminal Records and the Rehabilitation of Offenders Act 1974

● The Rehabilitation of Offenders Act 1974 is aimed at enabling reformed offenders to 'live down' their past.

● Broadly speaking, the Act provides that a person who is convicted of a criminal offence and receives no further *convictions* during a set period, called the *rehabilitation period*, becomes a rehabilitated person and their *conviction* becomes *spent*. This means that it need not be revealed.

● The *rehabilitation period* runs from the date of the *conviction* and its length depends on the sentence that was received. Some examples are shown on the table on the next page.

● Under the Act a *spent conviction*, or failure to disclose a *spent conviction*, is not usually a proper ground for denying a person a job or dismissing them *(see generally Chapter 58, Working, heading (e) in relation to unfair dismissal)* or excluding them from any profession, occupation or employment.

● However there are certain exceptions and the fact of the *spent conviction* and the details of the offence will have to be disclosed.

Sentence	Rehabilitation periods for	
	Adults	Under 018s
Detention in a young offender institution* for between 30 months and 6 months	10 years	5 years
Detention in a young offender institution* for less than 6 months	7 years	5 years
Detention in a young offender institution* for more than 30 months	Never	Never
Detention during Her Majesty's pleasure	Never	Never
A life sentence	Never	Never
A fine, a probation order and a community service order	5 years	2.5 years
A supervision order and a conditional discharge	The date it finishes or one year, whichever is the longer	
An attendance centre order	1 year after the order expires	

* or imprisonment including a suspended sentence, in the case of a person aged 21 or over.

The people who must disclose *spent convictions* include solicitors, barristers, judges, police officers, prison officers, doctors, dentists, opticians, nurses, midwives, accountants, teachers and probation officers.

● In addition, a *spent conviction* need not be mentioned when making an application for credit or insurance.

● At the request of the social services department of a local authority or a family health services authority, the police are able to make checks into the backgrounds (which includes any *spent convictions*) of those who work with children, notably social workers, staff of children's homes and nurseries, childminders and foster parents.

The address of NACRO, the National Association for the Care and Resettlement of Offenders, is given in Part Three, Where to Go for Information and Help, under heading (W) Other Useful Contacts.

(b) Fingerprints, photographs and body samples

The powers of the police to take these as part of their investigations into particular criminal offences are dealt with in Chapter 40, under heading (e).

● If you have been *convicted* of a criminal offence or if you receive a formal *caution (see further Chapter 16, Criminal Proceedings, heading (b))* for a criminal offence, fingerprints, photographs and body samples taken from you during the investigation may be kept by the police as records to assist them in the future in establishing the identities of people responsible for committing criminal offences.

● If you are *prosecuted* for the offence concerned and cleared, or not *prosecuted* (unless you admit the offence and are *cautioned* for it), the fingerprints, body samples and all copies must be destroyed as soon as practicable.

● The same applies to photographs, all negatives and copies, except if you have a previous conviction for a *recordable offence (see further below)*.

● Body samples need not be destroyed if they were taken for the purpose of the investigation of an offence for which another person has been *convicted* and from whom a sample was also taken. The idea is for all samples to be available if there is later found to have been a miscarriage of justice. In this situation, the police are not supposed to use the body samples or information obtained from them for the purpose of investigating other criminal offences or in evidence against you in relation to other criminal offences.

● You can witness the destruction provided you ask to do this within 5 days of being cleared or informed that you will not be *prosecuted*.

● If you have been convicted of a *recordable offence*, in certain circumstances, you can be required within 1 month of the date of the conviction to attend the police station for your fingerprints or a non-intimate sample (for example, hair from your head, fingernail scrapings, saliva, swabs taken from the mouth and any other part of the body (except the ears, nose, anus or a girl's vagina) and footprints) to be taken.

- *Recordable offences* are, broadly, those punishable with imprisonment in the case of an adult and certain non-imprisonable offences (for example, soliciting for prostitution and having an article with a blade or sharp point in a public place).

- The circumstances are

  o in the case of fingerprints

  - you were not kept in police detention at any stage, for instance because you were *summonsed* rather than arrested and charged *(see further Chapter 16, Criminal Proceedings, heading (c)); and*

  - you have never had your fingerprints taken;

  o in the case of non-intimate body samples

  - you have not had such a sample taken from you; *or*

  - such a sample was taken but it was unsuitable or insufficient for analysis.

- In either case, you should be given at least 7 days notice of when you have to attend the police station. If you do not attend you can be arrested.

- Both fingerprints and non-intimate body samples can be taken in these situations without consent, using reasonable force if necessary.

(c) Access to information held about you by officials

(1) Computer files

- Today, a great deal of information is held about people, on computers. If it is entered wrongly, is out of date or is mixed up with somebody else's information, this could result, for example, in you being wrongly refused a job, welfare benefits or a place at college.

- The Data Protection Act 1984 gives you the right to see most of the information held about you in *computer files* or in a computerised system, for example by

  o central government departments, for example relating to income support payments, taxes and passport applications;

- the Driver Vehicle Licensing Authority relating to car owners and driving licence holders;
- the Police National Computer relating to convictions for criminal offences;
- local authority departments, for example relating to those involved with social services, council tenants and those receiving housing benefit;
- organisations like British Gas, electricity companies and British Telecom; *and*
- banks and credit card companies.

● Every organisation, body or company that holds personal information on computer must place on the *Data Protection Register* the kind of files they hold, how they collect information and what they use it for.

● You can look at the Register

- at the *Data Protection Registrar's* office;
- by writing to the Data Protection Registrar and asking for a certified copy of the entry for the organisation, body or company concerned; *and*
- in many public libraries.

● The right of access to this information relates only to computer files as opposed to *manual files* in other words, those held on paper.

It also relates only to your own computer file and not to anybody else's, although parents can apply on behalf of their children who are under the age of 18.

● If you are under the age of 18 information will only be made available to you if the holder is satisfied that you understand the nature of the request.

● There may be a fee payable.

● You may need to make a written request to the organisation, body or company concerned and you may have to complete an application form providing details about yourself.

- They must send you a copy of the file within 40 days.

- If the information contained in a particular computer file is inaccurate or misleading, you have a right to request directly that it be corrected.

If you do not succeed, you can apply to the Registrar and, if that fails, you can make an application in the county court *(see Chapter 15, The Courts and the Legal System, heading (b)(3))*.

- The Registrar and the county court have power to award compensation if you suffer damage because of the inaccuracy of information held about you and/or if information about you is being, or has been, misused.

(2) Files held by social services

- You have a right to see *social work files* about you.

If the file is on computer you should apply to see it under the Data Protection Act 1984.

If it is a manual file, you are entitled under the Access to Personal Files Act 1987 to see information which has been recorded since 1 April 1989.

- You need to write to the social services department concerned which has 40 days to reply.

- A fee is payable.

- The right to see information is restricted in certain situations, notably, if

  ○ disclosure could lead to the identification of another person, for example an adoptive parent, foster parent or childminder, who has not consented to disclosure; *or*

  ○ it refers to your physical or mental health and the doctor, health visitor or psychiatrist who gave it considers that disclosure is likely to cause serious harm to you or to another person's physical or mental health; *or*

  ○ it is considered by the social services department that disclosure is likely to prejudice their work by seriously harming your physical, mental or emotional condition, or that of another person.

● If the information contained in a manual file is inaccurate or misleading you have a right to request directly that it be corrected.

If you are dissatisfied with the response you can ask within 28 days for the decision to be reviewed by a committee of 3 councillors.

● If you are under the age of 18 you can apply to see your own files provided that the social services department is satisfied that you understand the nature of the request. Otherwise a parent may apply on your behalf.

● A parent may be prevented from receiving information about you if it is likely to result in serious harm to your physical or mental health or emotional development.

● The Access to Personal Files Act 1987 applies in respect of manual files kept by *housing departments.*

(3) Medical records

● Under the Data Protection Act 1984 you are entitled to see your *medical records* if they are held on computer by a health professional but not otherwise. A health professional includes a doctor, dentist, psychologist, optician, pharmacist, nurse midwife and health visitor.

● The health professional is entitled to withhold information if its disclosure is likely to cause serious harm to your physical or mental health.

● If you are under the age of 18 the record holder must be satisfied that you are capable of understanding the nature of the application.

● You are also entitled, if you request this, to see any medical report prepared by your doctor for insurance or employment purposes before it is sent.

Chapter 44

● Your parents decide what religion you should follow until you are old enough to decide for yourself.

● Your parents have no legal duty to bring you up with any religious beliefs and/or to provide you with any religious instruction.

● If, for example, your parents are Jehovah's Witnesses and do not believe that you should have a blood transfusion, the High Court (*see Chapter 15, The Courts and the Legal System, heading (6)(4)*) has the power to override their objection if your life is in danger.

● If your parents divorce or separate and there is a dispute about religion, the court will not force the parent with whom you live to bring you up in a particular religion. If you feel strongly about a matter of religion, your wishes may be taken into account.

● You can decide to follow any, or no, religion. If you freely decide to follow a different religion to that of your parents, there is little that they can do to stop you.

However, if you are under the age of 18 and you join a sect whose practices could be harmful to you, your parents could try to force you to give up your membership by applying to make you a *Ward of Court (see Chapter 56, Wardship).*

See also Chapter 35, Medical Treatment; Chapter 38, Parental Responsibility and Decisions About Your Life and Your Upbringing; Chapter 56, Wardship. Religious assembly and instruction in school is dealt with in Chapter 25, under heading (d). The position regarding your religion if you are the subject of a care order is dealt with in Chapter 9, under heading (e).

Chapter 45

(a) The age of consent for girls

● A girl cannot lawfully consent to sexual intercourse until she has reached the age of 16.

She, herself, will not be committing any criminal offence if she does have sexual intercourse under this age *(see further heading (c) below)*.

● There are no laws about when a girl can consent to lesbian sex. Lesbian sex has never been illegal except at one time in the armed forces although it may be an indecent assault *(see further heading (c) below)*.

● Girls under the age of 16 cannot lawfully consent to an indecent assault.

(b) Men, heterosexual and homosexual sex

● It used to be the law that a boy under the age of 14 was not considered physically capable of having sexual intercourse. This has now changed and a boy aged 10 or over can commit any form of sexual offence. If he is under the age of 14 the prosecution must prove that he knew that what he was doing was seriously wrong.

● The age of consent for homosexual sex has recently been reduced from 21 to 18. The situation now is that homosexual acts between 2 men

○ both aged 18 or over;

○ who both consent; *and*

○ which take place in private, do not amount to a criminal offence.

● Boys under the age of 16 cannot lawfully consent to an indecent assault.

(c) Sexual offences

(1) Unlawful sexual intercourse

● If a man has sexual intercourse with a girl who is under the age of 16, he commits a criminal offence regardless of whether she actually consents.

● If the girl has not yet reached 13 there is no possible defence.

● If she is aged 13 or over, but has not yet reached 16, he may have a defence if

○ he reasonably believes they are validly married; *or*

○ he is under the age of 24 and has not previously been charged with a similar offence and he reasonably believes the girl to be aged 16 or over.

Otherwise, his belief that the girl is aged 16 or over, even if it is reasonable, is no defence.

(2) Rape

● Rape is defined as sexual intercourse by a man with a woman (whether vaginal or anal), and by a man with another man, where the other person (the victim), at the time of the intercourse, does not consent to it and, at the time, he knows that the victim does not consent or he does not care whether or not they consent.

- There has to be some penetration of the man's penis into the vagina or anus. Forced penetration by objects and forced oral sex are not included but this would be an indecent assault *(see further below)*.

- If the man uses force, or deliberately gets the victim drunk, the victim will not be consenting.

- In law, a woman cannot rape a man although it could be an indecent assault.

(3) Indecent assault

- This includes acts short of sexual intercourse such as touching somebody else's genitals or rubbing up against them. It includes forced penetration of the vagina or anus and forced oral sex.

- It can be committed by, or against, a female or a male of any age.

- There is a defence if the other person consents but a boy or girl under the age of 16 cannot lawfully consent.

- The belief that the other person is aged 16 or over, even if it is reasonable, is no defence.

(4) Gross indecency

- The offence of gross indecency with, or towards, a child under the age of 14 covers the situation where there is no assault but the person tries to persuade the child to touch them indecently, for example stroke their penis.

(5) Buggery

- Buggery (penile penetration of the anus) is no longer illegal between a heterosexual couple where both are aged 18 or over, they both consent to it and it takes place in private.

- It is still an offence to commit an act of buggery with somebody who is under the age of 18.

(6) Incest

- Incest involves sexual intercourse between people who are not permitted to have a sexual relationship regardless of age and consent.

- A man cannot have a sexual relationship with his mother, sister, half-sister, daughter or granddaughter.

● A woman cannot have a sexual relationship with her father, brother, half-brother, son or grandson.

(7) Indecent exposure

● If a boy or man exposes his penis with intent to insult a female or to the annoyance of others, he commits a criminal offence.

(8) Indecent photographs

● It is a criminal offence to take an indecent photograph of somebody who is under the age of 16.

This includes films and videos.

(9) Prostitution

● It is a criminal offence for a boy or a girl to approach a man and offer to have sex in return for money.

(d) Being a victim of a sexual offence

● If you have been raped or indecently assaulted, you should immediately contact a rape crisis centre for confidential advice and support.

The telephone number for London is given in Part Three, Where to Go for Information and Help, under heading (B), Children and Young People in Danger or Distress.

● You should report the offence to the police without delay.

● You should not wash yourself as you may destroy vital evidence such as semen or blood, and you should not change the clothes you are wearing.

● Somebody from the rape crisis centre should go with you to the police station to give you support.

● If you are a girl, you will be medically examined by a woman doctor and interviewed by a woman police officer.

The police now receive special training in how to deal sensitively with these situations so as to try to make the ordeal less upsetting for you.

The position if the offender is prosecuted and you have to attend court as a witness is dealt with in Chapter 16, Criminal Proceedings, under heading (g). The victim of a sexual offence has the right to remain anonymous.

If you need urgent help or counselling, the organisations and bodies listed in Part Three, Where to Go for Information and Help, under headings (B), Children and Young People in Danger or Distress, (C), Youth Services, (D), Family and Personal (Support and Counselling Services) and (J), Victims of Crime, may be able to give some assistance.

See also Chapter 1, Abortion; Chapter 2, Abuse and Child Protection Procedures; Chapter 13, Contraception; Chapter 34, Marriage.

Chapter 46

● A shopkeeper will commit a criminal offence if he or she sells cigarettes (and also cigars, loose tobacco and cigarette papers) to a young person under the age of 16 whether or not for their own use.

● It is not a criminal offence for a person under the age of 16 to smoke or be in possession of cigarettes but a police officer has a duty to confiscate cigarettes if he or she sees somebody who appears to be under 16 smoking in any public place.

● If an adult gives a cigarette to somebody who is under 16, the adult does not commit any criminal offence.

Smoking can affect your health.

Chapter 47

It will help you to understand this section if you first read Chapter 11, heading (a), which sets out the thinking behind the Children Act 1989.

(a) The provision of services

● The social services department of the local authority have a general duty to safeguard and promote the welfare of all *children in need* within their area and to help the families of such children to bring them up in their own homes wherever possible by providing a suitable range of services.

● A *child in need* is somebody under the age of 18 who is unlikely to achieve or maintain a reasonable standard of health or development or whose health or development may suffer if he or she does not get the help required and includes disabled children *(see further Chapter 18, Disability, heading (b))*.

● The range of services that must be provided for use by children and young people under the age of 18 and their parents includes

243

- ○ advice, guidance and counselling;
- ○ leisure activities and clubs;
- ○ home helps;
- ○ assistance for families to have a holiday;
- ○ the establishment of family centres to provide occupational, social, cultural, and recreational activities and to give advice, guidance and counselling; *and*
- ○ the provision of accommodation *(see further Chapter 9, Care Orders and Accommodation – Being Looked After by the Local Authority, heading (b))*.

● The social services department must publish and distribute booklets and leaflets listing the services available.

> You should be able to find these in your local library, your local Citizens' Advice Bureau and doctors' surgeries. If you cannot find the information you require and if you need to talk to a social worker about something, you should telephone or visit the social services office covering your area. You will find the details in your local telephone directory under the name of your local authority. The listing will usually be 'Social Services, Children and Families'.

(b) Complaints

● The social services department must establish and publicise a procedure for considering representations (including complaints) about the way in which they carry out their duties.

● Any child in need can make a complaint if the services to which they are entitled are not provided, for example

- ○ if you wish to see a social worker and nobody is prepared to give you any time; *or*
- ○ a reasonable request to attend a family centre for advice, guidance and counselling is denied.

The procedure for making complaints is dealt with in Chapter 9, Care Orders and Accommodation – Being Looked After by the Local Authority, under heading (g).

Details of various organisations providing assistance to children and young people in care, and which also look after the interests of all children in need, are given in Part Three, Where to Go for Information and Help, under heading (P), Children and Young People in Care.

See also Chapter 2, Abuse and Child Protection Procedures; Chapter 9, Care Orders and Accommodation – Being Looked After by the Local Authority; Chapter 11, The Children Act 1989; Chapter 18, Disability; Chapter 31, Housing and Homelessness; Chapter 33, Leaving Home and Running Away. Your right to access to information about you held in social services files is dealt with in Chapter 43, under heading (c).

Chapter 48

SOLICITORS AND LEGAL AID

(a) Sources of legal advice and representation

● There are other sources of legal advice apart from solicitors but, if you have a court case, you will probably have to *instruct* a solicitor because a solicitor has *rights of audience* which means that he or she can represent you in court.

● You can usually get general advice and legal advice at the following places

(1) Citizens' Advice Bureaux (CABs)

● These are mostly staffed by unpaid volunteers. They are normally a good place to start. You will find your local CAB listed in your local telephone directory or ask at your local library. CABs provide free advice and information on every subject. If they cannot deal with your problem they will direct you to the nearest local source of specialist advice. CABs normally keep lists of local solicitors and what they do. Some CABs have special sessions in which local solicitors give free legal advice.

(2) Law centres

●   These are usually staffed by a mixture of paid workers including qualified lawyers and unpaid volunteers. Your nearest law centre should be listed in your local telephone directory or ask at your local library. Law centres provide free legal advice and representation on a wide range of subjects particularly welfare benefits, housing and employment matters. Normally, they will only advise and represent people who live locally and will not become involved in civil cases where legal aid is available *(see further below)* or in criminal cases.

(3) Neighbourhood advice centres

●   There may be an advice centre near to where you live. The set-up depends on the particular advice centre but they tend to be a cross between a CAB and a law centre. They are aimed at serving the needs of the people in the local community.

(4) Solicitors

●   Solicitors are legally qualified. To become a solicitor a person must usually have a law degree from a university and then go to Law School for a year, followed by 2 years training in a firm of solicitors, although there are other routes to becoming a solicitor.

●   Some firms of solicitors employ *legal executives.* They do not have to have law degrees or go to Law School, but they must pass the examinations set by the Institute of Legal Executives and gain practical experience in a firm of solicitors.

You are entitled to ask about the qualifications of the person you are seeing.

●   If you need to find a solicitor, ask your family and friends to recommend one or ask at the CAB. *The Law Society* publishes *regional solicitors' lists* for England and Wales setting out the names and addresses of local solicitors, which areas of law they specialise in, and whether they represent people who are eligible for legal aid. These lists are generally available at CABs, law centres and your local library.

●   The Law Society has specialist panels of solicitors who do particular kinds of work, such as personal injury actions *(see further*

Chapter 3, Accidents and Negligence), and acting on behalf of children and young people in private and public law family cases. You can contact The Law Society for details.

● Solicitors specialising in family law are often members of the *Solicitors' Family Law Association* (SFLA). The SFLA has recently published guidelines for its members about how they can best represent children and young people. You can contact the SFLA for details.

> The relevant addresses and telephone numbers are given in Part Three, Where to Go for Information and Help, under heading (A), Legal and General.
> You should also read Part Four, Making the Law Work for You, heading (1), General advice and getting the most out of your solicitor.

(5) Barristers

● Your solicitor may arrange for you to see a barrister, also known as counsel, in conference, to advise you about your legal position and/or to help in the preparation of your case for court. Only a barrister can represent you in most of the cases that are heard in the Crown Court, High Court, Court of Appeal and House of Lords *(the various courts are dealt with in Chapter 15, The Courts and the Legal System, under heading (b))*. A barrister may sometimes represent you in other courts, particularly if it is a complicated case.

● To become a barrister, a person must usually have a law degree from a university and then go to Bar School for a year, followed by 1 years training, called 'pupillage' in a barristers' chambers, although there are other routes to becoming a barrister.

● Members of the public cannot normally go to barristers directly. This will be organised through your solicitor.

(b) Forms of legal aid and assistance

● The easiest way of finding out if a particular firm of solicitors represents people who are eligible for legal aid is to look in their window to see if there's a sign saying 'legal aid' (although not all firms undertaking legal aid work display this sign). Alternatively you can look in the *regional solicitors' list (see heading (a)(4) above)*.

- There are various forms of legal aid according to the nature of your case. If you are legally aided you do not have to pay for some, or all, of the costs of preparing the case before you go to court and of your representation in court. Instead, these will be paid by the tax-payer, but, as will be explained below, legal aid isn't necessarily completely free. Moreover, if you win a civil case, some of your costs may have to be deducted from any money you are awarded.

(1) Initial interviews

Some firms of solicitors will give you half an hours' interview and advice for no fee or only a small fee. *You must make it clear before-hand that this is what you want otherwise you could be charged the full rate.*

(2) The Green Form Scheme

- This enables a solicitor to give you a limited amount of advice and assistance either orally or in writing. For example

  ○ interviewing you and advising you on your rights;

  ○ writing letters on your behalf;

  ○ carrying out negotiations; *and*

  ○ drafting certain documents.

- The solicitor will probably use the Green Form Scheme to assist in the completion of an application for full legal aid.

- You can apply under the Green Form Scheme in your own right if you are aged 16 or over. Before then, unless there are exceptional circumstances, your parent (or guardian) should sign the form.

The Green Form Scheme is means-tested and is only available if your income and savings come within certain limits. The solicitor will advise you about this.

If you are on income support *(see Chapter 57, Welfare Benefits, heading (b))* or disability working allowance *(see Chapter 18, Disability, heading (f))* it will be free.

If you have savings of more than £1,000 and/or income of more than £72 per week when all your other expenses are paid you will not qualify.

(3) Legal aid in criminal cases

● Criminal legal aid is granted by the court. The solicitor will have the necessary forms and will complete these on your behalf, or help you to complete them.

You will need to sign the forms.

● It must be in the interests of justice to grant you legal aid, for example because

- ○ its a serious case and you could lose your liberty; *or*
- ○ there's a substantial question of law involved; *or*
- ○ witnesses have to be traced and interviewed on your behalf; *or*
- ○ the case is a very complicated one, for example involving mistaken identity.

● Your income and savings must be within the limits.

If you are under the age of 16 the financial position of your parents (or guardian) may be taken into account.

If you are aged 16 or over only your financial position will be taken into account and you will have to complete and sign a *statement of means.*

● If you are on income support *(see Chapter 57, Welfare Benefits, heading (b))* legal aid will be free.

If you have savings of more than £3,000 and income of more than £47 per week when all your other expenses are paid you may have to make a contribution towards your legal aid.

If you are found not guilty or the case against you is dropped, it is likely that any contribution you have had to pay will be returned to you.

● If legal aid is refused your solicitor may be able to challenge this.

(4) Duty solicitor schemes

● Most youth courts run a *duty solicitor scheme*. The duty solicitor will be a solicitor who practices locally and is not attached to the police or the court.

● The duty solicitor will give you free legal advice and may speak for you in court.

It would be appropriate to ask for the duty solicitor in a short case where you might not qualify for legal aid, for example if you are pleading guilty to drink driving where you were only just over the limit *(see further Chapter 22, Driving, heading (c)(6))* or if you are at risk of losing your liberty because you have not paid a fine.

● A different *duty solicitor scheme* operates 24 hours a day in police stations *(see further Chapter 40, The Police: Their Powers and Your Rights, heading (d)).*

(5) Legal aid in civil cases

● Civil legal aid is granted by the *Legal Aid Board.* The solicitor will have the necessary forms and will complete these on your behalf. Your parent (or guardian) will need to sign them if you are under the age of 18.

● Civil legal aid is both merits and means-tested. You must have reasonable grounds for being a party to the proceedings and it must be reasonable in all the circumstances for you to be granted civil legal aid. This means that you must have a good claim or a good defence. You cannot usually get legal aid if you are suing somebody for less than £1,000 because the *small claims* procedure applies *(see further Chapter 51, Suing and Being Sued, heading (c)).*

● You must complete and sign a statement of means.

It is your financial position which is taken into account and your income and savings must come within certain limits.

If you get income support you will be eligible financially.

The other rules about financial eligibility for civil legal aid and the contributions system are quite complicated. Your solicitor should be able to advise you about these.

● It takes time for the application to be processed, usually at least a month. In urgent cases an *Emergency Legal Aid Certificate* can be granted over the telephone.

● When the full certificate is granted it may be limited up to a certain stage in the proceedings at which point a barrister may have to advise whether it is justifiable for you to continue receiving legal aid.

● If legal aid is refused your solicitor may be able to challenge this.

● The *statutory charge* applies in most civil cases. *Your solicitor should explain this carefully to you and if you don't understand, don't be afraid to ask.* The general rule in civil proceedings is that the loser pays the winner's legal *costs.* However, there may be a shortfall between the amount that the loser is ordered to pay and the amount that it actually cost to bring your case. The Legal Aid Board is entitled to recover this shortfall from any *damages* you receive. This means that at the end of the day, you may not get the full amount of *damages* that were awarded in your favour (this puts you in exactly the same position as somebody who is paying privately).

See also Chapter 12, Compensation, heading (b), Awards of damages by the civil courts; Chapter 51, Suing and Being Sued.

---

(6) Legal aid in family cases

● If you are the subject of a public law family case *(see generally Chapter 15, The Courts and the Legal System, heading (a)),* for example the local authority is making an application for a *care order (see Chapter 11, The Children Act 1989, heading (c)(5), and further Chapter 10, Care Proceedings)* or a *supervision order (see Chapter 11, heading (c)(6)),* the court must appoint a solicitor for you. In these situations you are automatically entitled to free legal aid which is neither merits nor means-tested.

● If you are making your own application for a *section 8 order* in a private law case *(see further Chapter 11, The Children Act 1989, headings (b) and (d), and Chapter 20, Divorce and Separation, heading (c)),* the rules about civil legal aid apply *(see above).*

● So, if the Legal Aid Board does not consider that it is reasonable, for example, for you to make an application for a *specific issue order* to enable you to be known by another name, legal aid will be refused.

If legal aid is refused your solicitor may be able to challenge this.

● In financial cases *(see generally Chapter 20, Divorce and Separation, heading (d))* the *statutory charge* does not apply to any maintenance that is ordered to be paid by one parent either directly to you or to the other parent on your behalf.

However it does apply to lump sums over £2,500. You are allowed to keep the first £2,500 of any lump sum awarded but the excess attracts the *statutory charge*.

Chapter 49

SOLVENT ABUSE

● The most common forms of solvents giving off fumes which can be inhaled or sniffed in order to achieve a high are glue, paint, aerosols and lighter fuel.

● It is a criminal offence to supply, or offer to supply, a person under the age of 18 with a substance which the supplier knows, or has reason to believe, will be inhaled for the purpose of causing intoxication.

● The law is aimed mainly at shopkeepers but is wide enough to cover all adults and also children over the age of 10 and young people under the age of 18 who supply solvents for profit.

● It is not a criminal offence to sniff or be in possession of a sniffable substance although, occasionally, the police do arrest young people for public order offences *(see generally Chapter 41)* if they are caught using them in a public place.

> It must be emphasised that sniffing is very dangerous.
> If you have a problem with solvents see Part Three, Where to Go for Information and Help, under heading (M), Solvents.

Chapter 50

● If your mother or father remarries, your step-parent does not acquire *parental responsibility* for you *(see Chapter 38, Parental Responsibility and Decisions About Your Life and Your Upbringing)*.

● If you are in the care of your step-parent, he or she can do whatever is reasonable for the purpose of safeguarding or promoting your welfare.

● If you have a close relationship with a step-parent who divorces, or separates from, your natural parent, the step-parent can apply to the court for a *residence order (see Chapter 11, The Children Act 1989, heading (c)(1))* if they wish you to live with them, or a *contact order (see Chapter 11, heading (c)(2))* if they wish to continue seeing you.

● A step-parent can be appointed to act as your guardian *(see further Chapter 30)*.

● It is possible to be adopted by a natural parent and a step-parent, but the court is more likely to make a *joint residence order* in their favour instead.

If you are facing a problem caused by the presence of a step-parent at home, details of organisations that may be able to assist are given in Part Three, Where to Go for Information and Help, under the heading (D), Family and Personal (Support and Counselling Services).

See also Chapter 4, Adoption, heading (a), Being adopted; Chapter 20, Divorce and Separation; Chapter 36, Names; Chapter 38, Parental Responsibility and Decisions About Your Life and Your Upbringing.

Chapter 51

It will help you to understand this chapter if you first read Chapter 15 which gives an outline of the courts and the legal system and the nature of civil proceedings.

(a) What happens in the county court if you sue?

● As the majority of cases are heard in the county court, this chapter does not go into High Court procedure although, in fact, it is broadly similar to county court procedure.

● *Suing* means bringing a civil claim.

● The person *suing* is called the *plaintiff* (or sometimes the *applicant*) and the person being sued is called the *defendant* (or sometimes the *respondent*).

● In order to *sue* you must have a good *cause of action*, in other words, a claim which the law recognises against

    ○ another person;

    ○ a firm;

○ a limited company, for example a chain store; *or*

○ an organisation or other body, for example a local authority, for something they have done, or not done, to you.

● The county court deals with cases in which *plaintiffs sue defendants* for *damages* to compensate them, for example for being injured in an accident or having bought faulty goods which cost money to repair.

As well as claiming *damages, injunctions* may also be sought to prevent certain types of behaviour, for example assault, trespass or nuisance.

(1) The limitation period

● All cases must be brought within set time limits. For example

Action	Period from which time runs
Breach of contract (including debts)	6 years from breach
Torts	6 years from date tort commited (such as trespass) or from date damage occurred (such as nuisance)
Personal injury cases (excluding assaults)	3 years from date of accident, or from date of knowledge of injuries (if later). In exceptional cases can be over ridden (see further below)
Fatal accident cases	3 years from date of death. In exceptional cases can be overridden (see further below)

● If the case is not brought within the appropriate time limits, the general rule is that it cannot be brought at all. However, the time limits can be extended in certain circumstances.

In particular, if you were under the age of 18 when the cause of action arose, you have 6 years from your 18th birthday to bring a claim in your own right for breach of contract or in tort, and 3 years from that date in respect of personal injury and fatal accident cases. You can bring a claim earlier but you must do so through a *next friend* *(see further below).*

- In personal injury cases other than where the injuries are caused by an assault, the date of knowledge of the injuries is relevant if they did not become apparent until some time after the accident. For example
  - when you were 15 you were knocked over by a car and broke your arm, you will have 3 years from your 18th birthday to *sue* the driver;
  - say, instead of breaking your arm, back problems develop when you are 19, you have 3 years from the date when the back problems first started to *sue* the driver.

- Sometimes, in respect of personal injury and fatal accident claims, people fail to realise that they have a good cause of action until after the limitation period has expired. In these circumstances, the court has the power to extend the time limits to 3 years from the date the *plaintiff* became aware, or ought reasonably to have become aware, of their right to *sue* the *defendant*.

- The factors to be taken into account by the court in making that decision are:
  - the length of and reasons for the delay on the *plaintiff's* part;
  - whether evidence still exists;
  - the *defendant's* conduct;
  - the extent to which the *plaintiff* acted promptly and reasonably once he or she appreciated that there might be a cause of action; *and*
  - the steps taken by the *plaintiff* to obtain medical, legal or other expert advice.

(2) Issuing proceedings

- If you are under the age of 18, except for wages owed to you, you cannot issue proceedings in your own right but must have a *next friend*, normally one of your parents (or your guardian) or another responsible adult. *This is not the same person as the next friend in family proceedings. That kind of next friend is dealt with in Chapter 11, The Children Act 1989, heading (d).*

- The *next friend* has *conduct* of the proceedings on your behalf. This includes giving *instructions* to the solicitor and agreeing any *settlement*.

- Proceedings are normally issued in the county court nearest to where the *plaintiff* lives or to where the cause of action arose. If the *defendant* defends the case, it will be transferred to his or her local county court if that is a different court.

- An issue fee may be payable.

The amount of the fee depends on the nature of the case and the amount being claimed.

(3) Default actions

- Cases in which a debt and/or *damages* are being claimed are usually begun by *particulars of claim* which is a written summary of how the cause of action arises and the amount being claimed.

- The *defendant* has 14 days from the date this is received to file a *defence* and any *counterclaim* which must also be in writing.

- If the *defendant* admits the claim or fails to defend it, the *plaintiff* can apply to enter *judgement* and for legal *costs*.

(4) Fixed date actions

- Generally, where an *injunction* is being claimed the court staff will fix a *return date*.

If the *defendant* does not appear, an *injunction* can be made in his or her absence (provided that the case can be proved).

- As well as the particulars of claim, it is necessary to have a *notice of application* which should be supported by an *affidavit*, that is, a sworn statement of evidence.

(5) Directions

- The court has power to give directions about all sorts of matters that may arise while the case is being prepared for trial, in particular, about questions relating to the evidence.

These directions will usually be given by the *district judge (see below)*.

- There are some new procedural rules. For example

  o in most cases both sides must file written statements of the evidence upon which they intend to rely; *and*

○ unless the court has directed otherwise, the case must be set down for trial within 15 months from the filing of the defence otherwise it will be *automatically struck out.*

(6) The trial

● Cases where more than £1,000 is being claimed and/or those involving *injunctions* are normally, but not always, heard by a *circuit judge.*

● It is usual for the *plaintiff's* solicitor or barrister to begin by telling the judge what the case is about and by taking him or her through any documents. The *plaintiff* and the *plaintiff's* witnesses will give evidence followed by the *defendant* and the *defendant's* witnesses.

● You can give evidence if you are under the age of 18. If the judge does not think that you understand the nature of the *oath*, that is, what it means to swear to tell the truth, you can give *unsworn evidence*. The judge must still be satisfied that you know the difference between the truth and a lie.

● There are many rules about *hearsay* and other forms of evidence.

Basically, if you say something that the judge should not hear, for example because its a rumour based on what a neighbour told your mother, the *defendant's* lawyer will stand up and object.

● After the evidence has been completed, the lawyers will then make speeches.

● After speeches the judge will give a full judgement setting out his or her reasons.

(7) Costs

● The usual rule is that the loser pays the winner's legal *costs* but there are all sorts of exceptions.

● If you are under the age of 18 and you lose, your *next friend* is responsible for any *costs* that you may be ordered to pay.

You should always talk to your solicitor about costs. If you are legally aided the Legal Aid Board's statutory charge may affect the amount of damages you receive (see further Chapter 48, Solicitors and Legal Aid, heading (b)).

(8) Damages

> See generally Chapter 12, Compensation, heading (b)(2) in relation to damages, how they are worked out and what happens to them if you are under the age of 18.

● Even though you may get judgement in your favour, if the *defendant* doesn't have any money, or refuses to pay, you may not get all, or any, of the sum awarded.

● The court does not automatically collect *damages*, and an application must be made to the court to *enforce the judgment*. There are various ways this can be done, including

○ ordering the *defendant* to pay in instalments;

○ if the amount is sufficiently large, by making an adult *defendant bankrupt* (that is, the court takes over his or her property and debts; it is usually necessary to go to the High Court to do this);

○ if the *defendant* is working, obtaining an *attachment of earnings order* (that is, on each pay day the *defendant's* employer will deduct from his or her wages a set sum of money to be paid to you);

○ by issuing a *warrant of execution* so a *bailiff* can seize the *defendant's* goods and sell them to pay the damages.

Again, you should talk to your solicitor about the various options.

(b) What happens in the county court if you are sued?

● It is fairly unusual for children and young people under the age of 18 to be *sued* as they are unlikely to have the money to pay any *damages*.

● If you are *sued* while you are under 16, except for a debt that you owe, the proceedings must be brought against you through your *guardian ad litem*, normally one of your parents (or your guardian) or another responsible adult. *This is not the same person as the guardian ad litem* in care proceedings. That kind of guardian ad litem is dealt with in Chapter 10, *Care Proceedings, heading (b)*.

● If no suitable adult is prepared to act as your *guardian ad litem*, an application must be made to the court to appoint somebody.

● In a default action *(see further heading (a)(3) above),* if the proceedings were not brought through a *guardian ad litem* because it was not appreciated that you are under the age of 18 and you failed to file a defence and judgement was entered against you, you are entitled to have this judgement set aside.

● Although your *guardian ad litem* has *conduct* of the proceedings on your behalf, which includes giving instructions to the solicitor and offering any settlement, you must take responsibility for any *damages* that may be awarded against you, not the *guardian ad litem*.

● If you lose, your *guardian ad litem* is not responsible for any *costs* that you may be ordered to pay unless he or she incurred them by personal negligence or misconduct.

(c) The small claims court

● In the county court there is a special procedure for *district judges* to hear cases where less than £1,000 is being claimed.

● This procedure is designed to deal with quite straightforward cases, for example faulty goods, bad workmanship, small loans, unpaid wages and minor accidents.

● The idea is that members of the public should be able to bring small claims themselves without the need for a solicitor.

● Legal aid is not generally available. You can pay a solicitor privately but, even if you win, you are unlikely to recover the *costs*.

● The hearing will be less formal and the district judge can hear any evidence he or she chooses whether or not it is in the correct form and/or *hearsay*.

● If you are under the age of 18 you still require a *next friend* if you are suing or a *guardian ad litem* if you are being *sued* in the same way as with all other county court (and High Court) cases.

Every county court has booklets and leaflets explaining about small claims and the necessary forms that you will need to complete in order bring a small claim. It is a good idea to visit your local Citizens' Advice Bureau, law centre or neighbourhood advice centre for assistance. Some may even be prepared to do the necessary paperwork and to represent you.

See also Chapter 3, Accidents and Negligence; Chapter 12, Compensation; Chapter 14, Contracts; Chapter 29, Goods and Services; Chapter 48, Solicitors and Legal Aid. Accidents at school are dealt with in Chapter 25, under heading (i); accidents at work are dealt with in Chapter 58, under heading (f). Injunctions are covered in Chapter 21.

Chapter 52

The nature and effect of supervision orders

● Under a *supervision order*, you live at home with your parents or with another adult family member or friend and you have a social worker to advise, assist and befriend you. The social worker should make regular visits and ensure that you are safe.

● Only the local authority or the NSPCC can apply for a *supervision order*.

● Although both *care orders* and *supervision orders* are made in favour of the local authority, the major difference between them is that with a *supervision order* the local authority does not have *parental responsibility* for you *(see Chapter 38, Parental Responsibility and Decisions About Your Life and Your Upbringing)*.

● No *supervision order* can be made once you have reached the age of 17, or 16 if you are married.

● A *supervision order* lasts for up to 1 year and can be extended by the court to a maximum period of 3 years (or your 17th birthday if that is sooner).

- A *supervision order* may require you to
  - ○ keep the supervisor informed of any change of address; *and*
  - ○ allow the supervisor to visit you at the place where you are living.

- The supervisor can require you to live in a particular place or take part in particular activities for a period of up to 90 days, for example attend residential or day training courses.

- A *supervision order* may require you to submit to a medical or psychiatric examination.

However, where you have sufficient understanding to make an informed decision, the court must have your consent, and there must be satisfactory arrangements for the examination. You do not have to consent if you do not want this.

In addition, you can only be required to attend as a residential patient in a hospital, or mental nursing home, if the court is satisfied, on the evidence of a doctor that

- ○ you may be suffering from a physical or mental condition that requires treatment; *and*
- ○ a period as a residential patient is necessary if the examination is to be carried out properly.

- *The procedure on an application for a supervision order is identical to the procedure on an application for a care order. The rules about what happens in court, your representation – the guardian ad litem and your solicitor, the threshold criteria and significant harm, and interim orders, are dealt with in Chapter 10, Care Proceedings.*

Chapter 53

TATTOOS

● You cannot have a tattoo until you have reached the age of 18 except where this is performed for medical reasons by a doctor.

● A reputable tattooist should refuse to tattoo you unless you have proof that you are aged 18 or over.

You should always go to a tattooist who is registered with the local authority. A certificate should be displayed in the shop. You should check that the needles are sterilised and fresh needles and inks are used for each customer. Otherwise you risk infection from HIV.

See also Chapter 35, Medical Treatment.

Chapter 54

TAX AND NATIONAL INSURANCE

(a) National Insurance (NI)

● Everyone has a national insurance number and you will normally receive yours in the post just before your 16th birthday. You will be sent a *national insurance number card* which you should keep somewhere safe.

● From the time you are 16, provided your earnings are over a certain limit, you should pay NI whether you work full-time or part-time.

● NI contributions are deducted by your employer direct from your wages.

The amount you pay depends on how much you earn.

Your employer also makes contributions on your behalf.

● NI guarantees certain benefits you may need in your working life such as unemployment benefit, incapacity benefit and a pension when you retire.

How much you get depends on the contributions you have made.

If you are under the age of 18 and you lose your job, you are unlikely to qualify for unemployment benefit because you will not have made enough contributions.

● If you are on youth training (YT) *(see Chapter 59)* you will not pay NI.

(b) Income Tax

● Income tax helps to pay for the services the government provides, such as the National Health Service and state education as well as things like income support and legal aid.

● If you are on YT, you will not pay income tax.

● Normally, you don't have to pay income tax until you start work.

● If you earn above the personal allowance during the tax year, which runs from 6 April to 5 April of the following year, you must pay income tax.

● The personal allowance for a single person is presently £3,445.

● Income tax is generally deducted by your employer direct from your wages under the PAYE scheme.

The amount you pay depends on how much you earn but the basic rate applies to most young people.

● If it is your first job since leaving full-time education or YT, you complete a form P15 and your employer sends it to the tax office. You then get a PAYE code based on your personal allowance and your employer will work out how much tax to deduct (together with NI).

● If you leave your job, you get a form P45 from your employer which shows your PAYE code, your total earnings and the tax you have paid to date.

● You must give your P45 to your new employer so that he or she knows how much tax to deduct. If you do not have a P45 you will be taxed at an emergency rate until it is sorted out. You need a P45 to claim unemployment benefit.

● At the end of the tax year your employer gives you a form P60 showing how much tax and NI you have paid. You may also have to fill out your own tax return and send it to the tax office.

● The tax office confirms that you have paid the correct amount of tax. If you have paid too much, you will get a repayment. If you have paid too little, it will be deducted from next year's wages.

● Interest on bank or building society accounts becomes taxable when you start working so you must tell your branch immediately.

Chapter 55

THE UNITED NATIONS CONVENTION ON THE RIGHTS OF THE CHILD AND THE EUROPEAN CONVENTION ON HUMAN RIGHTS

(a) The United Nations (UN) Convention on the Rights of the Child

● The UN Convention is an international agreement designed to protect the rights of children and young people. The United Kingdom government has agreed to be bound by the UN Convention. It sets out rights which all children and young people under the age of 18 should have. These rights should apply to all children and young people equally, wherever they live and whatever their race, sex, religion, language, disability, opinion or family background.

● The UN Convention provides that when adults, organisations, official bodies and courts make decisions about children and young people, their best interests must be a primary consideration. It also provides that you must be given the opportunity to be heard. If you are capable of forming your own views, you should have a right to express them freely in all matters affecting you, and they must be given due weight according to your age and maturity.

The main rights that the UN Convention gives to children and young people are

- the right to life and the best possible chance to develop fully;
- the right to be given a name at birth and to be able to become a citizen of a particular country;
- the right to be cared for by your parents;
- the right to an adequate standard of living, if necessary with assistance from the government to your parents;
- the right to be cared for properly on a daily basis and the government should provide your parents with suitable help;
- if you cannot be looked after by your family, you must be properly looked after by another family or in a children's home;
- the right not to be separated from your parents against their will except if it is in your best interests and, if you are separated, to be able to keep in touch with your family unless this would not be in your best interests;
- governments must take steps to stop you from being taken out of the country illegally;
- the right, if you are unwell, to be given good healthcare;
- disabled children and young people must be helped to be as independent as possible and to be able to take a full and active part in everyday life;
- the right to live in a safe, healthy and unpolluted environment with good food and clean drinking water;
- the right to free education up to primary school level and the provision of a range of secondary schools;
- schools should help children to develop their skills and personality fully, teach them about their own and other people's rights and prepare them for adult life;
- the right to rest and play and the chance to join in a range of activities;

- the right to express what you think and feel so long as you do not break the law or affect other people's rights;

- the right, subject to guidance from your parents, to choose your own religion and to hold your own views as soon as you are able to decide for yourself;

- the right to join organisations and take part in meetings and peaceful demonstrations, so long as they are not against the law and you do not affect other people's rights;

- the right to personal privacy, for example not having your letters opened or phone calls listened to;

- the right of access to a wide range of information, especially any which would make life better for you;

- the right to be protected from all forms of violence, be kept safe from harm and be given proper care by those looking after you;

- the right not to be punished cruelly or treated humiliatingly. You must not be locked up unless the law permits this. If you are locked up lawfully, you must be treated with respect, be able to receive legal advice and have your case heard and decided as quickly as possible;

- if you have been badly treated you must be given help to recover;

- if you get into trouble with the law you must be treated in a way that is suitable to your age and you are to be treated as innocent until you are found guilty. You must be able to get legal advice and be represented by a lawyer. Wherever possible you should be dealt with other than through the courts. You should not be deprived of your liberty unless there is no other suitable sentence and only for the shortest time possible;

- the government must protect you from doing work which could be dangerous or harm your health or interfere with your education;

- the government must also protect you from dangerous drugs, sexual abuse and being abducted or sold.

- Every 5 years the government must send the UN Committee on the Rights of the Child a report explaining how it is putting the Convention into practice.

> If you, or any child or young person, is not being given the rights spelled out in the Convention, you can tell your MP, local council-lor, the relevant government department and interested children's organisations, for example The Children's Legal Centre.
> Their details, and those of the Children's Rights Development Unit, which monitors the UN Convention, are given in Part Three, Where to Go for Information and Help, under heading (A), Legal and General.

(b) The European Convention on Human Rights

- The European Convention sets out certain fundamental human rights which contracting states including the United Kingdom must maintain for everyone within their jurisdiction. These include the rights to

  - life;
  - freedom from torture, inhuman or degrading treatment or punishment;
  - freedom from slavery and forced labour;
  - liberty and security of the person;
  - a fair and public hearing before an independent and impartial tribunal;
  - privacy and respect for family life;
  - freedom of religion and conscience;
  - freedom of expression;
  - freedom of assembly and association;
  - freedom to be able to marry and have a family;
  - peaceful enjoyment of possessions;
  - education.

● These rights are to be enjoyed without discrimination on any ground such as sex, race, colour, language, religion, political or other opinion, national or social origin, association with a national minority, property, birth or other status.

● To ensure that these obligations are being met, individuals including children and young people can make complaints alleging violations of the European Convention to the European Commission of Human Rights. The Commission can then refer the case to the European Court of Human Rights, as can a contracting state, but an individual cannot go to the Court directly.

● The Commission can only hear complaints after you have pursued the matter as far as you can through the English legal system and within 6 months from the date on which the final decision was taken.

● The complaint must be in writing giving full details of what has happened.

● A report is made to the Commission which may then make a full investigation in order to try and reach a solution.

● Legal aid is not available.

The address of the European Commission of Human Rights is given in Part Three, Where to Go for Information and Help, under heading (A), Legal and General.

See also Chapter 11, The Children Act 1989.

Chapter 56

WARDSHIP

● If you are made a *Ward of Court*, you are put under the protection of the High Court *(see Chapter 15, The Courts and the Legal System, heading (b)(4))* until you are 18 and no important step can be taken in your life without the permission of the court.

● Wardship is no longer very common but, if you are aged between 16 and 18, your parents can apply to make you a *Ward of Court* in certain situations, for example

○ to put an end to an undesirable relationship;

○ if you join a religious sect whose practices could be harmful to you, to force you to give up your membership;

○ if you are refusing to consent to medical treatment which it would be in your best interests to have;

○ to stop you from leaving home, but the likelihood of your parents' succeeding is not very great unless you are exposing yourself to considerable risks.

See also Chapter 1, Abortion; Chapter 33, Leaving Home and Running Away; Chapter 34, Marriage; Chapter 35, Medical Treatment; Chapter 38, Parental Responsibility and Decisions About Your Life and Your Upbringing; Chapter 44, Religion.

Chapter 57

WELFARE BENEFITS

(a) General

● The rules about being able to claim various welfare benefits are quite complicated. You will have to fulfil certain conditions in order to qualify. Broadly speaking, benefits are either *means-tested* (that is, how much money you have is taken into account) or *non-means-tested*.

● The main means-tested benefits that you are likely to wish to claim in your own right are income support *(see further heading (b) below)* and housing benefit *(see further heading (c) below)*.

You may also qualify for free NHS prescriptions, dental treatment, eye tests and glasses *(the rules about these are dealt with in Chapter 35, Medical Treatment, under heading (d))* and for free school meals.

● Non-means-tested benefits are either *contributory* or *non-contributory*. Most young people under the age of 18 do not qualify for contributory, non-means-tested benefits such as unemployment benefit and incapacity benefit because they will not have paid enough national insurance *(see Chapter 54, Tax and National Insurance)*.

● *Non-contributory benefits for disabled children and young people are dealt with in Chapter 18, Disability.*

● In order to make a claim for benefits you will need to fill out a fairly detailed application form.

> If you think you may be eligible, or if you need help in completing the application form, you should go to your local Benefits Agency Office which deals with claims or to your local Citizens' Advice Bureau, law centre or neighbourhood advice centre.
>
> Your local Benefits Agency Office will be listed in your local telephone directory under 'Benefits Agency'.
>
> The telephone numbers of the free DSS helplines and the address of Child Poverty Action Group are given in Part Three, Where to Go for Information and Help, under heading (H), Welfare Benefits.
>
> In Part Three, under heading (C), Youth Services, organisations marked (WB) give specialist advice about welfare benefits.

(b) Income Support (IS)

The Benefits Agency pays money to people who don't have enough to live on – this is called income support.

(1) Who qualifies?

● You are not entitled to IS in your own right until you are 16.

Furthermore, the restrictions that apply to most 16 and 17 year olds mean that, generally, you have to be aged 18 or over to qualify for IS.

This is because at 16 or 17 if you are not working or in full-time education, you have a right to offer of a place on a youth training (YT) programme *(see Chapter 59)* and, normally, you will not get IS if you are on YT.

● As a general rule you cannot qualify for IS unless

  ○ you (and any partner with whom you are living as though husband and wife) are not working or are working less than 16 hours a week; *and* o   you are available for work or YT, and actively looking (but there are exceptions, *see further below*); *and*

o   you (and any partner) have savings of less than £8,000 (savings between £3,000 and £8,000 will affect the amount that you get); *and*

o   you must not be in full-time education at school or college (but there are exceptions if you have to live independently, *see further below*).

●   If you are working part-time and have a low income, IS tops you up to a certain level.

Having no income or a low income is not enough to make you eligible unless you meet the other conditions.

(2) 16 and 17 year olds entitled to income support

You may be able to get IS if you fall into any of the following special groups

●   If you have left school or college and you cannot work or go on YT because you are

o   a parent looking after your child; *or*

o   expecting a baby in 11 weeks or less for the period up to 7 weeks after the birth, or ill and unable to work because of pregnancy; *or*

o   so ill or disabled that your doctor says that you are incapable of working or going on YT for at least 1 year; *or*

o   registered blind; *or*

o   looking after an ill or disabled member of your family who cannot look after themselves; *or*

o   you've been temporarily laid off work but are intending to go back to the same job.

–   you are entitled to IS as long as the relevant condition is satisfied.

●   If you are still at school or college in full-time education and you are

o   a parent looking after your child; *or*

○ disabled; *or*

○ an orphan and there is nobody acting as your parent, for example you do not have a guardian; *or*

○ forced to live away from your parents and they are not keeping you, for example, because

– you've fallen out with them and they've thrown you out; *or*

– you left because you were in physical or moral danger or there was a serious risk to your physical or mental health; *or*

○ living separately from your parents and they cannot support you, for example, because they are very sick, mentally or physically disabled or in prison; *or*

○ living independently and have just left care

– you are entitled to IS until the end of the holiday after your last school or college term but you may be able to keep claiming IS if you register for YT.

● If you have just left school or college, are not living at home and have applied at the *Jobcentre* or *Careers Office* for a job or a YT place, and have not yet found something, you may be able to get IS for a limited period, namely

○ from the first Monday in September to the end of the year if you leave in the summer;

○ from the first Monday in January for 12 weeks if you leave at Christmas;

○ from the first Monday after Easter for 12 weeks, if you leave before Easter.

If at the end of this time you don't have a job or a YT place you may qualify for IS because of *severe hardship (see further below).*

The conditions are that

○ you are married and your husband or wife is over 18 or registered for work or YT or eligible for IS; *or*

○ you are an orphan and there is nobody acting as your parent; *or*

○ you have no choice but to live apart from your parents, for example, because

– you are under the supervision of the probation service or a local authority; *or*

– you left to avoid physical or sexual abuse; *or*

– you need special accommodation due to mental or physical illness or handicap; *or*

○ you are forced to live away from your parents and they are not keeping you, for example, because

– you've fallen out with them and they've thrown you out; *or*

– you left because you were in physical or moral danger or there was a serious risk to your physical or mental health; *or*

○ you are living separately from your parents and they cannot support you, for example, because they are very sick, mentally or physically disabled or in prison; *or*

○ you were in care just before you were 16.

● If you have just left care or a young offender institution and are living independently, you may be able to get IS for up to 8 weeks while you try to get a job or a YT place.

● Even if you don't fall into any of these special groups you may still be able to get IS if it is the only way of preventing *severe hardship*.

There are no set rules about what severe hardship is. Each case is looked at on its own merits. The circumstances that will be taken into account include whether

○ you have any money;

○ you can expect to get a job or a YT place;

○ you have anyone else who can help you;

○ you are threatened with homelessness or are already homeless;

○ you have an illness or a disability or are vulnerable; *and*

○ your parents are on welfare benefits and have difficulty supporting you.

● If you get IS because of severe hardship it will usually be for only a limited period while you are trying to get a job or a YT place.

(3) How much will you receive?

The amounts that are paid are fixed by the government every year.

● Everyone who qualifies is entitled to a *personal allowance*. The amount you get depends on your circumstances.

● You are also entitled to receive extra sums if you have a dependent child or children. The amount depends on their ages.

● There are set *premiums*, that is, additional amounts on top of your personal allowance, for families and lone parents.

● There are premiums for people with disabilities. The amount depends on your circumstances and the extent of your disability.

● The figures for April 1995 onwards are shown in the table below:

Personal allowances	Current weekly rates
Single person aged 16 or 17	£28.00
Single person aged 16 or 17 living apart from parents with good cause	£36.85
Couple both under 18 and eligible	£55.65
Couple where one is under 18	depends on their situation
Child under 10	£15.95

Premiums	Current weekly rates
Family	£10.25
Lone parent	£5.20
Disability	
Single person	£20.00
Couple	£28.55
Severe disability	
Single person	£35.05
Couple (lower rate)	£35.05
Couple (higher rate)	£70.10

● If you are on YT you may be able to get IS to top up your *training allowance* in some circumstances, for example if you are aged 16 and living independently and your *training allowance* is lower than IS.

● IS is paid fortnightly in arrears.

● If you don't have enough money to live on until your first payment (and you are aged 16 or over) you may be able to get a *crisis loan* from the *social fund*.

Crisis loans will only be paid if it is the only way to prevent serious damage or risk to your health or safety.

You will be expected to pay back the crisis loan although interest will not be added to the repayments.

(4) Making the claim

● You will be asked for some formal proof of your identity and age, for example, your birth certificate, passport or driving licence. You should also take your *national insurance number card (see Chapter 54, Tax and National Insurance)*. Documents such as your NHS medical card or a travel pass will not usually be sufficient.

● If you have left school or college and cannot work or go on YT or if you are still at school or college and are eligible, you will need to visit or telephone your local *Benefits Agency Office* and say you want to claim IS.

They will give you an application form which you will need to fill out and return to them, together with any necessary medical certificates.

● In all other cases you must first register as available for work or YT with the *Jobcentre* or *Careers Office*.

You will then need to go to your local *Unemployment Benefit Office* and say you want to claim IS.

They will give you an application form which you will need to fill out and return to your local *Benefits Agency Office*.

You will then be interviewed about your circumstances.

You should keep in contact with the *Careers Office* and you may be required to sign on once a fortnight at the *Unemployment Benefit Office*.

● The decision about whether you are entitled will be made by an officer from the *Benefits Agency Office* where you made the claim (except for *severe hardship* payments which are decided by the *Secretary of State*).

You should be notified in writing of the decision.

● You can challenge the decision by seeking a review, for example because there was a mistake about the facts.

You can seek a review at any time in writing.

● You can also appeal to a *Social Security Appeal Tribunal* (except for *severe hardship* payments) where you will have an opportunity to be heard.

You must appeal in writing giving reasons within 3 months of the decision.

In your local telephone directory you will find

■ your local Benefits Agency Office listed under 'Benefits Agency';

■ your local Careers Office listed under 'Careers Service', or under the name of your local authority;

■ your local Jobcentre and your local Unemployment Benefit Office listed under 'Employment Service'.

You should take the advice of your local Citizens' Advice Bureau, law centre or neighbourhood advice centre on the question of appealing.

(c) Housing Benefit (HB)

● If you have to pay any rent for the place where you live you may be able to claim HB from your local authority (the council) to help meet the rent payments.

● HB can only be paid in respect of rent that you pay to your landlord. If for example you pay a weekly sum to your parents for your keep you cannot get HB. However, if, for example, you rent a room in a house, share a rented flat with others, or are staying in a hostel or bed and breakfast hotel, you may be eligible for HB.

- HB is payable whether you rent from the council, a housing association or a private landlord.

- Rent means payment for your accommodation.

  HB does not cover any charges for food or laundry and any gas and electricity bills.

- HB may not cover the full amount of your rent if it is considered that your accommodation is too large or too expensive for your needs.

- There are no age limits to qualify.

- Most full-time students cannot get HB. The main exceptions are if you are

  o receiving IS; *or*

  o under the age of 19 and on a non-advanced course of education (that is, not at university or the equivalent); *or*

  o a lone parent looking after your child, or one of a couple both of whom are student with a child; *or*

  o disabled.

- The council will look at how much money you have coming in to your household. You (and any partner) must not have savings of more than £16,000 (savings of under £3,000 are ignored and savings between £3,000 and £16,000 will affect the amount that you get).

- You can also get HB if you are on IS, have low earnings, work part-time or are doing YT and receiving a *training allowance (see Chapter 59, Youth Training).*

- HB payments may be made either to you or direct to your landlord.

- HB is awarded for limited periods at the end of which you have to make a fresh claim.

- If you make a claim for IS you can claim HB at the same time.

  There is a separate form to claim HB (and *council tax benefit*) inside your IS claim form.

  You should return all the forms to your local *Benefits Agency Office* and they will pass on the HB form to the council.

If you are not claiming IS you should go to your local *neighbourhood housing office* (if there is one) or ask at the town hall, to obtain a form for HB (this is a more detailed form).

● You will need to provide proof of your address and the amount of the rent. If you have a written tenancy agreement or licence agreement *(see further Chapter 31, Housing and Homelessness, heading (b))* you should take this along, or ask your landlord to write a letter setting out the position.

● If you are refused HB you are entitled to a written statement of reasons. There is no independent appeal to a tribunal from a refusal of HB but an internal review can be requested in writing within 6 weeks of the decision.

● If you are still not satisfied with the outcome you have the right to request a *Housing Benefit Review Board* hearing. You must apply in writing giving your reasons within 4 weeks of the internal review.

● If you qualify for IS and/or HB you will also get help meeting any *council tax* payments for which you are responsible, called *council tax benefit.*

Council tax has replaced the community charge and pays for local services.

How much you pay depends largely upon the value of your home and each council sets the level for its own area.

● Normally, HB cannot be backdated. The council must be satisfied that there was 'good cause' for not claiming before.

Your local neighbourhood housing office will be listed in your local telephone directory under the name of your local authority.
You should take the advice of your local Citizens' Advice Bureau, law centre or neighbourhood advice centre on the question of appealing.

If you have any questions or problems about HB, most local authorities have housing advice centres or housing aid centres which may
be able to help you. To find their details, look in your local telephone
directory under the name of your local authority. Alternatively, you
could go to your local Citizens' Advice Bureau, law centre or neighbourhood advice centre.

Details of organisations that may be able to give you general advice
about HB are given in Part Three, Where to Go for Information and
Help, under heading (R), Housing and Homelessness.

*See also Chapter 31, Housing and Homelessness. The position of
disabled young people in relation to welfare benefits is dealt with in
Chapter 18, heading (f).*

Chapter 58

There are many rules about taking jobs. The younger you are, the greater protection you are entitled to as far as your welfare is concerned. For example, if you take a part-time job when you are 13 there are limits on the number of hours you can work and the kinds of work you can do. However, you do not have the same rights that an adult in full-time work may have in relation to job security and if a 13 year old is sacked from their part-time job for no good reason, there is little that can be done about it.

(a) When you can take full-time and part-time jobs and the sorts of work you can do

(1) Full-time jobs

● You cannot legally take a full-time job until you are no longer of compulsory school age. *When you can actually leave school is dealt with in Chapter 25, Education, under heading (a)* but, for the purpose of this chapter, 16 is taken as the relevant age.

● Once you have reached the age of 16, there are no limits on the number of hours you can work or on working night shifts but there are still certain jobs you cannot do. *(See further (4) below.)*

(2) Part-time jobs and work you can do at any age

● There are no restrictions if the person employing you is not in business. Therefore you do not need to be any particular age to do odd jobs such as cleaning cars and gardening for family and friends and to receive payment from them. You may also be able to baby-sit for another child. It is up to the adult to decide if you are sufficiently responsible to do the job. It is unlikely that you would be allowed to baby-sit before you are 14.

● You can do these sorts of jobs as often as you like provided that you do not take time off school.

(3) Part-time jobs and work you cannot do until you are 16

● If your family has a shop, restaurant or other business, and even if you don't receive any payment, you can legally work only the same hours and do the same things as somebody of the same age employed by a stranger.

● The basic rules are
  ○ you must be aged 13 or over;
  ○ you cannot work before 7 am or after 7 pm on any day;
  ○ you cannot work for more than 2 hours on any school day and any Sunday;
  ○ you cannot do any job requiring you to lift, carry or move anything heavy which is likely to injure you.

● The local authority has the power to make bye-laws altering these rules, for example children under the age of 13 may be allowed to be employed by their parents in light agricultural or horticultural work. These bye-laws can also prevent you from working at particular jobs or at particular times, for example cleaning windows more than 10 ft above the ground or delivering milk after 11 am on a Sunday.

● If you are thinking of taking a part-time job you should check with the *education welfare department* of your local authority as to what you are entitled to do in your area.

● There are many other rules prohibiting many other forms of employment. Some notable ones are

If you are under the age of 14

○ you cannot drive or ride an agricultural tractor or machine.

If you are under the age of 16 you cannot work for example

○ on board a ship (except a family or training one);

○ in industry, mining or manufacturing (except a factory where only members of your family work);

○ in demolition, building or transport, for example on the roads or railways;

○ as a street trader, for example selling newspapers or flowers busking, or shoe shining, except if local bye-laws allow you to be employed in this way by your parents once you have reached 14;

○ as a collector of money;

○ selling scrap metal;

○ in a fairground.

There is other work that you cannot do including operating a circular saw or handling poisons.

(4) Work you cannot do until you are 18

Until you are 18

○ you cannot work in a betting shop;

○ you cannot work in a bar during opening hours whether or not you are being paid (so, if your parents have a pub you cannot help out behind the bar). You can work in other parts of licensed premises, for example serving meals in a restaurant;

○ you cannot sell alcohol in an off-licence or supermarket unless the sale is approved by the licensee or another employee aged 18 or over;

○ you cannot clean any machine in motion or any part of a machine if it would expose you to risk of injury from any moving part;

○ you must not work at any dangerous machine unless you have received full training about the dangers, the precautions to be observed and you are properly supervised. There is a long list of dangerous machines, including power presses, meat mincing machines washing machines and garment presses in laundries.

(b) Working under the age of 16

● Your employer should ask for proof of your age before taking you on.

● Your employer has a duty to register you with the *education welfare department* of your local authority.

● You should be issued with an *employment card* or *work permit* which tells you the work you may do and the hours you may work.

● If you are employed illegally (for example because you are under-age or doing work you're not allowed to do) your employer's insurance may not cover you if you have an accident and it may be difficult for you to get any compensation.

● The *education welfare officer* (EWO) is responsible for ensuring that the rules about children and young people under the age of 16 who work are obeyed. However, the EWO does not have any power to enter premises where people under the age of 16 might be working illegally.

● If the EWO does find out that you are working illegally your employer can be prosecuted for a criminal offence.

● The EWO can order you to give up your job if it is affecting your health or stopping you from getting the full benefit of your education.

● You, yourself, can make a complaint to the EWO if you are being asked to work too many hours or to do something dangerous.

> The problem is that if you complain you may well lose your job but you have to consider the fact that you could be seriously injured. The risks of working illegally are generally far greater than the short-term advantage of having some cash in your pocket.

(c) The contract of employment

● Your contract of employment *(see further Chapter 14, Contracts)* concerns the work you do in return for the wages you receive. The sort of work you do and the amount you are paid are matters to be agreed between you and your employer.

● Both you and your employer have general duties.

You must

○ act responsibly and do your job to a reasonable standard;

○ obey reasonable instructions; *and*

○ be honest and trustworthy.

Your employer must

○ provide you with safe working conditions;

○ pay the agreed wages; *and*

○ not require you to do anything dangerous or illegal.

● The contract of employment does not have to be in writing (although contracts of apprenticeship must be written).

It can be a spoken agreement or contained in a letter offering you the job.

● If you work more than 8 hours per week and you do not have a written contract of employment within 2 months of starting the job you have a right to receive a *written statement of the main terms and conditions of your employment,* including

○ your job title or description;

○ the date your employment began;

○ your pay;

○ your hours of work;

○ your holiday entitlement;

○ any sick pay;

○ the notice period on both sides; *and*

○ details of the disciplinary and grievance procedures that apply.

● This statement is not your contract of employment, but it can be used as evidence. If your employer refuses to give you a statement, you can go to an industrial tribunal *(see further heading (i) below)*.

● You and your employer are at liberty to agree any other terms you choose.

(d) Hours of work and pay

● If you are aged 16 or over you can work any number of hours.

You *must* sort out these things with your employer before you take the job as there is no automatic entitlement to paid or unpaid holidays other than public holidays, nor to paid or unpaid sick leave.

● Moreover, the minimum wages that used to be set by the government, for example in shops and catering, have now been abolished. It is an unfortunate fact that many young people in menial full-time and part-time jobs are very badly paid and this is a situation that they cannot alter as the employer has all the power.

● You cannot usually be made to do over-time unless this is part of your contract of employment or an emergency arises.

● If you work more than 16 hours per week, or more than 8 hours per week in a company with 20 or more employees, you are entitled to an *itemised pay statement* showing your gross and net pay and any deductions for income tax and national insurance *(see Chapter 54)*.

● There are special rules about *maternity leave* which provide that all pregnant women employees regardless of their length of service and/or hours of work are entitled to a total of at least 14 weeks unpaid time off. In addition, women who have worked for the same employer for a long enough period have the right to return to work within 29 weeks after the baby is born. There are various requirements about notice. A dismissal on the grounds of pregnancy or having had time off to have a baby may amount to an unfair dismissal *(see further below)*.

These rules are quite complicated and you should check the position with your trade union representative (if you have one) or at your local Citizens' Advice Bureau, law centre or neighbourhood advice centre.

(e) Dismissal

(1) Notice

You and your employer can agree the notice period.

If you have worked more than one month but less than 2 years, you are entitled to a minimum of one week's notice, although probably not if you are taken on for an agreed temporary period.

You are entitled to 2 weeks notice after 2 years, three weeks after 3 years.

● You must be paid all your wages up to the date you leave.

If you are told to go on the spot you must receive wages for the notice period.

If you are not paid you can *sue* your employer for your wages in the county court *(see Chapter 15, The Courts and the Legal System, heading (b)(3))* in your own right *(see further Chapter 51, Suing and Being Sued, heading (a))*.

(2) Unfair dismissal

Your employer should have good reason before he or she sacks you, for example if your work is often of a low standard or you are continually late. A dismissal on the grounds of pregnancy is automatically unfair *(see further below)*.

● If you have been dismissed and have completed 2 years continuous employment with the same employer you are entitled to request a *written statement of reasons for dismissal*. If your employer refuses to give you one you can go to an industrial tribunal *(see further heading (i) below)*.

● If you are sacked without any justification, or if you leave because your employer's conduct towards you was in breach of your contract of employment or otherwise made it intolerable for you to remain (this is termed *constructive dismissal*), you may be able to bring *a claim for unfair dismissal in an industrial tribunal (see further heading (i) below)*.

● In order to bring a claim you must have completed 2 years continuous employment with the same employer and have worked for more than 16 hours per week.

If you work for a fewer number of hours, the position is complicated and you should take independent advice.

There are exceptions to the requirements relating to length of service. For example if the dismissal was for

   ○   a refusal to do something dangerous or unsafe;

   ○   trade union membership or non-membership *(see further below)*;

   ○   pregnancy, maternity or related grounds.

● You will need to complete an application form within 3 months from the date of the dismissal.

● The remedies for unfair dismissal are

   ○   an order for reinstatement or re-engagement although the order is not actually enforceable; *and/or*

   ○   compensation.

> If you feel that you have been unfairly dismissed you should talk to your trade union representative or go to your local Citizens' Advice Bureau, law centre or neighbourhood advice centre without delay.

(3) Redundancy

● Examples of *redundancy* are if a business closes down or if fewer employees are needed to do the same work. However, you cannot get a redundancy payment if you are under the age of 18. Furthermore, you must have been employed by the same employer for at least 2 years and no part of any period that you worked while you were under 18 counts towards this.

(4) Trade unions

● *Trade Unions* exist to protect and promote the rights of their members and they negotiate pay and hours of work.

- You can generally join when you are 16.

- If you are dismissed because you join or refuse to join a trade union this would be unfair dismissal *(see further above)*.

(f) Safety at work

- All employers must ensure that you are reasonably safe at work by providing safe working conditions, including

  o a safe system of work; *and*

  o safe premises and equipment; *and*

  o competent fellow employees; *and*

  o adequate supervision; *and*

  o proper instruction.

- If you are injured at work because it is unsafe, through faulty equipment or the fault of a fellow employee you may be able to *sue* your employer for damages for negligence in the civil courts *(see further Chapter 3, Accidents and Negligence; Chapter 51, Suing and Being Sued, heading (a); Chapter 12, Compensation, heading (b); and Chapter 48, Solicitors and Legal Aid)*.

- *Industrial Injury Compensation* may be payable by your employer. The amount you get depends on how badly you are injured or disabled and on the degree of your employer's negligence.

- If you become disabled through an accident at work, you may be able to get *industrial injuries disablement benefit*. You must be at least 14% disabled in order to qualify and you may be able to get allowances for reduced earnings, constant attendance and exceptionally severe disablement.

There are newspaper reports that this scheme is likely to be abolished by the government and you will need to check whether it is still in existence.

If you do have an accident, you should talk to your trade union representative or go to your local Citizens' Advice Bureau, law centre or neighbourhood advice centre, or see a solicitor without delay.

Details of the Law Society's Accident Line are given in Part Three, Where to Go for Information and Help, under heading (U), Accidents.

You should also read Part Four, Making the Law Work for You, heading(4), which deals with personal injuries.

(g) Discrimination at work

See generally Chapter 19, Discrimination.

Your employer must not treat you less favourably on the grounds of your colour, race, ethnic or national origin or nationality, or your sex or marital status.

● The rules apply to all people of all ages, whether they work full-time or part-time and however long they have been there.

● The employer must not discriminate in any of the following ways

   ❍ the selection of job applicants, for example rejecting suitably qualified people because they are black and/or women;

   ❍ the way people are treated at work, for example refusing to allow women to go on training courses or not promoting any Asian employees;

   ❍ making a dismissal, for example only making women employees redundant.

● Employers cannot label jobs for only men or women or for only white people or black people. There may be an exception if race or sex is a genuine occupational qualification, for example acting or modelling jobs, an Indian waiter in an Indian restaurant and a female attendant in a women's lavatory.

● If you are the victim of unlawful discrimination at work you can make a complaint to an industrial tribunal *(see further heading (i) below)* within 3 months from the date of the incident. If you are sacked or constructively dismissed on the grounds of race or sex this may also amount to an unfair dismissal *(see further heading (e)(2) above)*.

● The Equal Pay Act 1970 provides that women are entitled to equal pay with men when doing work that is the same or broadly similar for the same employer or an associated employer at a separate establishment.

In a recent court case women canteen workers and cleaners employed by British Coal were able to show that they were being treated less favourably than male surface mineworkers.

● You can make a complaint to an industrial tribunal about unequal pay at any time while you are still in the job, or within 6 months from the date you left.

The addresses of the Equal Opportunities Commission and the Commission for Racial Equality are given in Part Three, Where to Go for Information and Help, under heading (Q), Discrimination.

(h) Sexual harassment at work

The rules apply whether you are female or male.

● If you are subjected to sexual harassment, for example being touched in an unwelcome way, having to listen to crude remarks or being told that granting sexual favours will help your career, this is a form of discrimination.

● If your employer does this, you can go to an industrial tribunal *(see further heading (i) below)*. Your employer will also be responsible for the behaviour of managers, supervisors and other employees where their behaviour has caused you a disadvantage unless the employer took all reasonable steps to prevent this from happening.

● You should make a careful record of what has happened and complain to somebody more senior, or the personnel officer if the company has one, or your trade union representative.

● Your company may have a policy on sexual harassment and its own complaints procedure and you should find out about this.

It is always a good idea to put your complaint in writing. Sexual harassment is upsetting and humiliating. You shouldn't do it to anybody else and nobody should have to put up with it.

(i) Industrial tribunals

See generally Chapter 15, The Courts and the Legal System, heading (c).

● Industrial tribunals are independent judicial bodies which hear complaints from individual employees including claims for unfair dismissal.

● You will need to complete an application form which can be obtained from your local *Jobcentre. This will be listed under 'Employment Service' in your local telephone directory.*

● The case is usually decided by 3 people. The chairman is legally qualified and the 2 other members of the tribunal are drawn from employers' and employees' organisations.

● The procedures the tribunal follow are usually informal and flexible.

● Full legal aid is not available for industrial tribunal hearings, but a solicitor may be able to assist you in preparing the application under the *Green Form Scheme (see further Chapter 48, Solicitors and Legal Aid, heading (b)).*

● You can pay privately for your own solicitor to represent you at the hearing or, instead, you are allowed to be represented by a worker from a law centre, a trade union official or a friend.

● In certain circumstances a tribunal can review its decision and change it if it is wrong, but not simply because you disagree. You must apply in writing within 14 days after the decision was received by you.

● You have a right to appeal to the *Employment Appeal Tribunal* only on a point of law or because the decision was perverse by giving written notice that you wish to appeal within 42 days of the decision.

● If you are dissatisfied with the hearing and/or the appeal, you may be able to complain to the *Council on Tribunals.*

The address is given in Part Three, Where to Go for Information and Help, under heading (V), Consumer Protection.

If you require help in drafting and preparing your claim, you should go to your local Citizens' Advice Bureau, law centre or neighbourhood advice centre, or see a solicitor (but bear in mind that you may have to pay for a solicitor).

Details of organisations and bodies that may be able to assist you in dealing with problems related to work, are given in Part Three, Where to Go for Information and Help, under heading (T), Work.

See also Chapter 59, Youth Training. The position of disabled children and young people in relation to employment matters is dealt with in Chapter 18, under heading (e).

Chapter 59

What Youth Training (YT) is and the rights you have

● YT is a way of acquiring work skills and qualifications. It has largely replaced apprenticeships.

● If you are aged 16 or 17 and you are not in work or full-time education, you have the right to an offer of a YT place.

● If you are disabled or sick and unable to take up a place, this right may extend beyond your 18th birthday.

● To get a YT place you must put your name down at your local *Careers Office*.

The Careers Office will be listed in your local telephone directory under 'Careers Service', or the name of your local authority.

● YT is a scheme run by the government. The work is provided in a variety of ways, for example, by local authorities, public companies and private businesses. The careers officer will have details of the opportunities available in your area.

● There is no guarantee that you will get a job at the end of your placement.

- The minimum *training allowance* is presently £29.50 per week if you are aged 16 and £35 per week if you are aged 17.

You do not pay national insurance or income tax *(see Chapter 54).*

Your travel costs should be paid.

- In special circumstances you may get income support (IS) and housing benefit (HB) *(see Chapter 57, Welfare Benefits),* as well as the training allowance. For example, if you are aged 16 and have to live independently and your training allowance is less than IS (that is, £36.85 pw), you will get a top up to the same level as IS.

If you qualify for *disability living allowance* (DLA) *(see Chapter 18, Disability, heading (f))* you will still receive DLA.

- At the start of your placement you will get an individual *training plan* setting out the length of your placement and your duties. You must also receive a *written statement of your rights and conditions of work.*

- You generally work a minimum of 30 hours per week.

You should not work more than 40 hours per week excluding lunch breaks.

Overtime is not allowed.

- You are entitled to 19½ days holiday per year plus public and bank holidays.

- You are entitled to paid time off to go on related courses, do examinations and attend job interviews.

- If you are sick you generally receive your training allowance for up to 21 days.

- You should be provided with protective clothing, tools and equipment necessary for the job.

- You must be provided with training in health and safety. You have the same rights about safety in the workplace as all other employees *(see further Chapter 58, Working, heading (f)* and, in particular, you must be properly supervised and any equipment must be properly maintained.

- If you are have an accident while on YT because it is unsafe or through the fault of somebody else also on YT, you may be able to *sue* the provider of the work for *damages* for negligence in the civil courts *(see further Chapter 3, Accidents and Negligence; Chapter 51, Suing and Being Sued, heading (a); Chapter 12, Compensation, heading (b) Chapter 48, Solicitors and Legal Aid).*

If you do have an accident you should talk to your Careers Officer or go to your local Citizens' Advice Bureau, law centre or neighbourhood advice centre, or see a solicitor without delay.

Details of the Law Society's Accident Line are given in Part Three, Where to Go for Information and Help, under heading (U), Accidents.

You should also read Part Four, Making the Law Work for You, heading (4), which deals with personal injuries.

If you are asked to do something dangerous you should discuss this with the Careers Officer.

● You have the same rights not to be discriminated against on the grounds of sex and race as all other employees *(see further chapter 19, Discrimination, and chapter 58, Working, heading (g)).* For example

○ a girl should not be refused a YT place as a mechanic;

○ a black person on YT should not be singled out to do all the menial tasks.

● If you are subjected to sexual or racial discrimination, you may be able to take your case to an industrial tribunal *(see further Chapter 58, Working, heading (i)).*

● In addition you must not be discriminated against in relation to YT on the grounds of disability.

If you are the victim of unlawful discrimination you should discuss this with the Careers Officer.

● Unlike certain other employees, you are not entitled to receive any notice or written reasons before being dismissed. Furthermore, if you are unfairly dismissed you cannot go to an industrial tribunal.

● You can leave at any time you want, for example to change to another YT place or because you have been offered a job. You do not have to give any notice.

- If you do not have a YT place or a job to go to after you have left your YT place, and you are not entitled to income support, you may be able to get a *YT bridging allowance* presently £15 per week or £3 per day.

  You must generally have had a good reason for leaving.

  This is payable for 8 weeks or 40 days in any 52 week period.

  You must register with the *Careers Office* as available for YT.

  The careers officer will give you a form to complete which you must take immediately to the *Unemployment Benefit Office (this will be listed in your local telephone directory under 'Employment Service').*

  You must sign on fortnightly at the *Unemployment Benefit Office* and you must not refuse another YT place without a good reason.

- You are entitled to join a trade union while you are on YT.

See also Chapter 58, Working. The rights of disabled young people in relation to YT are dealt with in Chapter 18, under heading (d).

PART TWO

Table of Minimum Ages

WHAT THE LAW SAYS YOUNG PEOPLE ARE ALLOWED TO DO AND WHEN

At any age

- A bank, building society or National Savings account can be opened in your name.

- You can own premium bonds.

- You can smoke cigarettes but you cannot buy them.

- You may be able to give consent to surgical, medical and dental treatment on your own behalf if you are considered to have sufficient maturity and intelligence to understand what is involved.

- You can make your own application for a *residence order, contact order, specific issue order* or *prohibited steps order* if you are considered to have sufficient understanding to make the proposed application.

- If you make one of these applications you can apply for legal aid on your own behalf and you will be assessed on your own means.

- You can change your name.

- You can apply for access to personal information held about you on computer files provided that the holder is satisfied that you understand the nature of the request.

- Subject to certain exceptions, you can apply for access to personal information held about you in social services files provided that the social services department are satisfied that you understand the nature of the request.

- You may be given access to your health records provided that the holder is satisfied that you are capable of understanding the nature of the application.

- You can *sue* for *damages* but you must bring the proceedings through a *next friend* except if you are suing for wages owed to you.

- Your *next friend* makes any application for civil legal aid on your behalf, but it is your means that are taken into account.

- You can make a binding contract for necessaries.

- You can be *sued* for *damages* but the proceedings against you must be brought through a *guardian ad litem.*

- You can make a complaint if you believe that you have been discriminated against on the grounds of colour, race, ethnic or national origin or nationality, or sex or marital status.

- You can make a complaint against the police.

- You can baby-sit for another child (if you are felt to be sufficiently responsible) and receive payment.

- You can do odd jobs, such as cleaning cars and gardening for family and friends and receive payment.

- You can have your ears and nose pierced but you may have to be accompanied by a parent.

At 5 years old

- You must receive full-time education.

- You can drink alcohol in private.

- You have to pay a child's fare on trains, buses and the underground.

- You can see a U or PG category film at the cinema unaccompanied (provided the manager is prepared to let you in).

- You can buy or rent a U or PG category video (again, it is up to the shopkeeper).

At 7 years old

- You can open your own National Savings or Trustee Savings Bank account and pay money in and draw money out yourself.

At 10 years old

- You can be convicted of a criminal offence provided that the prosecution can prove that you actually knew that what you were doing was seriously wrong.
- Upon conviction for certain criminal offences you can be made the subject of a *supervision order* or an *attendance centre order*.
- You can be fined up to £250 for certain criminal offences.
- If you are convicted of murder, you can be detained during Her Majesty's pleasure.
- Upon conviction for a grave crime the Crown Court can order your long-term detention.
- You can open your own bank or building society account at the discretion of the manager.

At 12 years old

- You can buy a pet.
- You can see a 12 category film at the cinema and buy or rent a 12 category video.
- You can be trained to take part in a dangerous performance with a licence from the local authority.

At 13 years old

- You can take a part-time job but only for a limited number of hours and you can only do certain kinds of work.

- If you are being looked after by the local authority, if certain conditions are fulfilled, you can be placed in secure accommodation.

At 14 years old

- You have full criminal responsibility for your actions.
- You can be fined up to £1,000 for certain criminal offences.
- Your written consent, as well as the written consent of a parent, is generally required before the police can take body samples, fingerprints and photographs (under this age only the written consent of a parent is required).
- You can go into a bar but you cannot buy or drink alcohol.
- You no longer need to wear a safety helmet when riding a horse on a road.

At 15 years old

- If you are convicted of an imprisonable offence you can be sent to a *young offender institution*.
- You can see a 15 category film at the cinema and buy or rent a 15 category video.

At 16 years old

- You can leave school.
- You can work full-time if you have left school.
- You will get a national insurance number.
- You may be entitled to claim income support.
- You have to pay NHS prescription charges and for dental treatment, eye tests and glasses unless you are in full-time education or getting income support or have a low income.
- You can leave home, although your parents may be able to stop you by obtaining a court order.

- You cannot be made the subject of a fresh *residence order*, *contact order*, *specific issue order* or *prohibited steps order* unless there are exceptional circumstances although an existing order can be varied or discharged.

- You can get married with parental consent.

- If you are married, you can no longer be made the subject of a *care order* or a *supervision order*.

- You can change your name by *enrolling a deed poll*. Your parents cannot enrol a deed poll without your consent.

- A girl can consent to sexual intercourse.

- A girl can have an abortion without parental consent.

- You do not need parental consent for surgical, medical and dental treatment.

- You can receive contraceptive advice and supplies without parental knowledge and consent.

- You are entitled to apply for access to your school records.

- If you are convicted of certain criminal offences, you can be made the subject of a *probation order*, *community service order* or a *combination order*.

- You can apply for criminal legal aid and receive legal advice under the *Green Form Scheme* on your own behalf and will be assessed on your own means.

- You can hold a licence to drive an invalid carriage, moped, mowing machine or pedestrian controlled vehicle.

- You can be served beer or cider with a meal in a restaurant.

- You can buy liqueur chocolates.

- You can buy cigarettes, cigars, loose tobacco and cigarette papers.

- You can buy fireworks.

- You have to pay full fare on trains, buses and the underground.

- A boy can join the armed forces with parental consent.

- You will be deleted from your parent's passport and you must have your own passport in order to travel abroad (the written consent of a parent is required before a passport will be issued to you).
- You can join a trade union.

At 17 years old

- You can be interviewed by the police without an *appropriate adult* being present.
- Only your written consent is required by the police to the taking of body samples, fingerprints and photographs.
- You can no longer be made the subject of a *care order* or a *supervision order.*
- You can hold a licence to drive a motor car, motor cycle, scooter, small van, minibus or tractor.
- You can hold a pilot's licence.
- You can take part in public and dangerous performances without a licence from the local authority.
- A girl can join the armed forces with parental consent.

At 18 years old

- You can no longer be made a *Ward of Court.*
- You can no longer be adopted.
- You can get married without parental consent.
- You can leave home without parental consent.
- You can adopt your own child.
- A man can consent to a homosexual act with another man (also over 18) in private.
- Criminal charges against you will be dealt with in the adult courts.
- If you are convicted of a criminal offence, you can be fined up to whatever is the maximum fine for that particular offence.

- You can vote in general and local elections.

- You can serve on a jury.

- You can apply for your own passport on your own behalf.

- You can make a will.

- You can own land in your own right, hold a tenancy and take out a mortgage.

- You can make binding contracts in your own right.

- You can sue and be sued in your own right.

- You can apply for civil legal aid on your own behalf and will be assessed on your own means.

- You can hold a cheque guarantee card and a credit card.

- You can have an overdraft.

- You can take out a loan and enter into a hire purchase agreement or credit agreement.

- You can buy alcohol in a bar or from an off-licence. You can drink alcohol in a bar and you can work in a bar.

- You can enter a betting shop and place a bet and you can work in a betting shop.

- You can hold a licence to drive a small lorry.

- If you are adopted, you can apply for a copy of your original birth certificate and for your details to be placed on the *Adoption Contact Register.*

- You can see an 18 category film at the cinema and buy or rent an 18 category video.

- You can be tattooed.

- You can be hypnotised in public.

- You can donate blood and organs.

- You can join the armed forces without parental consent.

At 21 years old

- You can become a Member of Parliament.

- If you receive a custodial sentence, you will be sent to prison.

- You can receive a suspended sentence of imprisonment.

- You can hold a licence to drive a large lorry, bus or coach.

- You can apply for a licence to sell alcohol.

- You can adopt a child.

- You can supervise a learner driver if you have held, and still hold, a full licence for that type of motor car for at least 3 years.

PART THREE

Where to Go for Information and Help

The details of various organisations and bodies that may be able to give you assistance in dealing with different kinds of problems are listed under the following headings

(A) Legal and General

(B) Children and Young People in Danger or Distress

(C) Youth Services

(D) Family and Personal (Support and Counselling Services)

(E) Abortion and Contraception

(F) Health

(G) Disability

(H) Welfare Benefits

(I) Victims of Domestic Violence

(J) Victims of Crime

(K) Alcohol

(L) Drugs

(M) Solvents

(N) Gambling

(O) Adoption

(P) Children and Young People in Care

(Q) Discrimination

(R) Housing and Homelessness

(S) Education

(T) Work

(U) Accidents

(V) Consumer Protection

(W) Other Useful Contacts

(A) Legal and General
The Children's Legal Centre
20 Compton Terrace
London N1 2UN

Adviceline 0171–359 6251   2pm – 5pm   Monday – Friday

* Independent national organisation concerned with law and policy affecting children and young people. Offers free, confidential advice and information by telephone and letter on a wide range of subjects.

Law Centres Federation
Duchess House
18–19 Warren Street
London W1P 5DB

0171–387 8570

* Contact the Law Centres Federation for details of your local law centre or look in your local telephone directory or ask at your local library. Law centres provide independent, free legal advice and representation on a wide range of subjects, particularly welfare benefits, housing and employment matters.

Citizens' Advice Bureaux
You will find your local CAB listed in your local telephone directory or ask at your local library. CABs provide free, confidential and impartial advice and information on every subject. If they cannot deal with your problem they will refer you to the appropriate organisation in your area. Some have special sessions providing free legal advice.

Law Society
113 Chancery Lane
London WC2A 1PL

0171–242 1222

* Publishes lists of the names and addresses of all solicitors, their specialisations and whether they represent people who are eligible for legal aid.

Law Society's Children Panel

See entry under Law Society above

* If you wish to make your own application under the Children Act 1989, there are solicitors with special training and experience in this kind of work. The Law Society can help you to find a Children Panel solicitor in your area.

Solicitor's Family Law Association (SFLA)
PO Box 302
Orpington
Kent BR6 8QX

01689–850227

* Keeps a list of members specialising in private and public law family cases.

The Accident Line

See entry under heading (U), Accidents

Rights of Women
52–54 Featherstone Street
London EC1Y 8RT

0171–251 6577

Telephone advice line	7pm – 9pm	Tuesday, Wednesday & Thursday;
	Noon – 2pm	Tuesday, Thursday & Friday;
	3pm – 5pm	Wednesday

* Provides a legal advice service for women.

Gay Legal Advice (GLAD)
2 Greycoats Place
London SW1 1SB

0171–976 0840   7pm – 9.30pm Tuesday – Friday

* Provides a telephone service for lesbians and gay men giving legal advice and information about how the law affects them.

Liberty (National Council for Civil Liberties)
21 Tabard Street
London SE1 4LA

0171–403 3888   10am – 1pm;   2pm – 5.30pm
                                 Monday – Friday

* Independent political campaigning organisation working to defend and extend civil liberties.

Children's Rights Development Unit
235 Shaftesbury Avenue
London WC2H 8EZ

0171–240 4449

* Independent organisation monitoring the UN Convention.

INTERIGHTS – International Centre for the Protection of Human Rights
33 Islington High Street
London N1 9LH

0171–278 3230

* Provides advice on international human rights law and practical help in appealing, for example to the European Commission.

European Commission of Human Rights
Council of Europe
F–67075
Strasbourg
Cedex France

(B)   Children and Young People in Danger or Distress

You will find your nearest social services office in your local telephone directory under the name of your local authority; the listing will usually be 'Social Services, Children and Families'.

Childline

Freepost 1111
London N1 OBR

Freephone 0800–1111   24 hrs   Daily

* Free national helpline providing 24 hour confidential information and counselling for children and young people in trouble or danger, and with any problems they may be having.

NSPCC

NSPCC National Centre
42 Curtain Road
London EC2A 3NH

0171–825 2500

Child Protection Helpline Freephone 0800–800500
      24 hrs   Daily

* National organisation undertaking work to protect and support abused and neglected children and their families. Runs many projects including family centres.

The Samaritans

* Free helpline providing 24 hour confidential emotional support and advice to suicidal and despairing people. Look inside the front cover of your local telephone directory for your local helpline number or ring the operator.

London Rape Crisis Centre

Helpline 0171–837 1600   10am – 10pm   Monday – Friday;
      9am – Noon;   6pm – 11pm
      Saturday & Sunday
      24 hr answerphone

* Free confidential helpline run by women for women and girls who have been raped or sexually assaulted.

(C) Youth Services

National Youth Agency (NYA) (Head Office)
17–23 Albion Street
Leicester LE1 6GD

0116–2856789

* NYA is dedicated to making information available to young people about all issues affecting their lives, including education, employment and training, family and relationships, health, housing, justice and equality, money, sport, leisure, travel, Europe and the environment, and to giving them the support and power to act on this information. Information Shops for Young People have already been set up in various parts of the country and new ones are opening all the time, as well as Information Points. Contact the NYA for further details and the address of your nearest Information Point.

Information Shops for Young People can be found in the following locations

24 Market Street
The Wool Exchange
Bradford
BD1 1LH
01274–752431/2

Orchards Youth Club
25 Carnbrook Road
Kidbrooke
London SE3 8AE
0181–319 2112

2 Frederick Street
Widnes
Cheshire WA8 6PG
0151–420 7888 (general)
0151–420 7555 (counselling)

16 East Street
Horsham
West Sussex RH12 1HL
01403–270345

3 Abbey Street
Accrington
Lancs
BB5 1EN
01254–385050

Hunslet Library
Waterloo Road
Hunslet
Leeds LS10 2NS
0113–2713220

Central Library
West Gate
Mansfield
Notts NG18 1NH
01623–657077

93 Westminster Road
Morecambe
LA4 4JE
01524–831978

24–32 Carlton Street
Hockley
Nottingham
NG1 1NN
0115–9585111

Publicity House
235a High Street
Rochester
Kent ME1 1HQ
01634–811900

86 Victoria Road
Romford
Essex
RM1 2LA
01708–768512

Broad Leas Centre
Broad Leas
St Ives
Huntingdon
Cambs PE17 4QB
01480–386011

2 St Paul's Parade
Sheffield S1 TLG
0114–2700298

British Youth Council (BYC)
57 Chalton Street
London NW1 1HV

0171–387 7559

* Acts as the voice of young people aged 16–25 in the UK, representing their views to government and decision-makers. BYC is run by young people and has twice yearly Council meetings, and other events. Also provides information and advice on how to develop young people's partcipation in society and on a range of other issues affecting them.

NSPCC

See entry under heading (B), Children and Young People in Danger or Distress.

Barnardo's
Tanner's Lane
Barkingside
Ilford
Essex 1G6 1QG

0181–550 8822

* Runs various projects throughout the country and provides services including fostering, adoption, emergency accommodation, education and training and also respite care for disabled children and young people.

NCH – Action for Children
85 Highbury Park
London N5 1UD

0171–226 2033

* Runs projects throughout the country, including family centres. Works with vulnerable children and young people and their families including young offenders, victims of child sexual abuse and children with disabilities.

The Children's Society
Edward Rudolf House
Margery Street
London WC1X OJL

0171–837 4299

* Independent charity with Christian values working to address poverty, homelessness and other problems affecting the lives of children, young people and their families and providing a range of services including safe houses for runaways under 17, family centres, drug centres and projects for young offenders. (H)

Youth Access
Magazine Business Centre
11 Newarke Street
Leicester LE1 5SS

0116–2558763   9am – 5.30pm Monday – Thursday;
                         9am – 4.30pm Friday

* Provides information on advice and counselling services available throughout the country for children and young people.

Resource Network for Adolescents
Mill Lane
Warford
Alderley Edge
Cheshire SK9 7UD

01565–873929

* Organisation concerned with young people and services provided for them in the public, voluntary and private sectors.

National Children's Bureau
8 Wakley Street
London EC1V 7QE

0171–843 6000

Information line 0171–843 6008 10am – Noon   2pm – 4pm
Monday – Friday

* Research organisation providing information about issues relating to children and young people.

National Council of YMCAS
640 Forest Road
London E17 3DZ

0181–520 5599

* Youth welfare charity providing housing for the homeless, training for the unemployed, counselling for the abused and sports facilities for all.   (H)

The Brandon Centre
26 Prince of Wales Road
London NW5 3LG

| 0171–267 4792 | 9.30am – 5.30pm Tuesday & Friday; |
| (appointment only) | 9.30am – 8pm Monday & Wednesday |

* Provides free advice, information and counselling on a wide range of personal and also medical problems for 12–25 year olds. There is about a 4 week waiting list for counselling.

London Connection
12 Adelaide Street
London WC2N 4HW

0171–321 0633 (no telephone advice)

10 – 11.30am   Monday,
Tuesday, Thursday & Friday

* Provides free advice, information and support for 16–25 year olds, particularly those homeless in the West End of London, including streetwork contacts, hostel places, careers and welfare benefits advice and practical services, for example, laundry. (H) (WB)

Basement Project
4 Hogarth Road
London SW5 OPT

0171–373 2335 (no telephone advice)

11am – 3pm   Monday, Wed. & Friday;
(women only)   Noon – 4pm Thursday

* Drop-in advice and counselling service for 16–30 year olds on a wide range of matters, for example housing benefit, drugs and streetwork. (WB)

Teenage Information Network
102 Harper Road
London SE1 6AQ

0171–403 2444

3pm – 6pm   Tuesday;
5pm – 7pm   Wed. & Thursday;
2pm – 4pm   Friday

* Provides free advice, information and counselling on a wide range of subjects for 13–25 year olds.

Anti-Bullying Campaign
10 Borough High Street
London SE1 9QQ

0171–378 1446

9.30am – 5pm Monday – Friday
& 24 hr answerphone

* Provides practical information and help in overcoming the problem of bullying in schools. (E)

Kidscape
152 Buckingham Palace Road
London SW1W 9TR

Helpline 0171–730 3300   9.30am – 5pm Monday & Wednesday

* Deals with bullying, getting lost, danger from strangers and threats of abuse from known adults. Provides books, videos and training programmes.   (E)

National Council for Voluntary Youth Services
Coburn House
3 Coburn Road
London E3 2DA

0181–980 5712

* Can help you find an appropriate youth organisation anywhere in England.

Kids Club Network
279–281 Whitechapel Road
London E1 1BY

0171–247 3009

(D) Family and Personal (Support and Counselling Services)
Institute of Family Therapy Family Mediation Service
43 New Cavendish Street
London W1M 7RG

0171–935 1651

* Offers skilled family therapists with particular experience in dealing with family conflicts and the needs of children in this situation. Will see parents and their children to obtain their views and help them come to terms with problems within the family.

National Family Mediation
9 Tavistock Place
London WC1H 9SN

0171–383 5993

* Has details of conciliation services around the country. Can help couples arrive at agreement on issues such as the future of their children and financial arrangements.

Family Mediators Association
The Old House
Rectory Gardens
Henbury
Bristol BS10 7AQ
0117–9500140

* Provides a solicitor and a family mediator who work as a team to help couples arrive at agreement on issues such as the future of their children and financial arrangements.

Survivors of Sexual Abuse
Feltham Open Door Project
The Debrome Building
Boundaries Road
Feltham TW13 5DT

Helpline 0181–890 4732   24 hr answerphone

* Provides counselling services, referrals and self-help groups.

Gingerbread
35 Wellington Street
London WC2E 7BN

Adviceline 0171–240 0953   11am – 2pm   Monday – Friday

* National organisation with self-help groups for lone parents and their children.

National Council for One Parent Families
255 Kentish Town Road
London NW5 2LX

0171–267 1361   9.15am – 5.15pm   Monday – Friday

* Provides advice and information on a wide range of issues affecting lone parents and their children.

National Stepfamily Association

72 Willesden Lane

London NW6 7TA

0171–372 0844

Helpline 0171–372 0846   2pm – 5pm; 7pm – 10pm
                             Monday – Friday

* Offers advice, support and information to all members of step-families.

Lesbian and Gay Switchboard

0171–837 7324   24 hrs   Daily

* Provides confidential advice, information, counselling and referrals to lesbian and gay people and their families and friends.

CRUSE – Bereavement Care

Cruse House

126 Sheen Road

Richmond

Surrey TW9 1UR

0181–940 4818

Helpline 0181–332 7227   9.30am – 5pm Monday – Friday

* Offers help to bereaved people through 192 local branches providing individual and group counselling and advice, with special counsellors for children and young people.

(E)   Abortion and Contraception

Family Planning Association

27–35 Mortimer Street

London W1N 7RJ

0171–636 7866   10am – 5pm   Monday – Friday

* Contact the FPA for details of your local family planning clinic or to be put through to a medical officer.

British Pregnancy Advisory Service (BPAS)
Austy Manor
Wootton Wawen
Solihull
West Midlands B95 6BX

01564–793225
Helpline 0121–455 7333 9am – 5pm Monday – Thursday;
9am – 3.30pm Friday

* Non-profit making charity with 25 branches and 7 clinics providing abortion advice, information and help, including pregnancy testing, counselling and performing abortions.

Brook Advisory Centres
165 Grays Inn Road
London WC1X 8UD

0171–833 8488
Helpline 0171–617 8000 24 hrs Daily

* 26 local centres provide free, confidential counselling and contraception service especially for young people, including prescribing contraceptives and pregnancy testing. Ring the helpline for details of your local centre.

(F) Health

You will find the details for your local family health services authority in your local telephone directory under the name of your local health authority.

Department of Health
Richmond House
79 Whitehall
London SW1A 2NL

0171–210 5983
Health Information Service 0800–665544

* For any health-related enquiry. You will be automatically switched through to the appropriate person in your area.

Health Literature Line 0800–555777

* To obtain publications on a wide range of health-related subjects.

Saneline

0171–724 8000 (London) 0345–678000 (out of London)

2pm – Midnight   Daily

* Provides confidential support and information on mental illness issues for sufferers, and their families and friends.

Mind

Granta House

15–19 Broadway

Stratford

London E15 4BQ

0181–519 2122

Legal Adviceline	2pm – 4.30pm Wednesday & Friday
Information Line	10am – Noon, 2pm – 4.30pm
	Monday – Friday

* National organisation with over 230 local associations providing a wide range of services for people with mental health problems and their families and friends.

Young Minds

22A Boston Place

London NW1 6ER

0171–724 7262   9.30am – 5.30pm   Monday – Friday

* National association producing information about emotional and behavioural problems affecting children and young people and about mental health professionals and services.

The National Advisory Service on AIDS

Freephone 0800–567123   24 hrs   Daily

Terrence Higgins Trust

52–54 Gray's Inn Road

London WC1X 8JU

071–831 0330	10am – 5pm	Monday – Friday
Helpline 0171–242 1010	Noon – 10pm	Daily
Legal Line 0171–405 2381	7pm – 9pm	Monday & Wednesday
HIV Legal line	7pm – 9pm	Monday – Wednesday

* Charity providing advice, information and counselling for people who are HIV positive or suffering from AIDS and their families and friends.

Positively Women
5 Sebastian Street
London EC1V OHE

0171–490 5515
Helpline 0171–490 2327   Noon – 2pm   Monday – Friday
* National charity providing a range of free and confidential support services to women with HIV and AIDS.

Body Positive
51b Philbeach Gardens
Earls Court
London SW5 9EB

0171–835 1045
Helpline 0171–373 9124   7pm – 10pm   Daily
The centre is open   11am – 5pm   Sunday, Tuesday,
                                         Wed. & Thursday;
                           11am – 9pm   Monday & Friday
Positive Youth   6pm – 9pm   Friday
* Provides information, support and social groups to people affected by HIV and AIDS issues, including 'Positive Youth' and various weekends for people aged between 16 and 25.

Eating Disorders Association
Sackville Place
44 Magdalen Street
Norwich
Norfolk NR3 1JU

Helpline 01603–621414   9am – 6.30pm Monday – Friday
Youth Helpline 01603–765050 (for those under 18)
                           4pm – 6pm   Monday – Wednesday
* Provides information and support to those suffering from bulimia and anorexia nervosa and their families and friends.

Enuresis Resource and Information Centre (ERIC)
65 St Michael's Hill
Bristol BS2 8DZ

Helpline 0117–9264920   9.30am – 5.30pm Monday – Friday

* National charity providing advice and information to children, young people and parents about bed-wetting.

(G) Disability

DSS Freeline Disability Benefits

0800–882200   8.30am – 6.30pm Monday – Friday
               9am – 1pm   Saturday

Disability Alliance
1st Floor East
Universal House
88–94 Wentworth Street
London E1 7SA

0171–247 8776
Social Security Rights Advice Line 0171–247 8763
                      24 hr answerphone

* Provides information for disabled people about their rights.

Disabled Living Foundation
380–384 Harrow Road
London W9 2HU

0171–289 6111
Information line   1pm – 3.55pm Monday – Friday

* Provides practical advice and information on all aspects of living with disability for disabled people and their carers.

Dial UK
Park Lodge
St Catherine's Hospital
Tickhill Road
Balby
Doncaster
S Yorks DN4 8QN

| 01302–310123 | 9am – 5pm | Monday – Thursday; |
| | 9am – 4pm | Friday |

* Headquarters of a network of 100 disability advice centres giving free independent advice on all aspects of disability.

RADAR (Royal Association for Disability and Rehabilitation)
12 City Forum
250 City Road
London EC1V 8AF

Information line 0171–250 3222 10am – 4pm Monday – Friday

* Seeks to remove barriers faced by disabled people; specialises in mobility, education, employment, social services, housing and social security matters.

Royal National Institute For Deaf People
105 Gower Street
London WC1E 6AH
0171–387 8033

Royal National Institute for the Blind (RNIB)
224 Great Portland Street
London W1N 6AA
0171–388 1266

Mobility Information Service
National Mobility Centre
Unit 2a
Atcham Estate
Shrewsbury SY4 4UG

01743–761889

* Provides advice to the disabled, driver assessments, a range of adapted vehicles and information packs for drivers.

(H) Welfare Benefits

In your local telephone directory you will find your local Benefits Agency Office listed under 'Benefits Agency'; your local Careers Office listed under 'Careers Service', or under the name of your local authority; your local Jobcentre and your local Unemployment Benefit Office listed under 'Employment Service'. CABs, law centres and neighbourhood advice centres generally have workers who specialise in giving advice and information about the range of benefits available and who can help you fill out the application form. It is often important to get independent advice, particularly if you wish to appeal a decision. Many local authorities have a Welfare Rights Service providing advice and representation.

DSS Freeline Social Security

0800–666555   9am – 5pm   Monday – Friday

DSS Freeline Disability Benefits

See entry under heading (G), Disability

* The helplines provide general advice and information about the range of benefits available.

Department of Social Security (general enquiries)

Richmond House
79 Whitehall
London SW1H 9JS
0171–210 3000

Child Poverty Action Group

1–5 Bath Street
London EC1V 9PY

* Produces various publications, including 'National Welfare Benefits Handbook' and 'Rights Guide to Non-Means-Tested Benefits' if you wish to read more about the various state benefits that are available, but does not give advice to members of the public directly.

See further under heading (C), Youth Services entries marked (WB).

(I)   Victims of Domestic Violence

Your local police station, or CAB, will have details of organisations in your area providing emergency temporary accommodation for abused women and children.

Refuge

Crisisline 0181–995 4430   24 hrs   Daily

* Offers safe, emergency, temporary accommodation for women and children escaping from domestic violence and a range of services.

Women's Aid

0171–251 6537 (London);
0117–9633542 (Bristol);
0161–839 8574 (Manchester)
01222–390874 (Cardiff)

London times: 10am – 2pm   Monday – Friday;
                              7pm – 10pm   Monday – Thursday

Other areas times vary – 24 hr answerphone on each of the numbers provides emergency details.

* Run by women for women. Provides free, confidential advice, information and counselling and safe, emergency, temporary accommodation.

(J)   Victims of Crime

Criminal Injuries Compensation Board

Tay House
300 Bath Street
Glasgow G2 4JR

0141–331 2726

Victim Support

National Office
Cranmer House
39 Brixton Road
London SW9 6DZ

0171–735 9166   9am – 5pm   Monday – Friday

* Independent charity offering free, confidential emotional support, information and advice for victims of any crime with branches throughout the country.

332

Victims' Helpline

0171–729 1252   24 hrs   Daily

* Offers 24 hour free, confidential help for victims of crime and anyone in a crisis.

(K) Alcohol

Alcohol Concern
Waterbridge House
32–36 Loman Street
London SE1 0EE

0171–928 7377

* Gives details of local agencies across the country for people with drink problems.

Drinkline
13–14 West Smithfield
London EC1A 9DH

0171–332 0150
Helpline 0171–332 0202   9.30am – 11pm Monday – Friday;
                             6pm – 11pm   Saturday & Sunday
0345–320202   out of London callers
0500–801802   dial and listen tapes on alcohol related issues

* Provides advice, information and counselling for people with drink problems, and support for their families and friends.

Alcoholics Anonymous
Stonebow House
Stonebow
York YO1 2NJ

01904–644026
Helpline 0171–352 3001   10am – 10pm   Daily

* Self-help groups for people with drink problems who want to stop drinking.

Al-Anon & Alateen

61 Great Dover Street
London SE1 4YF

Helpline 0171–403 0888   10am – 4pm   Monday – Friday;
24 hr answerphone

* Alateen provides confidential help and support for 12–20 year olds who have a family member or friend who is an alcoholic.

(L) Drugs

Standing Conference on Drug Abuse (SCODA)

Waterbridge House
32–36 Loman Street
London SE1 0EE

0171–928 9500

24 hr drugline – dial 100 and ask for Freephone Drug Problems

* Answerphone message giving details of local drug services across the country.

Narcotics Anonymous

PO Box 1980
London N19 3LS

0171–272 9040
Helpline 0171–498 9005   10am – 8pm   Daily

* Self-help groups for people with drug problems who want to stop using drugs.

Families Anonymous

Unit 37
Doddington & Rollo Community Association
Charlotte Despard Avenue
London SW11 5JE

0171–498 4680   1pm – 4pm   Monday – Friday
24 hr answerphone

* Self-help groups for those affected by drug abuse or the related problems of a relative or friend. Call for a group in your area.

ADFAM
5th Floor
Epworth House
25 City Road
London EC1Y 1AA

Helpline 0171–638 3700   10am – 5pm   Monday – Friday

* Offers confidential support and information for the families and friends of drug users.

Release
388 Old Street
London EC1V 9LT

0171–729 9904   10am – 6pm   Monday – Friday
Helpline 0171–603 8654   24 hrs   Daily

* Provides free, confidential advice and information on problems with drugs and legal problems relating to drugs for drug users and their families and friends. Produces leaflets about a wide range of drugs.

Drugs in Schools Helpline
0345–366666   10am – 5pm   Monday – Friday

* Provides confidential information, support advice and assistance to pupils, parents and teachers in dealing with drug related incidents in schools.

Turning Point
101 Back Church Lane
London E1 1LU

0171–702 2300

* National charity helping people with drink, drug and mental health problems, offering residential rehabilitation, day care and advice.

(M) Solvents
Re-Solv
30A High Street
Stone
Staffordshire ST15 8AW

01785–817885   9am – 5pm   Monday – Friday
                        24 hr answerphone

* Charity concerned with providing information and assistance in over-coming solvent abuse.

(N) Gambling
Gamblers Anonymous & Gam-Anon
PO Box 88
London SW10 0EU

Helpline 0171–384 3040   24 hrs   Daily

* Self-help groups for people with gambling problems. Gam-Anon pro-vides support for families of compulsive gamblers.

(O) Adoption
Office of Population Censuses and Surveys
General Register Office
Adoption Centre
Smedley Hydro
Trafalgar Road
Birkdale
Southport PR8 2HH

* For information and applications about access to birth records and the Adoption Contact Register.

**National Organisation for Counselling Adoptees
and their Parents (NORCAP)**
3 New High Street
Headington
Oxford OX3 7AJ

Adviceline 01865–750554   10am – 4pm   Monday, Wednesday
                                           & Friday

* Provides information, support and counselling for people who have been adopted and their families, and helps with searching for birth families.

Post Adoption Centre
Torriano Mews
Torriano Avenue
London NW5 2SG

0171–284 0555   10.30am – 1.30pm Monday, Tuesday,
                                               Wednesday & Friday;
                               5.30pm – 7.30pm Thursday

* Provides information, advice and counselling for people who have been
adopted.

(P) Children and Young People in Care
Advice, Advocacy and Representation Service for Children (ASC)
1 Sickle Street
Manchester M60 2AA

0161–839 8442
Helpline Freephone 0800–616101   24 hrs   Daily

* Charity providing independent, confidential representation for children
and young people in care or receiving services from social services departments who need to make their wishes and feelings known.

Voice For The Child In Care
80 White Lion Street
London N1 9PS

0171–833 5792   9am – 5pm   Monday – Friday

* Provides advocates for children and young people in care who wish to
make a complaint, and those in secure accommodation.

Independent Representation for Children in Need (IRCHIN)
23A Hawthorne Drive
Heswall
Wirral
Merseyside L61 6UP

0151–342 7852

* Provides advocates for children and young people in care who wish to
make a complaint, and those in secure accommodation.

Family Rights Group
The Print House
18 Ashwin Street
London E8 3DL

Advice/Helpline 0171–249 0008 1.30pm –3.30pm Monday – Friday

* Offers free, confidential advice and information by telephone and letter on issues relating to children in care, or involved with social services, or child protection procedures.

'Who Cares Trust?'
Kemp House
152–160 City Road
London EC1V 2NP

0171–251 3117   9am – 5pm   Monday – Friday
                                 24 hr answerphone

* Provides advice and information for children and young people in care, and those who work with them, on health, education and employment issues.

(Q) Discrimination
Equal Opportunities Commission
Overseas House
Quay Street
Manchester M3 3HN
0161–833 9244

Commission For Racial Equality
Elliot House
10–12 Allington Street
London SW1E 5EH
0171–828 7022

(R) Housing and Homelessness

You will find the details for your local housing department and Neighbourhood Housing Office in your local telephone directory under the name of your local authority.

Most local authorities have Homeless Persons Units and Housing Advice Centres or Housing Aid Centres, which may be able to find you a home or a hostel place and help you with housing benefit. Housing advice and aid centres also give advice to people who are having problems with their landlords. Look in your local telephone directory under the name of your local authority to find the details.

Shelter
88 Old Street
London EC1V 9HU

0171–253 0202	10am – 1pm	Monday – Friday

Emergency London Nightline Freephone 0800–446441

6pm – 9am	Monday – Friday;
24 hrs	Sat. & Sunday

* Has 29 housing advice centres outside London providing advice, information and practical help and can assist with temporary, emergency accommodation in London.

Centrepoint
Bewlay House
2 Swallow Place
Oxford Circus
London W1R 7AA

0171–629 2229

Centrepoint Soho (emergency shelter)
25 Berwick Street
London W1V 3RF
0171–287 9134   24 hrs   Daily

* Provides temporary, emergency accommodation for single, homeless young people in London. Also gives advice on jobs, training, health care, housing and legal matters.

SHAC (London)
Kingsbourne House
229–231 High Holborn
London WC1V 7DA

0171–404 7447

Housing Advice Line 0171–404 2610   10am – 1pm
                                            Monday – Friday

* Provides emergency housing advice and has a single homeless project.

Alone In London
188 King's Cross Road
London WC1X 9DE

0171–278 4224   9am – 4pm   Monday, Tuesday,
                                           & Friday;
                           9am – 1pm   Wednesday;
                           Noon – 7pm   Thursday

* Provides advice and counselling for young people aged 16–21 and has
an advocacy service.

CHAR (Campaign for Single Homeless People)
5–15 Cromer Street
London WC1H 8LS

0171–833 2071

See further under heading (C), Youth Services, entries marked (H).

National Missing Person's Helpline

Freecall 0500–700 700   24 hrs

* Helps to find missing people and provides counselling and support for
their families.

Message Home Service

Freecall 0500–700 740   24 hrs

* If you have run away from home and wish to let your family know that
you are well, but not where you are, you can leave a message which will
be passed on to them.

Squatters Advisory Service
2A St Paul's Road
London N1 2QN

0171–359 8814   2pm – 6pm   Monday – Friday

* Gives legal and practical advice to squatters and homeless people.

(S) Education

You will find your local education authority listed in your local telephone directory under 'Education Authorities', or the name of your local authority.

Department for Education
Sanctuary Buildings
Great Smith Street
London SW1P 3BT

0171–925 5000 (headquarters)
0171–925 6155 (Parents' Charter)
0171–925 5834 (Technology Colleges)

National Curriculum Council
15/17 New Street
York YO1 2RA

01904–622533

Grant-Maintained Schools Centre
36 Great Smith Street
London SW1P 3BU

0171–233 4666

Independent Schools Information Service
56 Buckingham Gate
London SW1E 6AG

0171–630 8793/4

Boarding Schools Association
Westmorland
43 Raglan Road
Reigate
Surrey RH2 ODU
01737–226450

Assisted Places Team
Department for Education
Mowden Hall
Staindrop Road
Darlington DL3 9BG
01325–392156/8

Advisory Centre for Education (ACE)
1B Aberdeen Studios
22–24 Highbury Grove
London N5 2EA

Helpline 0171–354 8321   2pm – 5pm   Monday – Friday

* Provides independent, free confidential advice on all aspects of the education service for parents of compulsory school-age pupils, including exclusions.

Mencap National Centre
123 Golden Lane
London EC1Y ORT

0171–454 0454   9am – 5.30pm Monday – Friday

* Organisation for people with learning disabilities and their families, providing services and support.

Network '81
1–7 Woodfield Terrace
Chapel Hill
Stansted
Essex CM24 8AJ

Helpline 01279–647415   11am – 2pm   Monday – Friday

* National network of parents of children with special educational needs, offering help and advice on statementing. You need to become a member.

British Dyslexia Association
98 London Road
Reading
Berks RG1 5AU
01734–662677
Helpline 01734–668271   10am – 12.45pm; 2pm – 5pm
                                                                          Monday – Friday
* Provides support and information to all those with dyslexia.

AFASIC
347 Central Markets
Smithfield
London EC1A 9NH
0171–236 3632   9am – 5pm   Monday –Thursday;
                                     9am – 4pm   Friday
* Represents children and young people with speech and language
impairments.

National Association for Gifted Children
Park Campus
Boughton Green
Northampton NN2 7AL
01604–792300
* Charity advising and assisting parents and teachers of gifted children
with branches throughout the country.

National Union of Students
461 Holloway Road
London N7 6LJ
0171–272 8900   10am – 5pm   Monday – Friday
See further under heading (C) Youth Services, entries marked (E).

(T) Work

Department of Employment
Caxton House
Tothill Street
London SW1H 9AT
0171–273 3000

Central Office of the Industrial Tribunals
100 Southgate Street
Bury St Edmunds
Suffolk IP33 2AQ
01284–762300

Advisory, Conciliation and Arbitration Service (ACAS)
Head Office
27 Wilton Street
London NW1 1AA
0171–210 3613

Health and Safety Executive
Baynards House
Chepstow Place
London W2 4TF
0171–243 6000

Trades Union Congress
Great Russell Street
London WC1B 3LS
0171–636 4030

Low Pay Unit
27–29 Amwell Street
London EC1R 1UN

0171–713 7616
Adviceline 0171–713 7583   9.30am – 5.30pm   Monday – Friday
* Provides advice and information to low paid workers on their rights at work.

Youthaid
409 Brixton Road
London SW9 7DQ

0171–737 8068   2pm – 5pm   Monday – Thursday
* National charity providing information and advice for unemployed young people, including welfare benefits, training and employment.

(U) Accidents
Motor Insurer's Bureau
152 Silbury Boulevard
Central Milton Keynes MK9 1NB
01908–240000

The Accident Line
The Law Society
Freepost PO Box 61
London NW1 7QS

Freephone 0500–192939

* To help people injured in an accident, the Law Society offers a free consultation with a local, specialist solicitor who is part of the scheme.

(V) Consumer Protection
Solicitors Complaints Bureau
Victoria Court
8 Dormer Place
Leamington Spa
Warwickshire CV32 5AE

Helpline 01926–822007/8/9   9.30am – 4pm Monday – Friday

Bar Council

3 Bedford Row

London WC1R 4DB

0171–242 0082

* For complaints about barristers.

General Medical Council

44 Hallam Street

London W1N 6AE

0171–580 7642

* Keeps a register of all doctors showing their names, addresses and qualifications.

Police Complaints Authority

10 Great George Street

London SW1

0171–273 6450

Council on Tribunals

22 Kingsway

London WC2B

0171–936 7045

Banking Ombudsman

70 Gray's Inn Road

London WC1X 8NB

0171–404 9944

Building Societies Ombudsman

35 Grosvenor Gardens

London SW1X 7AW

0171–931 0044

Health Service Ombudsman
Church House
Great Smith Street
London SW1P 3BW

0171–276 2035

Insurance Ombudsman
City Gate One
135 Park Street
London SE1 9EA

0171–928 7600

Legal Services Ombudsman
22 Oxford Court
Oxford Street
Manchester M2 3WQ

0161–236 9532

Local Government Ombudsman

For Greater London, Kent, Surrey, East and West Sussex:
21 Queen Anne's Gate
London SW1H 9BU

0171–915 3210

For East Anglia, the South, the South West, the West and Central England:
The Oaks
Westwood Way
Westwood Business Park
Coventry CV4 8JB

01203–695999

For East Midlands and the North of England:
Beverley House
17 Shipton Road
York YO3 6FZ
01904–630151

Trading Standards Department

All local authorities have a Trading Standards Department. Trading Standards Officers investigate complaints about false descriptions, prices, weights and measures, safety of products, consumer credit and other things like cigarette sales to children.

Look in your local telephone directory under the name of your local authority to find the details or ask at your local CAB, law centre or neighbourhood advice centre.

National Consumer Council
20 Grosvenor Gardens
London SW1W 0DH
0171–730 3469   9am – 5.30pm   Monday – Friday
* Will provide telephone advice about your rights.

Consumers Association
2 Marylebone Road
London NW1 4DX
0171–830 6000   9am – 5pm   Monday – Friday
* Protects the interests of consumers and gives information and advice.

Office of Fair Trading
Field House
15–25 Breams Buildings
London EC4A 1PR
0171–242 2858

Advertising Standards Authority
Brook House
Torrington Place
London WC1E 7HN

0171–580 5555   10am – 4pm   Monday – Friday

Office of the Data Protection Registrar
Springfield House
Water Lane
Wilmslow
Cheshire SK9 5AX

01625–535777

Campaign for Freedom of Information
88 Old Street
London EC1V 9AR

0171–253 2445

(W) Other Useful Contacts

National Association for the Care and Resettlement of Offenders (NACRO)
169 Clapham Road
London SW9 OPU

0171–582 6500

Home Office
Lunar House
Wellesley Road
Croydon CRO 2BY

0181–686 0688

Passport Offices
5th Floor
India Buildings
Water Street
Liverpool L2 OQZ
0151–237 3010

Clive House
70–78 Petty France
London SW1H 9HD
0171–279 3434

Olympia House
Dock Street
Newport
Gwent NP9 1XA
01633–244500/244292

Aragon Court
Northminster Road
Peterborough PE1 1QG
01733–895555

* Application forms are available from post offices.

The Child Abduction Unit
The Lord Chancellor's Department
81 Chancery Lane
London WC2A 1DD
0171–911 7045/7047/7094

Reunite (National Council for Abducted Children)
PO Box 4
London WC1X 8XY

Helpline 0171–404 8356	11am – 2pm	Monday, Wed., Friday
	2pm – 5pm	Tuesday & Thursday

Joint Council for the Welfare of Immigrants
115 Old Street
London EC1V 9JZ

0171–251 8708

Adviceline 0171–251 8706   2pm – 5.30pm Monday, Tuesday
                                                                 & Thursday
Personal calls without appointment   10 am – 12.30pm
                                              Monday, Tuesday & Thursday

* Advises and represents people with problems caused by immigration and nationality laws.

United Kingdom Immigrants Advisory Service
County House, 2nd floor
Great Dover Street
London SE1

0171–357 6917
Emergencies 0181–814 1559 24 hrs   Daily

Refugee Council
Bondway House
3–9 Bondway
London SW8 1SJ

Adviceline 0171–582 6927

* Provides advice, guidance and training for refugees.

Refugee Legal Centre
Sussex House
39–45 Bermondsey Street
London SE1 3XF

0171–827 9090

* Provides legal advice and representation.

Driver and Vehicle Licensing Authority (DVLA)
Customer enquiries, Drivers, DVLC,
Swansea SA6 7JL

01792–772151

PART FOUR

Making the Law Work for You

TIPS ON THINGS YOU CAN DO TO PROTECT YOUR POSITION

(1) General advice and getting the most out of your solicitor

■ In some situations you may be able to solve your problem without seeing a solicitor.

■ In any event, it is often a good idea to start by visiting your local *Citizens' Advice Bureau* where they will give you free advice and information about your position. They will usually write letters on your behalf or help you to draft them. *Law centres* and *neighbourhood advice centres* may also be helpful, especially if you have the sort of problem that a solicitor won't normally deal with, for example welfare benefits or employment matters or if you buy faulty goods and the value of the item is too small to enable you to qualify for legal aid. *See further Part One, Chapter 48, Solicitors and Legal Aid.*

In Part Three you will find a list of addresses and telephone numbers of various organisations and bodies offering specialist information and help.

- *You must act quickly* - never ignore a problem. It is unlikely to go away of its own accord and you will probably make things worse for yourself by delaying.

- If you do have to see a solicitor, you should make an appointment as soon as possible. Remember that the law is complicated these days and most solicitors don't do everything (or, if they do, they may not be very good!). Instead, most solicitors specialise in a particular area of law, such as family, crime, personal injuries or housing. Larger firms will have different solicitors dealing with different matters.

- If you don't know a suitable solicitor, ask your family and friends to recommend one or ask at the Citizens' Advice Bureau. The *Law Society* publishes regional solicitors' lists for England and Wales setting out the names and addresses of local solicitors, which areas of law they specialise in, and whether they represent people who are eligible for legal aid. These lists are generally available at CABs, law centres, neighbourhood advice centres and your local library. The Law Society has specialist panels of solicitors who do particular kinds of work, such as personal injury actions and acting on behalf of children and young people in private and public law family cases. You can contact the Law Society for details. Solicitors specialising in family law are often members of the *Solicitors' Family Law Association (SFLA)*. You can contact the SFLA for details.

The relevant addresses and telephone numbers are given in Part Three, Where to Go for Information and Help, under heading (A), Legal and General.

- When you make an appointment to see a solicitor, whether you go into the office or telephone, tell the receptionist, briefly and clearly, about the nature of your problem so that you can be seen by the most suitable person.

- *Don't be shy about asking about costs!* This is something that any responsible solicitor should discuss with you at the first meeting. You are entitled to know how much you are likely to have to pay in total. After all you're the customer! If you don't understand how the rules about legal aid work, ask for a further explanation.

■ If your solicitor uses legal jargon or expressions you don't understand ask for an explanation.

■ Think about the information and advice you need and the questions you want to ask. It may help if you write down a list and take it with you to remind yourself.

■ Tell your solicitor everything. It is a strict rule that whatever you say to him or her is completely confidential. Your solicitor may start off on the wrong track if you haven't given a true and complete picture.

■ Your solicitor will be greatly helped if you have all the relevant information available. You should always take with you to the first meeting any letters, receipts or other documents you have in your possession and show them to your solicitor. Your solicitor will decide whether or not they are relevant and this could save you valuable time and money in the long run.

■ Don't forget to ask the solicitor how long your case is likely to take. You will be amazed at how slow things like personal injury actions can sometimes be and how quickly certain criminal cases can be over!

■ At the end of the first meeting ask the solicitor to write you a letter setting out

– that he or she has taken on the work;

– the advice that you have been given;

– the name of the person who will actually be dealing with your case;

– when you will next hear from the solicitor;

– what the next stage is;

– an estimate of the costs and details of how legal aid works; *and*

– any further information the solicitor needs you to get, and by when.

■ It is very important that you keep in touch with your solicitor and let him or her know if you change your address so that you can easily be contacted. You must keep your solicitor informed of any relevant changes in your personal circumstances.

(2) Complaining and letter writing

■ Be polite, but firm. Never make violent threats and try not to get emotional if you want to be taken seriously. Do not allow yourself to be intimidated.

■ If you speak to somebody in person or on the telephone, ask for their name so that you can refer to it in later letters.

■ If you need to complain about something you must do it quickly.

■ It is generally better to put it in writing.

■ Always put your full name and address at the top of your letter, date it and sign it.

■ Make sure your letter is easy to read. A typewriter is best but otherwise use black ink and block capitals.

■ It is a good idea to send your letter recorded delivery so that you have proof that it was sent.

■ *Always make a photocopy of any letter you send and keep it in a safe place.*

■ Always keep any letters you receive in a safe place.

■ Your letter should be polite, short and simple. Try to get your facts in the right order. Come to the point as soon as possible. People get bored by long, rambling letters.

■ If you receive an official letter, you must deal with it immediately. The problem won't resolve itself.

■ If a large organisation, such as a bank or insurance company, writes to you, always quote their reference at the top of your reply. If a named person signed the letter to you, clearly mark your letter and the envelope 'For the attention of ...' otherwise your letter might get lost in the system.

■ If you do have to *sue* somebody you should always write them a letter first setting out exactly what you are claiming and how the claim arises and stating that if you are not paid in full within a set time, you will *sue* them. This gives them an opportunity to settle the case without going to court. If you don't write a letter along these lines, even if you win the case you might be penalised in *costs*.

(3) Faulty goods

See Part One, Chapter 29, Goods and Services, heading (a) for the general position regarding your rights and remedies.

For example

❑ *you buy a new radio/cassette player from a high street branch of a well known chain store for £99.99. When you get it home and put a tape in it, it won't play and it chews up the tape. This happens with another tape.*

What should you do?

■ *You should always keep the receipt for anything valuable you buy* and also any packaging in case you have to take it back.

■ The machine does not comply with the Sale of Goods Act 1979 because it is not of satisfactory quality and it is not reasonably fit for its purpose, that is, it is defective because you can't play tapes in it.

■ Regardless of whether the shop gave you a separate manufacturer's guarantee, you are entitled to get your money back from the shop because the machine went wrong as soon as you used it.

■ You should take it back to the shop immediately, in its box, together with the receipt and the two chewed up tapes. If you delay, even though the machine is clearly faulty, you may lose your rights.

■ Ask to speak to the manager and make a note of his or her name. Tell the manager that you want a refund or to exchange the machine for an identical one. You should insist that the shop gives you compensation to cover the cost of buying replacement tapes.

■ If the manager says that the shop doesn't give refunds and they are only prepared to repair the machine, do not agree to this and do not leave it in the shop.

■ Go home and put the machine in a safe place. You should not use the radio part, otherwise you may lose your rights.

■ Write immediately to the shop's head office. You should give the make and model number of the machine and enclose a photocopy of the receipt. You should set out briefly when and where you purchased it, what is wrong with it, the manager's name and what he or she said to you. You should make it plain that you are rejecting the machine and it is available for collection by the company at any time. Again, you should seek a refund or a replacement and compensation for the tapes. Add a warning that you will bring proceedings in the county court unless the matter is resolved within 14 days.

■ If this does not prompt a satisfactory response, you will have to sue the shop by making a small claim in your local county court *(see Part One, Chapter 51, which deals with how you sue people in the county court)*. Remember that unless you are aged 18 or over you cannot do this in your own right and one of your parents or another responsible adult will have to issue the proceedings on your behalf as your *next friend*.

(4) Personal injuries

See Part One, Chapter 3, Accidents and Negligence; Chapter 51, Suing and Being Sued, heading (a); Chapter 12, Compensation, heading (b), Awards of damages by the civil courts; and Chapter 48, Solicitors and Legal Aid.

For example

❑ *you are riding along the high street on your bicycle when a car comes out of a side street without stopping and knocks you flying. The police and an ambulance are called. You are taken to hospital with a broken arm and bruising to your face. The front wheel of your bicycle is completely buckled and there is a long tear to the sleeve of your jacket.*

What should you do?

■ Avoid saying anything to the driver that could be used against you at a later stage to suggest that you admitted to having been at fault, such as 'I'm sorry' or 'I didn't see you'.

■ Try to get the name and address of the driver, the make of the car and registration number and details of the driver's insurance company. This will assist you in speedily making a claim for compensation against the driver or the driver's insurers or, if no *settlement* can be reached, in *suing* the driver in the county court for *damages*.

■ Try to get the name, number and police station of the police officers who come to the scene. Later on, your solicitor will be able to apply for a copy of any police *accident report book* which will contain the names and addresses of any eye-witnesses. Try to get the details of these people yourself as well.

■ * While things are still fresh in your mind, write down everything that happened and what was said by everyone involved in as much detail as possible. This will help your solicitor in writing letters on your behalf and drafting the particulars of claim should a county court action be necessary.

■ * While you still have the bruising get somebody to take a photograph of your face.

■ * Get the name of the doctor who saw you at the hospital. Later on, your solicitor will be able to obtain a formal medical report.

■ * You should also take photographs of your bicycle and jacket. Keep the jacket somewhere safe.

■ * If the bicycle can be repaired, you should have this done immediately, and you are entitled to be compensated by the driver or the driver's insurers. Keep the repair invoice somewhere safe.

■ * If the bicycle is damaged beyond repair, get the bike shop to put this in writing and keep the bicycle somewhere safe. You are entitled to buy another similar bicycle but not one that is more sophisticated or expensive, for example if you were riding an ordinary 5 year old pedal cycle, you cannot buy a brand new 18 speed mountain bike and expect to get the cost back. Keep the invoice for the replacement bicycle somewhere safe.

■ * If you cannot afford to buy a replacement bicycle and you need a bicycle, for example to get to school, college or work, you are entitled to hire another bicycle of a similar age and make while the matter is being sorted out. However, you will not be repaid in full where it would actually work out cheaper to buy a replacement immediately. In these circumstances you would be better advised to buy a cheap second hand bicycle to use temporarily. Keep any hire receipts and the invoice somewhere safe.

■ * You are entitled to buy another similar jacket but not one that is more expensive. Keep the receipt somewhere safe.

■ * While your arm is broken and you are unable to ride a bicycle, you are entitled to be compensated for your travel expenses. This does not mean that you can take taxis everywhere if you could get to where you want to go just as easily by public transport. Keep any receipts and expired travel passes somewhere safe.

■ Your solicitor will also find out if the driver is going to be prosecuted in the magistrates' court for a road traffic offence. If the driver is prosecuted and pleads guilty or is found guilty after a trial (in which you would probably have to give evidence *(see Part One, Chapter 16, heading (g))*, his or her insurers are almost certain to admit liability and pay you compensation. If the driver is convicted and you do have to *sue* him or her in the county court, you stand a good chance of winning.

Assuming that it was not a car that caused the accident, but a large pot-hole in the road this would be the responsibility of the local authority, but the points marked* apply equally.

■ You should also take a photograph of the pot-hole immediately before the council come along and repair it.

(5) Criminal proceedings

See Part One, Chapter 15, The Courts and the Legal System, heading (a) and (b)(1); Chapter 16, Criminal Proceedings; and Chapter 48, Solicitors and Legal Aid, for the general position regarding prosecutions, procedure in the youth court, sentencing and penalties and legal aid. The powers of the police and your rights are dealt with in Chapter 40.

- If it comes to a prosecution, go and see a solicitor immediately with one of your parents. You must do this well in advance of the hearing. If you don't, it is likely that the hearing will have to be put off to another day and you and your parents will have had a wasted journey and you could be criticised by the magistrates.

- You will receive a summons or charge sheet from the police. Read it carefully as it will tell you the date, time and name and address of the court you have to attend. Make a separate note of these details to remind yourself and give the summons or charge sheet to your solicitor as soon as you see him or her.

- If you have any witnesses of your own, give their names and addresses to your solicitor immediately. Tell the witnesses that your solicitor will be in touch shortly and they will have to make statements. Likewise, if you are saying that it is a case of mistaken identity and, at the time the crime took place, you were, for example at a football match, keep the programme and take it to your solicitor as proof.

- It is not for your solicitor to make a judgement about whether you are guilty or not guilty. Their duty is to advise you and to represent you to the best of their ability in line with your *instructions*, that is, what you tell your solicitor. Your instructions are confidential.

- If you tell your solicitor 'I did it', your solicitor has a duty to advise you to admit the charge and he or she is not allowed to make up a defence for you. In certain circumstances, you are entitled to put the prosecution to proof without giving evidence yourself. Your solicitor will advise you about this.

- If you say to your solicitor 'I did it, but I'm going not guilty', don't be surprised if he or she tells you that their firm can no longer act for you. Similarly, if you lie to your solicitor about something important and you're found out, the likelihood is that they will advise you to go to another firm.

- Try to get to court early, at least half an hour before the time given, so that you will have enough time to talk to your lawyer before the case is called on. Your solicitor may send another solicitor or a barrister to represent you in court so you need to have enough time to talk to that person.

■ Let the usher or other court official know that you have arrived.

■ The impression you make is important. Try to dress neatly and tidily. It is better not to wear a hat or cap unless you have to for religious reasons (being a Rastafarian is not always an acceptable reason). Stand up straight and look the magistrates in the eye. Do not chew gum or eat in court.

■ You must tell your lawyer everything you want said on your behalf. Your lawyer cannot guess what's in your mind.

■ At a trial, if you disagree with something said by a witness for the prosecution, tell your lawyer so that the witness can be challenged in cross-examination.

■ If you are being questioned stay cool, calm and collected. Listen carefully to the questions you are asked and answer as briefly and as accurately as you can. Remember your lawyer is on your side and the questions he or she asks are designed to get the best from you. The questions the prosecution lawyer puts to you in cross-examination are likely to be designed to trip you up, so say as little as possible and keep to the point.

■ Never answer a question with a question or a sarcastic comment. If you don't understand a question, don't worry about saying so.

■ If you admit the charge or it is proved against you, if there is something you disagree with in a *pre-sentence report* or something has been missed out, let your lawyer know so that he or she can deal with it when addressing the magistrates on your behalf.

■ When a *pre-sentence report* is made on you, be friendly, open and honest towards the person making the report. Answer all their questions and tell them everything about yourself. If you come over in a good light in the report and it contains a favourable recommendation, the court is likely to give you a less severe sentence.

PART FIVE

Quiz

Test your Knowledge of the Law

If you've read this book, you should be able to answer all the questions!

Questions

1 At what age can you get married with the permission of your parents?

2 At what age can you place a bet?

3 What are *damages*?

4 What is a *tort*?

5 At what age can you drink alcohol in a bar?

6 At what age can you buy a pet?

7 What is the age of criminal responsibility?

8 At what age can you make a will?

9 Can a woman rape a man? Can a man rape another man?

10 What is an *affidavit*?

11 At what age can you be sent to prison?

12 Is it illegal to possess anabolic steroids?

13 What is a *community service order*?

14 What is *parental responsibility*?

15 At what age can you have a tattoo?

16 Is it compulsory to go to school if you are under the age of 16?

17 What is the *Child Protection Register*?

18 At what age can you buy liqueur chocolates?

19 What is a *next friend*?

20 At what age can you become a Member of Parliament?

Answers

1 You can get married with the permission of your parents at the age of 16.

2 You can place a bet at the age of 18.

3 *Damages* are a sum of money ordered by the civil courts to be paid by a *defendant* to a *plaintiff* in order to compensate them for their losses, for example their personal injuries or damage to their property.

4 A *tort* is a civil wrong, for example assault, trespass or nuisance.

5 You can drink alcohol in a bar at the age of 18.

6 You can buy a pet at the age of 12.

7 The age of full criminal responsibility is 14. If you are aged 10 or over, but have not reached yet reached 14, you can only be convicted of a criminal offence if the prosecution can prove that you actually knew what you were doping was seriously wrong.

8 You can make a will at the age of 18.

9 A woman cannot rape a man, but a man can rape another man.

10 An *affidavit* is a sworn statement of evidence.

11 You can be sent to prison at the age of 21.

12 It is not illegal to possess anabolic steroids.

13 A *community service order* is a sentence passed by the criminal courts under which a person must perform a certain number of hours of unpaid work in the community.

14 *Parental responsibility* is the right, duty and power to bring up a child and make decisions about his or her life.

15 You can have a tattoo at the age of 18 or at any age if performed by a doctor for medical reasons.

16 It is not compulsory to go to school if you are under the age of 16. It is compulsory to receive education but this does not have to be provided in a school so long as the local education authority is satisfied with the arrangements that have been made.

17 The *Child Protection Register* is a register kept by the local authority of the names of all children in the area who have been, or are suspected of having been, abused or neglected in some way.

18 You can buy liqueur chocolates at the age of 16.

19 If you are under the age of 18, you cannot *sue* somebody else in your own right but must issue the proceedings through your *next friend* who will be one of your parents or another responsible adult.

20 You can become a Member of Parliament at the age of 21.